U. S. S. R.

Prut R.

MOLDAVIAN

Nistru R.

MOLDAVIA

MOLDAVIAN S. S. R.

(Dniester R.)

Iași

CARPATHIAN

Siret R.

Brașov

ALPS

Sinaia

govişte

Ploiești

Galați

Brăila

Petrești

Ialomița R.

BUCUREȘTI

Constanța

(Danube R.)

Dunărea R.

ARIA

Black
Sea

Kilometers

0          75

Miles

0          75

© 1991 A. Karl/J. Kemp

# KISS
# THE HAND
# YOU
# CANNOT
# BITE

# KISS THE HAND YOU CANNOT BITE

## THE RISE AND FALL OF THE CEAUŞESCUS

### EDWARD BEHR

VILLARD BOOKS    NEW YORK / 1991

Library of Congress Cataloging-in-Publication Data
Behr, Edward
    Kiss the hand you cannot bite : the rise and fall of the
Ceaușescus / by Edward Behr.
        p.   cm.
    Includes index.
    ISBN 0-679-40128-8
    1. Romania—History—1944   2. Ceaușescu, Nicolae.   3. Ceaușescu.
Elena.   I. Title.
DR267.B39   1991        949.8—dc20        90-22263
Design by ROBERT BULL DESIGN

For Ryszard Kapuściński

"Romania is like a foolish person who has inherited a great fortune. It is all dissipated like vulgar nonsense. You know the story we Romanians tell about ourselves: that God, when He had given gifts to the nations, found He had given to Romania everything—forests, rivers, mountains, minerals, oil and a fertile soil that yielded many crops. 'Hah,' said God, 'This is too much,' and so, to strike a balance, he put here the worst people he could find. The Romanians laugh at this. It is a true, sad joke!" said Klein but he told it without any sign of sadness.

Olivia Manning,
*The Great Fortune,*
(vol. 1 of
*The Balkan Trilogy*)

# FOREWORD

It's a good thing that this intelligent and fascinating book has been written. It's a good thing that it has been written by an author who can hold the reader's attention from the first page to the last, yet at the same time treat him seriously. This is not only a shocking account, full of revelations and scandals about the communist Dracula; it is also a probing and essential analysis of a system that could allow a grim and repellent regime, like that of Nicolae and Elena Ceaușescu, to exist for a quarter of a century without meeting any firm opposition in its own country and to enjoy the world's approval at the same time.

In his opening sentences Edward Behr draws us into the atmosphere of the famous Romanian events of December 1989: when the "Leader," "Conducător," "Genius," "Sun" appears on the balcony of his palace in Bucharest for the last time. The crowds, who in previous years welcomed the "Leader" with ecstasy and adoration, now greet him with hostile shouts and shaking fists. Startled and confused, Ceaușescu panics and escapes from the city in his helicopter. Three days later he, together with his wife—his "evil genie," as she is called—is sentenced in a hurriedly improvised trial and shot to death by a firing squad. But many people in the elite, in the *apparat* created by Ceaușescu, have remained in power. That is why Behr, whenever he writes about the Romanian revolution, puts the word "revolution" in quotation marks. Rightly so, because the case of the Romanian revolution is the case of an unfinished revolution. The leader has gone, but his people

remain. The leader has gone, but the world he has created—
or at least many, many of its structures, institutions, and
customs—lives on, very often to the astonishment and disillusionment of those who, fighting against it, had counted on a
quick and final victory.

I ask myself what is left now that the leader has gone.
What is left after the departures of Ceauşescu and Zhivkov,
Husak and Enver Hoxha? What will remain after the departures of Fidel Castro and Kim Il Sung? Unfortunately, much
will remain, and all of it bad. Today, judging by events since
the autumn of 1989, we know that politicians and their cliques
do not disappear without a trace. They leave behind them a
disfigured and shabby world, one that exists and will continue
to exist for a long time.

Both in the East and in the West there has dominated, up
till now, a simplified view of the communism reigning in Central and Eastern Europe. In the West it has been assumed that
communist dictatorships rule in Eastern Europe because they
rose to power with the help of Soviet tanks. It would be enough
to withdraw these tanks and overthrow the dictatorships, and
freedom, democracy, and prosperity would prevail in these
countries. In a somewhat different way, albeit with the same
conclusions, the same is assumed in Eastern Europe. It is
thought that one-party dictatorships, planted by Moscow, rule
over us; it would be enough for these dictatorships to lose
power, and we would live in the same prosperous and harmonious way as the West.

Reality, however, demonstrates something different. The
collapse of the communist system is of course a great step
forward, but it is only the beginning of a hard, painful, and
long road to the developed and wealthy civilization of the
West. The problem is that communism has not only taken root
in the institutions that have remained behind it, but that it has
formed the attitudes of the people, continues to influence
their behavior and habits, and determines their scale of values
and way of thinking. Soviet power no longer exists, but *Homo
sovieticus* lives on—we meet him only too often. This is the
cause of the disillusionment of those today who believed that
the fall of communism would immediately, and somehow au-

tomatically, open the gates to a civilized paradise for post-communist society. When over trusting hopes are thwarted, the result is the desire for a quick getaway. A good example is the Romania of today, Romania after the removal of Ceaușescu. The people abolished the dictator, not so that they could turn to the building of a democracy, but so that they could open up the borders and leave. Hundreds of thousands of Romanians are flooding into Europe today. They are emigrating because they do not believe in the chance of democracy and prosperity in their own country. That is one of the triumphs of communism: It knows how to plant in people the conviction that communism, together with its prisoners and poverty, is an enduring and indestructible structure, impossible to reform or change.

I am mentioning this because the great virtue of Behr's book is that it draws attention to the deep social and cultural roots of the Ceaușescu dictatorship. Of course, the author could have restricted himself to the accumulation and description of the unheard-of excesses, abuses, scandals, and pathological behavior characterizing the regime of the Romanian dictator. There would have been enough of this to fill several sensational and horrifying volumes. But Behr's ambitions go further. He wants to set the background for us, to create a clear and distinctive setting for the repelling yet engrossing spectacle that played itself out in Romania after the coming of Nicolae and Elena to power. Examine the context, the author urges us. Romania is situated in that part of Europe which was inhabited by peasant masses, ruled for centuries by sovereign lords, landlords, clan leaders, and autocrats. They held the power of life and death over their underlings. Being themselves the law, they were above the law. They were all-powerful and went unpunished. From ancient times these people were the objects of a blind and slavish worship. Ceaușescu belongs to this very tradition, fits into it, and is its product. His rule is notable only for its high level of degeneration, for the anachronisms that pervaded his fascist feudalism, and for an unprecedented falsehood when he defined his dictatorship as the rule of the people, as a model of democracy, and as socialism.

But then—how can one explain the long-lasting existence of the Ceaușescu regime? Let us name a few reasons. First, in countries like Romania, on account of their delayed development, there never arises a civil society, that is, one that could independently express its interests and opinions and— equally important—control the power and not allow it to be abused. There is the absence of a strong middle class, a bourgeoisie, and therefore that social force which represents private ownership, defends the rights of the individual, and believes in the individual's dignity and independence.

Second, dictatorships like that of Ceaușescu can exist only in an environment characterized by the low level of its culture. Culture is the greatest enemy of dictatorial power. These two forces are in continual conflict and locked in an implacable struggle. Behr portrays in detail the course of the war fought by Ceaușescu against the culture of his own country and against its representatives. He describes the destruction and the enormity of the devastation carried out by Ceaușescu. The comparison here between dictatorship and kitsch is very accurate. The descriptions in this book of the cheap and primitive tastes of the Ceaușescus and the interiors of their palaces, dripping with kitsch, are excellent. Each dictatorship not only surrounds itself with kitsch—it is in itself a vulgar political kitsch, unhappily often stained with blood. It is the triumph of tastelessness, not the harmless, containable kitsch of mass culture but an aggressive kitsch, which ruins the creative culture, poisons the social atmosphere, and has only hate and contempt for the individual.

Finally, the third reason for the duration of Ceaușescu's regime is self-interest. Many political experts have for years upheld a simplified theory of communism. Communism, this theory states, relies for its existence on terror, police, and fear. This is true, but it's not completely true. Communist power is maintained equally thanks to the fact that part of society has something to gain from it. Solzhenitsyn gave a picture of a similar situation in *The Gulag Archipelago*. During the years of Stalin's reign, he writes, "half the nation sat in prisons, while the other half walked the streets and cheered in honor of the leader" (I quote from memory). Exactly so. The cunning of communist leaders depended on creating a situation where the attainment of any one thing, no matter how meager and trivial, was seen by everyone as proof of the benevolence and generosity of the dictator. People were happy if they were given something, when anywhere else it would be their due! As a result, the feeling which they had toward the dictator became one of gratitude, sometimes even outright adulation. Poverty is terribly demoralizing. And Romanian society lived in poverty—it was possible to win someone's loyalty with a pair of shoes or a shirt. "I think in the West you have a somewhat romantic view of the system," the leading dissident architect, Mariela Celac, tells the author. In her case, when she began to criticize the complete destruction of Romanian architecture, "I don't think a phone call from a Party boss or from a Securitate official was required to get me fired from my job. My employers fired me as a kind of Pavlovian reaction." Yes, it wasn't only Ceaușescu, his entourage, and his police who built the dictatorship. Nearly everyone built it, very often adding their own brick at their own initiative. This eventually gave rise to mistrust and hostility among the people. No one was sure who was denouncing whom, who was digging a pit for whom.

Behr's book is also a crushing, and timely, indictment of nationalism. The author shows how nationalism was skilfully and cynically exploited by the "Conducător" for his own unsound and base aims. It was enough that from time to time he delivered an anti-Soviet tirade and could immediately count on the support of the West as well as the support of his own people. Everything was forgiven him. The parts of the book dealing with this issue are so convincing that it makes one want to exclaim: "People, stop and think! Don't you see how this miserable and unscrupulous tyrant is making use of your naïveté and your illusions, so that you don't stop him from committing his crimes in cold blood?" But nationalism can so drug and paralyze the mind that it becomes incapable of any critical judgment. Today Ceaușescu would be a very anachronistic figure. Neither anti-Sovietism nor anti-Americanism can help any dictator now. Politicians a hundred times more anti-Russian than Ceaușescu have empty pockets and empty bank

accounts, while anti-American dictators, in the shape of Sad-
dam Hussein, are isolated and condemned by the world.

Does this mean, then, that the case of Ceauşescu is now
only history? No. The actuality and universality of this book
are striking. The author returns to one idea all the time—and
rightly so: All forms of domination, oppression, and degra-
dation are bred wherever ignorance, irrationality, and indis-
crimination reign. In this excellent book Behr not only gathers
evidence for the accusations against our contemporary tyrant,
he also stresses the importance and power of thought, of the
necessity of being oneself and fighting for one's own dignity,
and of the art of walking with head held high in times of
rejection and nihilism.

There are chapters in this book that are ready-made film
scenes. I have in mind especially the chapter dedicated to the
building of the biggest palace in the world, which at
Ceauşescu's will was to stand in the center of Bucharest. The
minds of dictators are full of the most astounding paradoxes
and absurdities. On one hand, the dictator wants to appear
before us as a man eternally youthful and immortal. On the
other hand, he is aware that, unfortunately, he too cannot
escape the laws of nature. That is why, before his death, he
wants to leave some memorial behind him, some monumental
work, and the crazier and more eccentric this work is, the
better. In Ceauşescu's case, the monument (in which *nota bene*
himself was to live) was to be the House of the Republic, built
over many years. The pages of the book where Behr describes
Ceauşescu's ravings on the site of this monstrosity, which in its
sprawling hugeness and ugliness recalls the tower of Babel in
Brueghel's painting—how, torn by the nightmares of uncer-
tainty and beset with innumerable doubts, he orders whole
floors to be demolished in one place and put up in another;
how he orders alterations here, changes there, rearrange-
ments elsewhere; how he splutters and sweats, how he sulks
and flies into tantrums, how he storms, screams, and rages—
are real masterpieces.

After putting down Behr's brilliantly written book, an honest guide through the dark corridors and clandestine dun-

geons of Ceaușescu's murky world, one is reminded of the call which once burst forth from Goethe's lips: "Let there be more light!"

—Ryszard Kapuściński
November, 1990

# Acknowledgments

On Christmas Day, 1989, Anthony Geffen, with whom I had worked on *Hirohito—Behind the Myth*, the BBC-1 and P.B.S. television documentary, called to suggest that we make a film about the Ceauşescus. That was the genesis of this book, and it's unlikely I would have gone ahead without his considerable help and encouragement, and that of Sue Haycock, who, from the start, assisted me enormously. In all sorts of ways, their contribution was vital. Other members of the BBC's Elstree headquarters were also immensely supportive and I owe a great deal to them. I particularly wish to thank Dr. Dennis Deletant, who was kind enough to read the manuscript and, throughout, was unstinting in his generous help. My debt to Michaela Filip, who translated, interpreted, and probed so many interviewees with charm and persistence over a period of months throughout Romania, is incommensurable.

In Romania I talked to many people who gave up a great deal of their valuable time to talk to me at length. I especially want to thank Professor Ion Ardeleanu, the former director of the (now closed) Museum of the History of the Romanian Communist Party, and the leading specialist on the subject; also Gheorghe Apostol, Alex Bîrlădeanu, Ana Blandiana, Professor Dan Berindei, Eugen Bobu, Silviu Brucan, Nadia Bujor, Ion Caramitru, Florea Ceauşescu, Zoia Ceauşescu, Mariela Celac, Dr. Mircea Corciovei, Professor Dimonie, Corneliu Coposu, Doina Cornea, Dr. George Cosa, Dr. Zorel Filipescu, Professor Dinu Giurăscu, Eugen Iarovici, Mihai Ionescu, General (retired) Ştefan Kostyal, Gabriele Liecanu, William H. Luers, Mircea Malitza, Colonel Vasile Maluţan, Cătălin Mamali, Gheorghe Maurer, Dumitru Mazilu, Ginu and Alexandru Miron,

Dan Mizrahy, Ștefan Nicolescu, Anca Petrescu (architect), Dan
Petrescu (from Iași), Constantin Pîrvulescu, Mihai Popescu,
Gabriel Preda, Dr. Aurel Romilă, Rabbi Moses Rosen, Eugen
Rusu, Major Ion Secu, General Victor Stănculescu, Dumitru
Tinu, Dr. Theodorescu and his staff at the Romanian Televi-
sion Network, including Emanuel Valeriu, and many others,
including the editorial staff of *România Liberă*.

I would also like to thank the commander of the anti-
aircraft artillery regiment in Tîrgoviște for allowing me the full
run of the barracks to reconstruct the final days of the
Ceaușescus there; the director of the Doftana Museum, the
housekeepers of the many Ceaușescu homes and chalets
throughout Romania, Florea Fugaru, gamekeeper, and many
others once connected with the Ceaușescu regime who wish to
remain anonymous.

Paul Goma and Virgil Tănase in Paris, and ex-king
Michael of Romania (in Geneva) and Princess Margarita (in
Romania) were also patient, and generous with their time, as
were, in the USA, Ken Auchincloss, editor of *Newsweek* Inter-
national, Mircea Codreanu, Liviu Turcu, and Ambassador
David Funderburk.

I am not an academic, and bear witness to the thoroughness and skill of those real experts and professional historians
whose insights and scholarship revealed the Romanian past to
me in its fascinating whole. In particular, I would like to thank
Hannah Pakula, whose *Queen Marie of Romania* is not only an
extraordinary biography but one of the best works of history
on Romania's pre–World War II years; Ghită Ionescu, author
of *Communism in Romania*, Michael Shafir, George Schöpflin,
Vladimir Tismăneanu, and especially Mary Ellen Fischer,
whose monumental work *Nicolae Ceaușescu, a Political Biography* is admired and used as a work of reference by many of the
still living *dramatis personae* within the (now officially dis-
banded) RCP.

Several key witnesses to the recent and less recent past—
Ambassador David Funderburk, Ivor Porter (ex-SOE in wartime Romania), and my old friend and colleague Clare
Hollingworth—wrote fascinating books about their own earlier involvement in Romania, from which I have quoted

briefly. I would also like to thank President Valéry Giscard d'Estaing, John Simpson (BBC), and Chris Thau.

Last but not least, I want to thank Christiane, who fed me and nursed me through some obsessive months while I was wrestling with the subject, and Ed Victor, *agent extraordinaire,* who not only came to my house but invariably answered my calls.

Bucharest-Paris-Ramatuelle
November 1990

# CONTENTS

# KISS
# THE HAND
# YOU
# CANNOT
# BITE

# CHAPTER ONE
# THE END

**N**ICOLAE CEAUȘESCU'S LAST PUBLIC APPEAR-
ance followed a time-honored ritual. Several thousand
"reliable" factory workers were quietly bused into town,
spending the night under Party supervision in various Bucharest factory barracks and guest houses. On the morning of
December 21, as the crowds gathered, two Party hacks, whose
role was to warm up the proceedings, trotted out the now-
familiar slogans on the "counterrevolutionary agitators" responsible for Romania's problems and pledged their undying
loyalty to the Conducător. From the balcony of the Central
Committee building in the center of Bucharest, Ceaușescu
then stepped forward to face the battery of microphones and

began his speech. It got under way with the usual chorus of "spontaneous" interruptions—sycophantic slogans taken up from cheerleaders and disciplined, cued applause, punctuating his platitudinous remarks, heard ad nauseam in the last few years, about the glories of "scientific socialism" and Romania's brilliant achievements in every conceivable sphere. Then, eight minutes on, from the rear of the 100,000-strong crowd, came an interruption of another kind: the unprecedented rumble of boos and catcalls, and the chant of TI-MI-ŞOA-RA (Timişoara, where anti-Ceauşescu riots had ended in deaths and turmoil only a few days previously). Romanian Television, thanks to its fixed-camera emplacements on several sides of the square, continued filming the scene. There were a few tear-gas grenade explosions, and the angry ripple in the crowd grew and grew, with cries of "Ceauşescu, *we* are the people," "down with the murderers," "Romania awake," and the spirited singing of long-banned prewar patriotic songs. The TV cameras not only picked up all this but also revealed the confusion on the balcony: Ceauşescu faltering, nonplussed, and his wife, Elena, urging him, "Promise them something. Talk to them!"

Visibly disturbed, Ceauşescu interrupted his vituperations against hooligans to announce across-the-board wage, pension, and family-allowance hikes representing a two-dollar increase in the monthly minimum wage. The catcalls and boos increased, and Ceauşescu, utterly unprepared for the crowd's reactions, broke off his speech altogether. Romanian Television cameras caught his bewildered, haggard look. Viewers saw a burly uniformed figure take him by the arm and usher him away from the balcony. Then, incredibly, the Romanian screens went blank. When they came on again, about three minutes later, pandemonium raged in front of the Central Committee building.

The news of what was happening in front of the Central Committee building immediately spread throughout Bucharest, and people in their thousands now descended into the streets. "This, we knew, must be the end," said Michaela Filip, a museum official who watched Ceauşescu's last speech on her TV. "The entire town was in an uproar." Riots went on all night, and now sharpshooters from Securitate began shooting civilians at random. That night, eighty-five civilians were admitted to Bucharest hospitals with gunshot wounds, and scores more were shot dead. As in Timișoara, rumor quickly multiplied the deaths by ten, twenty, a hundred. Despite the shootings, crowds massed in front of the Party buildings, in University Square between the old university building and the Inter-Continental Hotel, and in front of the Romanian TV station in a quiet suburb. Shooting continued all night, but it was impossible to determine whether it was confined to Securitate killers or whether some army elements were firing on civilians as well. The confusion was complete, all the more so since certain Securitate units wore army uniforms. One of the more persistent rumors was that Ceaușescu had ordered into action a "killer commando" composed of Arabs undergoing terrorist training at the hands of Securitate. There was never any evidence of this, but it reflected a profoundly atavistic sentiment: Surely the sharpshooters gunning down civilians on the street at random could not possibly be Romanians . . .

Though only a handful of Romanians were aware of it at the time, the bulk of the wavering Romanian armed forces, excluding certain pockets of Securitate, rallied to the demonstrators that night. After weeks of unrest, violent anti-Ceaușescu demonstrations broke out in Timișoara on December 16. The following day (December 17), Ceaușescu accused general Vasile Milea, the defense minister, of disobeying orders, and threatened him with dismissal if he did not order Romanian troops to open fire on the crowds. The general had acquiesced, but only in front of Ceaușescu. He had not issued such orders, and by the morning of December 22 he would be dead, a "suicide," according to official reports, a victim of a Ceaușescu-ordered execution, according to others. Months later, the true circumstances of his death were still in doubt. What is certain is that Milea's death caused the senior-most commanders of all three services to realize, if they had not already done so, that Ceaușescu was now a lost cause. The head of Securitate, General Iulian Vlad, had already come to that conclusion.

On the morning of December 22, the day after Ceaușescu's

disastrous public appearance, a soldier on a tank in University Square ostentatiously removed the magazine from his submachine gun and waved both at the crowd. From then on, a new slogan could be heard all over Bucharest: "The army is with us."

That morning, the crowds were still in the square outside the Central Committee building and, incredibly, the Ceauşescus were still inside it. They had remained there all night, mulling over their options with their staff. The courtiers had stayed too. As one of those present later noted, everyone was watching everyone else. Anyone leaving would have been singled out as a traitor. General Vlad and other last-minute turncoats gave no inkling that they had written Ceauşescu off. Long groomed in the art of sycophancy, Vlad had no difficulty concealing his real feelings. It was, of course, far too risky to let on that he believed Ceauşescu's situation was hopeless—for some of the members of Ceauşescu's entourage still could not grasp the enormity of the situation. In any case, they knew about Ceauşescu's personal obsession for security and the tremendous precautions taken to ensure that he should never be taken by surprise. Though nowhere in evidence, a Delta Force–type unit of marksmen and crack NCOs had been raised to protect Ceauşescu, and as the world was soon to find out, a network of underground passages (some of them modified sewers) linked Ceauşescu residences and Party offices, complete with communications centers, bedrooms, and bunkers. Conceivably, the couple could have used the rabbit-warren complex beneath Bucharest to make a getaway. Why they waited so long inside the Central Committee building instead of making an earlier escape bid, why they decided to use a helicopter, and why they chose to leave virtually alone and unprotected when an eighty-man squad of crack security troops was standing by to protect them, concealed in the cellars of their habitual residence, the Spring Palace (Palatul Primăverii) in Bucharest, is a mystery only the Ceauşescus themselves could solve.

At 11:23 A.M. on December 22, helicopters made their first appearance over Bucharest, and one of them hovered over the Central Committee building, eventually landing on the roof. The helicopters, the anti-Ceaușescu demonstrators below assumed, must belong to Securitate and must be about to open fire. The crowd panicked. Some rioters ran down side streets, but others, encouraged by the new passivity of the army, which by this time was clearly, in its majority, on the side of the rioters, rushed the Central Committee building.

The helicopter that had landed on the roof was *not* from Securitate. The commander of its three-man crew, Lieutenant-Colonel Vasile Maluțan, the Ceaușescus' personal pilot since 1980, had been summoned to fly them to safety fifteen minutes previously.

"I was sent to the roof of the Central Committee to wait," Maluțan later said. "Originally there were supposed to be four helicopters, three in reserve to bring out the government. A fifth one was in the air, dropping tracts over the crowd, warning them not to be foiled by this latest 'imperialist conspiracy.' The mission of the other three helicopters was canceled, and I toyed with the idea of flying away from the Central Committee roof without picking anyone up. But I could see some Securitate sharpshooters on adjacent rooftops and feared that if they saw me taking off empty, they might try and shoot me down.

"I radioed my base: Do I stay here? The answer came back. Yes. Stay and wait. On the roof, there was in any case only room for two helicopters at a time. There was a Securitate man stationed on the roof, and I asked him, 'Why don't they come?' He replied that the demonstrators were inside the building, which was true, and that they were having discussions with the president, which was not." This may not have been a deliberate lie but merely the Securitate man's assumption, or it may have been what he had been told over his walkie-talkie. Maluțan was perfectly aware of the events taking place in the square below, for his radio link with his air force base was providing him with a running commentary of what most Romanians were in fact watching on their TV screens. Romanian Television, by this time, was on the air again and reporting the riots, with commendable bravery.

The Ceaușescus' decision to flee by helicopter rather than by tunnel was a fatal mistake. Probably the fact that some demonstrators were already inside the Central Committee building prompted them to go up and not down, but a special elevator was available to take them underground. In past years, the Ceaușescus' obsession with security had led them not only to build an extensive network of underground tunnels, with at least one exit far from the center of town, but their specially trained Securitate squad was supposed to be on standby twenty-four hours a day for their personal protection in any emergency. Stashed away in Swiss banks were hundreds of millions of dollars, and there were at least three countries— Iran, China, and Albania—that would have been happy to harbor them as exiles. But in the confusion and panic on the morning of December 22, as the mob converged on the Central Committee building (most of the demonstrators had no inkling that the Ceaușescus were actually inside), all their elaborate plans, if they had any, went awry. The pilot, Maluțan, would see to that.

Even before reaching the roof, they faced an unforeseen, ominous hurdle: The elevator doors on the top floor of the Central Committee building would not open. One of their security guards finally smashed his way through. Onto the roof, breathless, exhausted, and utterly bewildered, rushed Elena and Nicolae Ceaușescu, closely followed by two Securitate bodyguards and two of his most faithful henchmen, Manea Mănescu (deputy prime minister and one of Ceaușescu's brothers-in-law) and Emil Bobu, his prime minister. Close behind them, Maluțan sensed, rather than saw, were the first of the demonstrators who had burst into the Central Committee building. Maluțan said, "There's far too many of you," but the panic-stricken group paid no attention. It would have been useless at this stage for Maluțan to argue that the helicopter, with six passengers and a full tank, was grossly overloaded. He took off, barely clearing the roof. "Had we been on the ground," he said, "I don't think we would have been able to make it." As it was, the helicopter dipped but remained in the air, acquiring the necessary lift, up and away from the center of Bucharest. Listening to the helicopter's black box later, Maluțan realized he had been on the rooftop for only twenty-four minutes, "but it seemed much longer than that."

In the air, Maluțan turned to his passengers. Above the noise of the rotors, he shouted, "Where to?" "They didn't know," he recalled later. Nicolae and Elena Ceaușescu began an "animated discussion." Then Ceaușescu shouted, "To Snagov," a town some forty miles northeast of Bucharest where the Ceaușescus had one of their many palaces. He also shouted, "Try and get the Oltenia-region HQ on the radio." Maluțan tried to make the connection, but as he put it, "communications with the Oltenia region had to go through Securitate, and the Securitate communications center was not answering. I found out later they had all run away."

Minutes later, the French-built helicopter landed on the Snagov lawn. The six passengers got out, and Ceaușescu told Maluțan to come along as well, "and don't speak to anybody but me." The two crewmen remained behind in the cockpit.

Inside the palace, Ceaușescu made for the special secret VVIP phone linking him to key military, Securitate, and government installations. It wasn't working, so they moved to another phone, an ordinary line this time. "I want to talk to the commander of the air force," Ceaușescu told Maluțan. "Don't tell him where we are. I want him to meet us somewhere, with two helicopter loads of armed guards." Maluțan located the air force general at home and phoned him there. At first the general said he would put on his uniform and come straight to the base. Then, as the implications of Ceaușescu's flight registered, he changed his mind. There was not sufficient time, he said, to transmit the orders about the guards. "Talk to your own unit commander," he told Maluțan, "let him deal with it," and hung up. The air force, clearly, had already written the Ceaușescus off but was refusing to commit itself further at this stage. The buck was being passed.

Maluțan called his base commander. "No helicopters are taking off, they have all been grounded," his commanding officer told him. "You must try and manage on your own." In fact, though Maluțan never mentioned his location, he didn't have to: While the helicopter was still in the air, Maluțan had

informed his base they were on their way to Snagov. One of
the Securitate guards accompanying Ceaușescu also got into
the act. "Tell them to send a second helicopter," he said.

By this time the presidential phone was working again,
and Ceaușescu was making call after call. Maluțan could hear
him speaking to district secretary after district secretary, in
region after region all over Romania. "He kept asking the
same questions over and over again," Maluțan recalled.
" 'What are things like in your district? Is it calm? Are the
people quiet? Have there been any demonstrations?' "
Maluțan also heard him speak to a top official who had been
sent to put down the Timișoara demonstrations. To him,
Ceaușescu seemed intent on delivering the speech he had been
unable to make from the Central Committee balcony the day
before. "We must maintain our territorial integrity," he kept
saying. "We have sufficient comrade activists and devoted
workers who will serve the cause for another hundred years."
Suddenly, he turned toward Maluțan. "Do you serve the
cause?" he asked Maluțan. "I didn't know what to say," the
pilot recalled. "I was nonplussed, so I said nothing." Eventually, he countered with another, more practical question.
"What do you want to do?" he asked Ceaușescu. As Maluțan
later recalled, "I didn't want this trip to be my last."

Maluțan had, in fact, already devised a plan to ditch the
Ceaușescus and their party. He urged Ceaușescu to change
helicopters. Because of the strain imposed by the flight from
the Central Committee rooftop, he told Ceaușescu, he could
no longer guarantee the president's safety. Why not allow this
aircraft to return to base so that Maluțan could come back with
a safer craft? He had, of course, no intention of returning.

"I almost convinced Nicolae," said Maluțan, "but Elena
was more determined, more realistic. 'If you go away and
leave us,' she told me, 'we're done for. Who else is with us?' "
Maluțan knew his plan had failed but he was determined to
press home an initial advantage. "All right," he said. "I will
take off, but not with everyone. Where do you want to go?"
Ceaușescu said they would fly to Boteni, the military airport
thirty kilometers northwest of Bucharest. "I'll go prepare the
crew," Maluțan said, and went back to the helicopter.

"I wanted to reassure them," said Maluțan, "and I told them, 'I'll do everything in my power to see we get out of this unscathed, that this trip has a happy ending.' I told them to start up the engines. 'If they don't come aboard immediately,' I told the crew, 'we'll take off without them, even if the security men start shooting at us.' But as soon as they heard the sound of the engines revving up, they all scurried out of the palace and onto the lawn, scrambling aboard the helicopter." This was where Bobu and Mănescu were left behind. They said goodbye to the Ceaușescus inside the helicopter. Mănescu, Maluțan recalled, kissed Ceaușescu's hands.

"I didn't intend to go to Boteni," said Maluțan later. "We were still overloaded. I intended to fly back to my own air force base. By this time, it was around one P.M. The radio operator at the base was telling me to tune into the radio, and on the radio I heard that the Romanian TV station had been occupied by demonstrators, that the Ceaușescus had run away, and that the army was fraternizing with the mob. Now, even more than before, I wanted to get rid of the Ceaușescus." He could see Nicolae deep in heated conversation with Elena. Above the noise of the rotors, Ceaușescu again asked Maluțan: "Do you serve our cause?" and again Maluțan replied with a question of his own. "Where are you going? Do you really want to go to Boteni?"

Ceaușescu had changed his mind again. On the phone to the district secretariats, he must have realized that his best bet was to find an area that had not, so far, rebelled against him. He told Maluțan, "Fly to Pitești," a town 115 kilometers northwest of Bucharest. "I had heard him call Pitești," Maluțan recalled, "and overheard him saying it was quiet there." "Don't give away the flight plan to anyone," Ceaușescu shouted above the noise of the helicopter.

Maluțan, by this time, was determined to get rid of the Ceaușescus even if it meant taking considerable risks. He flew high, "so we could be seen by radar," and he banked steeply, intending to take the group back to his own air force base. But one of the Securitate guards spotted the maneuver and came up behind him, saying, "Vasile, what are you up to?"

"I replied, 'Let's all go home, I know the way home.' But

the guard just said, 'You must obey the president's orders.' I went back on course, thinking furiously, and took the plunge. I shouted to Ceauşescu, 'We've been spotted by radar. We could be shot down at any moment.' He suddenly looked very scared, and said, 'Let's go down then.' We were now close to Boteni military airport. I said, 'Do you want to go to Boteni?' He said, 'No. Land here, near the road.' We were almost above the main highway. The town called Titu was only four kilometers away. I landed the helicopter in a field very close to the road. One of the Securitate men, his submachine gun under his coat, walked out onto the freeway to stop a car. The rest of the party got out too. Ceauşescu beckoned me. I got out of the cockpit. He asked me again, 'Do you serve our cause?' I said, 'Whose cause? What cause?' He put out his hand and I shook it. We said good-bye. Elena Ceauşescu said nothing. I could see she was scared, but also very, very angry. It was clear that she loathed and despised me. Her security guard turned to me and said quietly, 'Don't you think you will have to face the consequences of your actions?' I said, 'Everyone has to do that.' He could have shot me on Ceauşescu's orders. We took off as quick as we could, and as we did so, I could see the Securitate man flagging down a small red car."

It took less than fifteen minutes to get back to base, Maluţan recalled. "Everyone knew what had happened, because they had been listening in on my frequency. Some rejoiced, some cried. For the first time I felt emotionally drained. I looked pale and was unsteady on my feet, on the point of collapse. Someone took me to the infirmary, where an army doctor took my blood pressure. It was abnormally high: 170/105, but I wasn't in the infirmary long." As Maluţan left the infirmary, a fellow officer came up to him and said, "This sort of thing isn't good for us at all, comrade." He was wrong: Three months later, Maluţan was promoted to full colonel. His last Ceauşescu mission had lasted less than three hours.

The tragicomic events that followed could have been devised by the Romanian-born playwright Eugène Ionesco, master of the theater of the absurd. For as soon as he had ditched the Ceauşescus, Maluţan had given his air force base commander the map reference of the spot on the road where he had left them and the number plate of the red car he thought had been flagged down. As it turned out, he had made a mistake: that first red car had not stopped.

The security guard, Marian Constantin Rusu, did flag down a second red Dacia car, the commonest type of car in Romania, made locally under license from Renault and the only Romanian-built car readily available to ordinary Romanians. Its terrorized owner, Dr. Nicolae Deca, took the Ceaușescus and one of the Securitate men, called Florian Raț, aboard. "I'll take you anywhere you want," the doctor said, fearful of being shot if he didn't. Rusu flagged down a second car and followed them. Ceaușescu was apparently unaware of Rusu's plan, for once inside the red car, the doctor later recalled, he said to Elena, "So Rusu has left us too." The trip didn't last long. The red Dacia owner claimed he was running out of gasoline, and stopped. Rusu also got out of the second car. Its driver, clearly relieved, drove off.

The requisitioned cars had stopped in a village called Văcărești, in front of a house belonging to a factory worker, Nicolae Petrișor. He was washing down his black car, and the only reason he was at home that midafternoon was because it was his thirty-fifth birthday and he had received permission to leave work early to be with his family. Someone in the Ceaușescu group—it may have been Ceaușescu himself—mentioned that Petrișor's car looked like a better bet than the doctor's and suggested that they drive off in it.

Florian Raț had already started siphoning gasoline out of the black car and into the red, using the time-honored suction method, with a piece of rubber tubing. While this was going on, the door of the red car opened and Petrișor caught sight of the Ceaușescus. As he told *România Liberă* later, in his excitement he shouted to his wife inside the house, "They're here! It's them!" Raț showed him his gun and told him to shut up.

It is difficult for anyone outside Romania to understand the extent of Petrișor's predicament. Afterward, he told a *Libération* reporter that he was "petrified," and that he believed that Elena, during the subsequent trip, held a gun at his head. But later reports, including those of a team of *România Liberă* reporters, give a slightly different version of events. "I'm a Seventh-day Adventist," he told the Ceauşescus. "I can save you." Whether he was intent on making a spectacular conversion or whether, fearful of reprisals, he wanted to make a show of loyalty is still not clear, and Petrişor has refused to elaborate. Whatever his motive, the Ceauşescus, and a remaining bodyguard—for Rusu took advantage of the halt to disappear—got into Petrişor's car and drove off. As they left, a small crowd of neighbors watched with incredulous amazement. One of them shouted, "Nicolae! Don't do it! They'll kill you!" Others called on their children to take a good look at "the tyrants." "I said good-bye to my wife," Petrişor said later, "and thought I would never see her again."

Inside the car, the Ceauşescus asked Petrişor where he worked and asked about his wife and children. "They seemed relieved," he said later, "that I was a Seventh-day Adventist." Then they talked, in hushed tones, to each other. Ceauşescu said, "We lost Maniu, we lost Maniu," noticing that Rusu had finally abandoned them. He told Petrişor to turn on the car radio. Romanian Radio was by now in the hands of the insurgents, and for the first time Ceauşescu learned that Don Iliescu, a veteran communist in semidisgrace for many years, was among them. He also heard the first few seconds of an impassioned speech by the dissident poet Mircea Dinescu. "Turn the damn thing off," he snapped.

Petrişor had promised to drive them to his workplace, a distribution center in the vicinity of Văcăreşti, but the Ceauşescus had other ideas. Elena wanted them to drive to Corbea, a wooded area where a loyal henchman, Ion Dincă, owned a country cottage. "It's too cold there, we'd freeze," Ceauşescu said. He suggested they head for Tîrgovişte. There was a showcase "special steels" factory near Tîrgovişte, a "Potemkin village" model factory much displayed to foreign VIPs. Its staff were privileged, loyal workers, and Ceauşescu had visited them several times with state guests. Surely they would be welcome there.

But at the factory gates they were turned away. Like all Romanian factories that day, it was on strike, and workers at the locked gates hurled stones at their car. Petrişor reversed and drove off fast. "They owe everything to me," Ceauşescu told Elena, "and look at them now."

Petrişor then drove toward the local Party headquarters, which Ceauşescu still believed to be "loyal"—on the basis of his phone calls in Snagov. Clearly, his information was out of date, for the streets surrounding it were in uproar. After some more aimless driving around, Petrişor took them to the Plant Protection Center in Tîrgovişte, another showcase establishment the Ceauşescus knew well. Having left them there, he made his escape.

The Ceauşescus were allowed to enter the Plant Protection Center. Its director, Victor Seinescu, was to become for a very short while something of a local hero. He told the media later that he had insulted and berated the Ceauşescus and tricked them into surrendering to the police.

What actually happened was that at 2 P.M., he called the militia to drive them to the safety of the local militia/Securitate headquarters in Tîrgovişte. A militia car arrived at 2:30 P.M., with two militiamen in uniform, and for the next four hours the Ceauşescus tried in vain to reach this HQ, which they believed was full of *Securişti* still loyal to them.

Because of the excited crowds on the streets of the city, they had to hide, driving down side street after side street, parking for hours in a dark spot near a small park. Surprisingly, no one at any time spotted them inside the militia car.

Equally surprisingly, the local militia commander who received the call from the Plant Protection Center kept the news of the whereabouts of the Ceauşescus to himself. The army barracks was only five hundred yards away, but no one there knew about the Ceauşescus in the militia car. The implication, of course, was that the militia commander, like so many other members of the Romanian security establishment, was still in doubt about the final outcome of the uprising and wondered whether the proper path to promotion might not be to help the Ceauşescus until the situation became clearer.[1]

Minute by minute, however, it was becoming clearer to those in the militia and Securitate alike that with the army firmly committed to the uprising and against Ceauşescu, they themselves were in trouble. They started leaving the militia building in droves, until by the middle of the afternoon there was no one left. Securitate cars, weapons, and munitions were also left behind.

The Tîrgovişte army commander, who headed the anti-aircraft artillery regiment housed in a barracks only five hundred yards away from the militia building, got wind of the desertions and immediately dispatched a squad of fifty officers and men to occupy the militia building. So when the Ceauşescus *did* finally make it into the building, at 6 P.M., they were immediately taken into the army's custody, bundled into a Securitate ARO (the Romanian equivalent of a Land Rover), and driven by a roundabout route to the army barracks. Three army officers sat with them, shielding them from the public's gaze—for angry crowds still roamed the streets. The ARO had no lights, and the streets were dark.

The drive took less than five minutes. On arrival, the Ceauşescus were immediately taken to the army office belonging to Captain Dabija, which was hastily transformed into two cubicles, separated by desks, with army beds and blankets. There was a large, hissing porcelain stove in one corner and a cold-water-tap washbasin in another. This ground-floor wing of the barracks was immediately placed out of bounds to all but a small group of handpicked officers and NCOs. One of them, Major Ion Secu, a career officer, was to remain with the Ceauşescus constantly for the next three and a half days.

On arrival, said Secu, "Ceauşescu behaved as though he were still the commander in chief. His first words were, 'Well, what's the situation? Give me your report.' I said, 'We are here to protect you from the mob, but we must obey the authorities in Bucharest.' This enraged him, and he began a long tirade against the traitors who had engineered this plot against him. Only gradually did he adjust to the fact that he was a prisoner."

For the next three days, Secu said, Ceauşescu alternated between bouts of deep, silent depression and moments of intense excitability, when he would rant about his "betrayal." "My fate was decided in Malta," he repeated over and over again, referring to the Gorbachev-Bush summit that had taken place there a few weeks previously.

Apart from the Ceaușescus' guards—one of whom slept in their room for the next three nights—none of the rest of the troops were aware of their prisoners' identity, though many suspected that some high dignitaries of the regime—perhaps including Prime Minister Emil Bobu—were being held there.

Captain Dabija first saw them as he entered the room with a tray of army food—salami and salted cheese. "I can't eat this," Nicolae Ceaușescu said, fingering the hunk of brown bread. "I told them that this was what we had been eating for years, these were regular army rations," Dabija said, but Ceaușescu snapped, "Don't give me that crap. This area has the best bread in Romania." "This stuff is inedible," Elena said, holding up the cheese and salami. "Don't you know the commander in chief doesn't touch salt?"

The tone was set for three days of nagging. "She complained all the time," Dabija recalled. "She was frightened but in a state of constant fury, and her rage was terrifying. She refused to go to the bathroom, so we had to bring her a chamber pot." Whenever Dabija addressed Ceaușescu, she snapped, "How dare you talk to the commander in chief like that?" "She demanded tea, and when it came, she said, 'Does it have sugar in it? My husband's a diabetic. How can you bring him tea with sugar?' She complained not only about the food but about the room, the bed, and the absence of clean clothes. She would swear at us, then try to wheedle things out of us. She demanded insulin for Ceaușescu, which was delivered on December 24, but once it was there, she wouldn't let him take it. They asked for apples, which they ate. 'How can we live like this?' she kept saying. 'At home we have proper food.' "

That first night, Secu recalled, Nicolae and Elena slept in the same bed, huddled together. "It was somewhat embarrassing," he said, "to have to be present in the same room with these two old people in each others' arms."

They talked, he recalled, in whispers, and though they kept hugging each other, they also kept on bickering softly. He heard Nicolae say, "If you'd only told me what was going on, I could have gotten rid of that Iliescu. I could have finished him off last summer. But you didn't let me. You knew about the plot and wouldn't let me touch them." Elena replied,

"It's all your fault. We shouldn't have come here in the first place. That was your responsibility." Secu also heard Nicolae say, "How could that oaf Mircea Dinescu [the famous Romanian poet and dissident whose speech they had heard in the car] have organized a revolution? The man's a nut."

Probably because of his diabetic condition, Secu recalled, Nicolae Ceaușescu made frequent visits to the evil-smelling toilet at the end of the corridor, always under guard. "He really did seem quite ill," Secu said. "We asked him whether he wanted to see a doctor, but he replied angrily that he had his own doctor in Bucharest, thank you very much, 'and he's the only man I trust.' "

They refused to eat anything but bread and apples and drank only unsweetened tea. Meals from the officers' mess were brought regularly (soups and stews) but were left untouched, as though they feared the dishes were poisoned.

Ceaușescu demanded to see the unit commander. "How can you arrest me?" he asked him. "I'm your commander in chief." He asked for money "to buy edible food in town. Don't worry, I'll reimburse you." The commander refused.

From their room, the Ceaușescus could hear Tîrgoviște demonstrators baying for their blood. Ceaușescu said, "Open the window. I must talk to the people." According to Major Dabija, he still believed he had sufficient authority to win over the crowd.

Because of the presence of Securitate sharpshooter squads around the barracks, which was right in the center of town and not easily defended, the commander of the artillery unit discussed with some of his officers the advisability of taking the Ceaușescus to Bucharest. But the firing died down slightly from December 24 onward, and later the army discovered that some of the noise made by Securitate had been recordings of bursts of machine-gun fire, beamed in the direction of the barracks and deliberately intended to confuse them. In all, five men were killed by sharpshooter fire from December 22 to December 25.

On the morning of December 23, with considerable firing taking place around the barracks, it was decided that—both to confuse Securitate, in the event they decided to overrun the barracks, and to make the couple more difficult to find—they should be dressed in army clothes. Ceaușescu was told to remove his dark overcoat and fur hat and wear an army uniform. He did so, but Elena refused. The army guards removed her fur-collared coat by force, wrapped an army greatcoat around her, and thrust an army cap on her head.

They remained in their improvised cell for the next day and a half. Then, at 11 P.M. on the night of December 24, they were hustled into an armored car, wearing their army greatcoats, and told to lie facedown on the floor. There they remained for the next five hours. At 4 A.M., the alert over, they were allowed to return to their room. That dawn, back in their room, when their meal was brought, Ceaușescu slammed his fist on the table. "How dare you bring me food like this!" he asked.

Ceaușescu made only one attempt to talk his way out of confinement. "One night," said Major Secu, "he noticed me dozing off. Elena was watching everything from her bunk, wide awake and very attentive. He said to me, 'Are you tired? You have every right to be tired.' He then asked me about my family. I told him I was married, with one child, and lived in a small apartment. 'That's tough,' Ceaușescu said. 'You deserve something better than that. Listen,' he said. 'You wouldn't be risking your life for nothing. I could get you a villa in Kiseleff [a fashionable part of Bucharest]. Seven or eight rooms, a garage, more if you like. And the car inside the garage needn't be an ordinary Dacia.' I said nothing, and Ceaușescu began again. 'If you take me out of here,' he said, 'and take me to the TV station, where I can address the people, I could see that you got one million, two million dollars. And until I have access to that kind of money, I know a cache near here in Voinești where I can lay my hands on hundreds of thousands of lei.' "

"I just stared open-mouthed," said Secu, "and said to myself, Is this really Ceaușescu, the man we have been trained to regard as a superman?"

Investigators later tried to follow up the Voinești money trail, but found nothing in that small village that indicated that Ceaușescu had secret funds stashed away there.

On December 25, from 9:45 A.M. for about an hour, the
Ceauşescus were again hustled into the armored car. While
they were still inside it, the first helicopters from Bucharest
arrived, with lawyers, prosecutors, and observers, including a
member of the newly constituted National Salvation Front,
Gelu Voican, and General Victor Stănculescu. These were the
real organizers of the trial. Stănculescu had made contingency
plans for an execution as well, for with him came four handpicked army men, specially selected by the general to act as
executioners. Dabija recalled that Stănculescu also, *before* the
trial began, selected the exact spot where the execution was to
take place—along the long wall on one side of the barracks
square.

By this time, the sporadic firing had stopped but tension
remained high. Throughout his telephone conversations with
the newly formed National Salvation Front in Bucharest over
the previous three days, the Tîrgovişte barracks commander
had deliberately concealed the Ceauşescus' whereabouts, telling the Defense Ministry only that they were under guard
"somewhere in a nearby wood." There were two reasons for
this: He feared his men might take the law into their own
hands and shoot the Ceauşescus out of hand if they realized
who the prisoners were; and he was aware that Securitate had
probably bugged his phone as a routine measure long before
the revolution. On arrival, General Stănculescu's first words
were "Take me to the wood." "They're in this armored car,"
the artillery commander replied, gesturing to the vehicle in
the yard. "Shall we put them on the helicopter and get them
back to Bucharest?" No, said Stănculescu. "The trial will take
place right here, so get everything ready." A schoolroom near
the office where the Ceauşescus were held was rigged up as a
tiny courtroom. It was the only secure place, Secu said. All the
larger rooms on that floor faced the street.

Now, for the first time, all the soldiers in the barracks
knew who the high-ranking prisoners were, for they had been
seen and filmed (by an army colonel also flown in with General
Stănculescu) stepping out of the armored car. They went
straight from the vehicle into the small schoolroom hastily
transformed into an improvised courtroom. The two defense

lawyers, chosen by Romania's bar association, talked briefly to the Ceaușescus, attempting to get them to plead diminished responsibility through insanity. The Ceaușescus snarled at them. "I do not recognize you, I do not recognize this court," Nicolae said. "I can only be tried before the Great National Assembly and before the representatives of the working class." He was to say this again and again throughout the trial. Before it began, he submitted to a brief medical examination, conducted by the same army doctor who had examined Maluțan three days previously. His blood pressure was as high as Maluțan's had been—170-107. Elena refused to be examined.

The trial lasted fifty-five minutes. It was public only in the sense that in the small courtroom, a handful of observers (including General Stănculescu and Gelu Voican, later deputy prime minister) sat with their aides to the right of the court. The Ceaușescus faced the president and his assessors. The observers were on their left, the prosecutor, the clerk of the court, and the lawyers on their right. Except for the two lawyers, the court officials were from the army, for this was supposed to be a military tribunal, but the prosecutor wore jeans and a crewneck sweater and seemed to have trouble pronouncing the long legal words in his prepared brief. Nicolae wore the dark overcoat he had fled in. He clasped his fur hat. Elena was in her coat with fur lapels. Along with her handbag, she carried a flat white-wrapped package. This was the insulin that had been sent to Tîrgoviște by the Defense Ministry at the Ceaușescu' request. In the videotape of the trial, a uniformed, mustachioed guard can also be seen, holding his submachine gun at the ready throughout the proceedings, tears streaming down his face.

Even by the standards of the infamous Stalinist trials of the thirties, the proceedings were farcical. As we now know, the trial's purpose was not to bring the Ceaușescus to justice but to provide a legal pretext for executing them as soon as possible. The Securitate sharpshooters would only give up, the leaders of the newly constituted National Salvation Front believed, once it was clear that the Ceaușescus were no longer alive. Speed was therefore essential, and the court members were also desperately anxious to leave Tîrgoviște as quickly as possible for safety reasons: The later their departure, the more hazardous the journey home through Bucharest's streets to the safety of the Defense Ministry. Their trip to Tîrgovişte had taken nearly two hours instead of a mere twenty minutes, for the helicopter pilots had been so fearful of a sneak Securitate attack by a loyalist Ceauşescu commando that they had taken a long, circuitous route, and this meant that on the way home, they would have to stop to refuel. Their fears were not unfounded. Nicu Theodorescu, the senior defense lawyer, was to be wounded in the back by a ricocheting bullet as he neared the ministry in an armored car later that night.

The president of the court (an army officer who was to commit suicide two months later, allegedly as a result of "deep depression") acted as much as a prosecutor as an impartial judge. So did the senior defense lawyer, Theodorescu, the only person in court who appeared to bask in the limelight and enjoy the proceedings. By far the most elegant individual in the room, in his heavily chalk-striped dark suit, Theodorescu displayed a patronizing bedside manner as he strode over to the Ceauşescus' table, urging them to plead insanity. Some of the charges, such as the "genocide" of Timişoara and Ceauşescu's alleged use of "foreign mercenaries" to kill demonstrators, were shortly afterward to be proved groundless. "This is outrageous, a provocation," Elena shouted back at the court when the charges were first aired. Nicolae patted her hand, urging her to calm down. The whole trial reflected the court's haste, and the sordid decor robbed it of any dignity. The president of the court had wanted to hold the trial in the more dignified surroundings of a house in the center of Tîrgovişte or, failing that, a larger room within the barracks. He had been overruled on security grounds. At times, the proceedings resembled a drunken argument, with both sides hating each other but too exhausted to come to blows.

From the start, a gaunt, hoarse, and clearly exhausted Nicolae Ceauşescu refused to be drawn into any kind of debate, rejecting the court's right to try him. "I recognize only the Great National Assembly and the representatives of the working class," he said again and again. "I will sign nothing. I will say nothing. I refuse to answer those who have fomented this coup d'état. I am not the accused. I am the president of the republic, I am your commander in chief. We have been working for the people since the age of fourteen." The so-called National Salvation Front, which had taken over in Bucharest, was nothing more than a "National Treason Front." "Those who usurped power, as has happened hundreds of times in past Romanian history, will answer before the people and the Great National Assembly. No one else in the world can sit in judgment on us."

The Great National Assembly had been dissolved, the president of the court replied. "No one has the right to dissolve it," Ceauşescu answered. "That's what the people are fighting for. That's why they will fight on till this band of traitors has been eliminated, the traitors who organized the coup with foreign help." His bravado was consistent. The time spent in the armored car and the sounds of firing at night may well have convinced him that a full-scale civil war was raging outside.

Though he refused to get drawn into any formal debate with the court, on several occasions, "speaking as an ordinary citizen," he tried to refute the charges against him. Asked whether he had "starved Romania," he shouted, "Nonsense. Speaking as an ordinary citizen I can tell you that for the first time in their lives the workers had two hundred kilos of flour a year and many additional benefits. All you allege are lies. As an ordinary citizen, I can tell you that never in Romania's history has there been such progress."

"What about the gold weighing machine with which your daughter used to weigh the meat she received from abroad?" the prosecutor asked.

"It's a lie," Elena shouted back. "She has an apartment, like everyone else, not a villa. Nothing was brought in from abroad. This is outrageous."

"You have always been wiser and more ready to talk, a scientist. You were the most important aide, the number two in the cabinet, in the government. Did *you* know about the genocide in Timişoara?" the prosecutor asked Elena.

"What genocide?" she said. "By the way, I won't answer any more questions."

"Did you know about the genocide, or did you, as a chemist, deal only with polymers? You, as a scientist, did not know about it?"

"Her scientific papers were published abroad!" Ceaușescu snapped.

"And who wrote the papers for you, Elena?" the prosecutor asked.

"Such impudence!" Elena Ceaușescu said. "I am a member and the chairwoman of the Academy of Sciences. You cannot talk to me like that."

"So she's an academician," said the president of the court, "and there's nothing more to say."

"By insulting us, you are insulting all the learned bodies throughout the world that conferred these degrees on us," Ceaușescu said. Again, he patted his wife's hand in a soothing gesture, as if to say, Don't even bother with people like that.

"What about your $400 million in foreign bank accounts?" the prosecutor asked.

"Show me proof, I want proof," Ceaușescu replied. "Confront me with the organizers of the coup. There are no such accounts. It's all lies. There's not a single dollar. I will file libel charges against this so-called prosecutor. He will have to answer for this before our legal appeals court, before the working class. All the presents we received from dozens of countries are in a museum and belong to the state. They have all been inventoried."

"What about the circumstances of General Milea's death?" the prosecutor asked. "Why don't you ask the coroner?" was Elena's shrill reply. Nicolae replied, "He committed suicide because he realized that he had shirked his responsibilities, that he was a traitor."

And why was he a traitor? "Because he refused to carry out orders, people came to him and convinced him to commit suicide," said Ceaușescu.

"Are you mentally defective?" the prosecutor asked him.

"This is outrageous," Elena shouted back. "How can you even ask such a question?"

"Let's get this over with," said Ceaușescu, and looked pointedly at his watch.

Captain Dabija, who listened to the proceedings from the corridor outside, believes the story that Ceauşescu was trying to activate a special device on his wristwatch to enable a Securitate rescue squad to locate him is "rubbish." It was an ordinary watch, he said, and Ceauşescu only consulted it ostentatiously to ape the president, who was nervously looking at *his* watch repeatedly during the proceedings. Major Secu confirmed this. "After washing his face and hands, once, Ceauşescu forgot to put his watch back on," he said. "I took a close look at it. It was quite an ordinary Swiss watch."

During the five-minute respite for "deliberations," one of the observers present closest to Ceauşescu leaned over and asked him why he had refused to accept the legality of the tribunal. "You're only making things more difficult for yourself," he said. Ceauşescu repeated that the court had no legal validity. The "observer," Major Mugurel Florescu, an aide to General Stănculescu, then asked him, "Why did you leave the Central Committee building by helicopter?" Ceauşescu glowered, looked hard at General Stănculescu, also in the row of "observers," and said darkly, "Because I was advised to do so by those who were plotting against me, and some of these traitors"—he fixed on Stănculescu fiercely again—"are right here in this room."

The Ceauşescus again refused to rise as the court's members entered the room after the recess. While the death sentence was being read, neither the president of the court nor any of the prosecution looked directly at the couple. Asked whether they wanted to appeal, the still-seated Ceauşescus, hunched against the small table, refused even to reply.

Under Romanian law, death sentences cannot be carried out until at least ten days after their promulgation, whether those sentenced appeal or not. The defense lawyers, however, kept silent. The tribunal was determined to bring about its "final solution," and legal niceties had already been disregarded on such a scale that this was, after all, only one more infringement. The four men brought in by General Stănculescu walked up to the Ceauşescus and started tying their wrists behind their backs. This was probably the first inkling they had that they were to die in the next few minutes.

There's no denying Nicolae Ceaușescu's dignity in those final fearful moments. "I don't recognize the legitimacy of this court," he shouted. "Whoever staged this coup can shoot anyone they want. The traitors will answer for their treason. Romania will live, and learn of your treachery. It is better to fight with glory than to live as a slave."

Elena was shrill to the end. "Everyone has the right to die as they wish," she screamed. Then, on the verge of hysteria, anger vying with panic, she shouted, "Don't tie us up. It's a shame, a disgrace. I brought you up like a mother. Why are you doing this? If you want to kill us, kill us together. We will always be together." Tears now streamed down Ceaușescu's face, but Elena was dry-eyed with rage. The four soldiers especially brought in for the purpose, who had bound their wrists, escorted them along the corridor, one on each side, out into the yard. There were soldiers watching, one of them so close that he bumped into Elena, shouting, "Lady, you're in real trouble." "You keep away from me, you motherfucker," she shouted.

Nicolae had started humming the opening bars of the "Internationale" as he left the courtroom. At this stage, said Secu, "he probably thought that despite the death sentence, the helicopters would take them back to Bucharest. It was only once they were in the open that they must have realized they were going to be shot right away." "Stop it, Nicu," Elena said. "Look, they're going to shoot us like dogs." Then, a few seconds later, she said, "I can't believe this. Is the death penalty still in force in Romania?"

The four executioners placed them against the wall, facing it. Their orders were not to fire at Nicolae above chest level, for he had to be recognizable in pictures taken after his death. No such orders applied to Elena. The Ceaușescus instinctively turned away from the wall, and as they did so, the four soldiers opened fire, firing at least thirty rounds each at the couple. On the wall behind them, months later, scars from over a hundred bullets were counted. The soldier whom Elena had sworn at rushed up to the wall and fired a burst at her. An army photographer and the colonel with the camera took pictures.

Months later, some French forensic experts, after studying the photos of the dead couple, noted a discrepancy in their rigidity and in the blood flow and theorized that while Elena had died from the shots, Nicolae had died several hours earlier of a heart attack and was shot after his death. "The fact was," said Major Secu, "that as soon as the firing started, Elena fainted and fell to the ground. She was shot as she was lying flat on the paving stones. Hence the trail of blood." Because Nicolae had been wearing a thick overcoat, he said, "the blood was absorbed by the clothing." He ridiculed the notion they had been shot separately. "Hundreds of soldiers saw it happen," he said, and even some local inhabitants, from the windows of their apartments overlooking the square across the street, witnessed the event.

The corpses were wrapped in tent cloth and bundled aboard a waiting helicopter. They were unloaded in the middle of a playing field in a sports stadium in a Bucharest suburb that had been used by the Defense Ministry as a helipad for the transport of all those connected with the trial.

The corpses promptly vanished. Army search parties scoured the area all night before finding them the following morning, near a shed within the stadium grounds. Who shifted the bodies, and for what purpose, was never satisfactorily established.

# CHAPTER TWO
# THE
# BEGINNING

66 "THE HISTORY OF THE ROMANIANS," wrote Nicolae Ceaușescu, "is the history of a settled people who developed in a unitary manner from the heart of ancient Dacia, building a thriving material and spiritual culture."

As William Boot's long-suffering editor in Evelyn Waugh's classic *Scoop* would have said: Up to a point, Lord Copper.

The thrust of Ceaușescu's history books, which he authored only in the sense that he graciously put his name to them (they were actually written by a team of professional historians only too happy to act as ghostwriters to the Conducător, or supreme leader, as Ceaușescu was known), was

■

that Romanian nationalism was justified and firmly rooted in
the past. All Ceaușescu-era history books established that the
Dacians—the original inhabitants of what is now Romania—
were far more advanced than other "aboriginal" European
races. In the eyes of the authors of these "officially approved"
histories, they were in many ways superior to the Romans
themselves, had resisted the Roman invasion with considerable heroism, and, after the Roman legions' withdrawal, had
managed to survive intact. Nicolae Ceaușescu was depicted as
the spiritual descendant of such mythical figures as the Dacian
warrior-kings Burebista and Decebal. Of Burebista,
Ceaușescu's stable of historians boasted that he had "unified
the country from the Slovak mountains to the Danube to the
Eastern shore of the Black Sea. Coming to rule people tired
because of many wars, Burebista so uplifted them through
drills, abstention from wine and obedience that in the space of
a few years he built a strong state. Even the Romans came to
fear him."[1]

"Long and tough was the road traversed by Burebista's
and Decebal's descendants," wrote another "official" historian.
"From centuries of strenuous battles and Dacian and Roman
civilizations, a new people came into being, *preserving and developing its forerunner's best features and virtues* [author's italics].
The Dacians offered to the Greeks and Romans alike a superior and very specific spiritual consistency, recorded in ancient
literature with astonishment and admiration—an almost fab-
ulous debt to (Dacian) bravery, wisdom and sense of justice."

In the numerous histories of Romania written during the
Ceaușescu years, only three kings were worthy of a mention
alongside the Conducător: Burebista, Decebal, and Michael
the Brave, the legendary prince who unified Walachia, Moldavia, and Transylvania, challenging the rule of the Ottoman
Empire—of which Romania was a vassal in 1600. As a foot-
note, Ceaușescu's historians always added that four of Michael
the Brave's captains had later settled in Scornicești,
Ceaușescu's village, the implication being that he was probably
one of their descendants. Robert Maxwell's Pergamon Press
biography of Ceaușescu, anonymously written and clearly
translated from the Romanian, makes almost no mention of

the later Romanian royal family, from Carol I (enthroned in 1881) to King Michael (deposed in 1947). At the time of its publication, there could be only one king. Indeed, apart from Romania's older generation, only a minority of Romanians who grew up since 1965 were aware of the existence of a royal family, and this in turn explained the general indifference that prevailed when the ruling post-Ceauşescu National Salvation Front banned ex-king Michael from visiting Romania prior to the May 1990 elections there. Ironically, the president of Romania's tiny royalist association today is a distant cousin of Elena Ceauşescu.

That the Dacians, or at any rate a hybrid Roman-Dacian intermixture, did survive after the Romans' departure in A.D. 271–274 is not disputed: The Romanian language, so close to Italian, is proof of that. "What happened is that the Daco-Roman race vanished after the Roman occupation for 1000 years, reappearing in the 13th and 14th centuries as 'voievo-date' (Governorships) of Walachia and Moldavia."[2] By this time, of course, as a "race," the Dacians no longer existed, for there had been successive invasions of Goths and Huns, while Bulgarians, Slavs, Hungarians, and Tatars, not to mention Jews and gypsies, had also entered the country in large numbers and settled in Romania. But Ceauşescu's official historians deliberately downplayed the intermarriages that took place and are evident in the physical characteristics of today's Romanians. That the myth of Dacian purity survived Ceauşescu's death was apparent immediately after his execution: When it became safe to do so, rumors immediately spread that he had been a Tatar or a gypsy—such a monster could not have been a real Romanian.

Without going to the demented lengths of Hitler and his obsession with the Aryan race, Ceauşescu related the survival of the Dacian "race" to modern Romania, just as the Dacian struggle to survive against the Romans was related to Romania's later history and to the way it had handled its Soviet links. Ceauşescu-era history books could not deny the existence of many different kinds of foreign invaders, but as Ceauşescu himself "wrote," in the turgid Marxist-Leninist style of his ghostwriters:

Hundreds of years passed, in which the Romanian community of economic interests, territory, culture and language got cemented. Conditions were provided in that period, although somewhat late, for the passage to a higher organization—the formation of the three Romanian Principalities: Valachia, Moldavia and Transylvania. As it is known, they came into being and developed in the struggle against foreign domination, for the union into a strong state, apt to face the foreign invasions, to ensure their own self-dependent development.

As another "official" historian put it, in even more excruciating prose,

The permanence of the autochthonous element after the Roman conquest was the very prerequisite of the process of ethnocultural intertwining of the Dacians and the Romans, which resulted in the formation of the Romanian people. The invasions, starting in the 3rd century AD by the migratory populations that had a lower level of evolution, caused damage and devastation, but they were, however, unable to change the community of life, language and culture of this people, its historic course towards superior forms of political and socio-economic organization.

The stress was not just on "purity" but on the parallels between ancient and modern history, so that ancient Romania's standoff against the Roman Empire could be interpreted as the prefiguration of gallant little Romania challenging the Soviet communist empire in the 1960s.

So total was the Romanian Communist party's (RCP) grip on education for over forty years that very few Romanians other than professional historians with access to specialized libraries have been able to learn the whole truth about their past. Unlike in Poland, where during the communist era history was taught at home to supplant the official, stereotyped school version imposed on the teachers, in Romania the official Ceauşescu-era history books became the gospel of schoolchildren.

The same woolliness and imprecision concerning the past also characterizes most of the "official" history-book references to Transylvania. In fact it was fought over, bartered, and ceded many times. In 1526, it became independent when Hungary was partitioned. In 1691, it was reunited with Hungary. From 1918 to 1940, it was part of Romania again, before its northern part became, briefly, and during the Second World War, Hungarian. The Romanian-speaking element under Hungarian rule suffered even more than the ethnic Hungarians: Not wanting to learn Hungarian and forbidden from learning Romanian in schools, they remained illiterate. The province of Bessarabia suffered the same *va et vient:* First a Turkish vassal (like the rest of Romania), it was annexed by Russia in 1812. In 1856 three of its southern provinces became Romanian. In 1878 they were returned to Russia. By the Treaty of Versailles after World War I the rest of Bessarabia was awarded to Romania, but Bessarabia did not remain Romanian for long: Annexed by Stalin in 1940, it became from then onward part of the now crumbling USSR, renamed the Moldavian People's Republic.

The crude nationalism Ceauşescu insisted should be taught in schools was understandable. With Romania's checkered record and hybrid antecedents, it was essential, in his eyes, to establish a clear sense of national identity. Like most of his endeavors, his heavy-handedness, and that of his sycophants, was counterproductive: Like so much of the Ceauşescu era, it all ended in a ridiculous overkill.

Romanian realities were very different from the carefully contrived *images d'Epinal* fostered by the official historians, including those on the team of General Ilie Ceauşescu, brother of Nicolae, who headed an Institute of Military History and also "wrote" books (but not, apparently, as many as he would have wished; the Conducător, jealous of the stature of all around him, including those of his family whose careers he advanced, saw to that). The Vlachs, as the Romanian population of Walachia and Moldavia were known in the thirteenth century, continued practicing their Christian religion under the Turks. These *hospodars* (princes) were constantly at war with one another, and intrafamily feuds were common. They paid tribute to the Turks, in exchange for physical control over the land and its people. The most famous *hospodar* was

Vlad (Dracula) the Impaler, who rebelled against the Turks and attempted to stamp out corruption. In Romania, he remains a hero.

The Turks, the *voievodate* (governors), and the predatory habits of the Greek Phanariot princes, whom the Turks, in the later stages of the occupation, allowed to run the Romanian provinces for them in exchange for hard cash, have all left their mark on present-day Romania. The Greek satraps took their name from the *phanar*, the lighthouse district of Constantinople that they were supposed to have come from, and their corrupt ways have had a lasting impact on Romanian life.

Conditions were equally unpalatable in the eighteenth and early nineteenth centuries. Native Romanian aristocrats bought and sold the right to rule their local fiefdoms from the Phanariots. The local gentry, "squeezed" in turn by the aristocrats, took it out on the peasants. "The lot of the Romanian peasant (in the eighteenth and early nineteenth centuries) was so miserable," wrote Hannah Pakula in her remarkable biography of Queen Marie of Romania,[3] "the tribute exacted so exaggerated, that he was known to kill his cow, or destroy his house to avoid paying the cow-tax or the so-called chimney tax. By skimming off all the profit from their labors, the Turks destroyed the Romanians' motivation to work, and the rich resources of the Principalities remained undeveloped. Walachia and Moldavia, one Russian general noted, were 'favored by nature but persecuted by fate.' " Much the same could be said, later, of Ceaușescu-era Romania.

For all their corruption and greed, the Phanariots brought culture and liberal notions to Romania, a love of the French language and literature, as well as the notion of nationalism. By this time, the crumbling Ottoman Empire was no longer able to maintain the credible pretense of suzerainty over the Romanian provinces, and other predators were gathering. The Austro-Hungarian Empire, not content with Transylvania, coveted Walachia and Moldavia as well, but the most serious contender was Russia. After repeated Russian invasions under Nicholas, all repulsed, a semblance of order came in the aftermath of the Crimean War. The existence of Moldavia and Walachia was guaranteed by Austria, Britain, France, Rus-

sia, Sardinia, and Turkey at the Treaty of Paris, and elections
were held to determine their future. The guarantors wanted
the provinces to remain separate, but the inhabitants of both
provinces turned the tables on them by voting for the same
popular native son, Colonel (and Prince) Ion Cuza. On December 23, 1861, Cuza announced that "the Romanian nation
is founded," adding, presciently, "I fear you will not be satisfied with me for long."

Prince Cuza's early promise as a statesman was belied by
later events. He and his wife rapidly became fascinated, and
corrupted, by the exercise of power. Their "regal" behavior,
and the ease with which they divorced themselves from the
preoccupations of ordinary Romanians, at first irritated then
infuriated their subjects. The historical parallel between the
Cuzas and the Ceauşescus is undeniable, the main difference
being that while Prince Cuza became increasingly remote and
preoccupied with protocol, his regime neither terrorized nor
starved the people and he was disposed of democratically, or
at least by political consensus. Five years after he came to
power, his country in ruins as a result of his mismanagement,
Prince Cuza was forced to resign.

European monarchies in the 1860s had a cachet they have
long since lost. Scions of royal families were in considerable
demand to lend the weight of their prestige to countries in
need of enhanced status. Ion Brătianu, the leading Romanian
Liberal politician of the time, set out to look for a prince to
reign over his country rather like a headhunter searching for
the CEO of a newly established company. The Belgian king's
younger brother turned him down, but Prince Karl of Germany, the second son of the reigning family of Hohenzollern-
Sigmaringen, cousin to King Wilhelm I and a serving army
officer, was tempted by the offer. He consulted Chancellor
Otto von Bismarck, who persuaded him to accept.

Contrary to what the silence and distortions of Ceauşescu's
version of history implied, Prince Karl's management of his
adopted country from 1866 onward represented a genuine
"great leap forward" for a backward, corrupt, and bankrupt
Romania. On the diplomatic, constitutional, and economic
fronts, this somber, humorless man, old beyond his twenty-

seven years, revealed himself an innovator and remarkable administrator, a patient diplomat, and eventually a great, if unloved, king. King Carol I, as he later became known, built roads, railroads, and factories, established a small industrial base and sophisticated trade relations with other European powers, modernized the army, and reduced the inefficiency of the proverbially corrupt administration. In short, he put Romania on the map.

To some extent, Russia helped him throw off the last remnants of Turkish suzerainty. In 1877, tsarist Russia was determined to push eastward and went to war with Turkey. Nicholas I's armies were allowed to pass through Romania, Prince Karl committed his army to the tsar, and together the Romanians and the Russians reached the gates of Constantinople (as Istanbul was then called). The Congress of Berlin, meeting in 1878, set its seal on the complete independence of Romania. But there was a price: In return for challenging the Turks, the tsar demanded, and was given, the rich Romanian province of Bessarabia. Not for the first time, Romanians joked that with an ally like Russia, who needed enemies?

Ceaușescu's historians, insofar as they mention this period at all other than in clichés, tend to stress its shortcomings: the parliamentary domination of landlords and aristocrats at the expense of the peasants and workers, the latent anti-Semitism, and the German flavor of the period (Karl had married a German princess, Elizabeth de Wied). No credit is given to King Carol I for his nation building or his attempts to introduce a measure of democracy to feudal Romania. In most of their books, he is not mentioned at all. When he first came to Bucharest, wrote Hannah Pakula, "Prince Karl asked where he was, and was told he had reached the royal palace. Looking at the building and thinking he had not heard correctly, Karl asked, '*Where* is the Palace?' His informant could only point in embarrassment to the low building that looked out on an undistinguished guardhouse and a gypsy camp, with its group of pigs wallowing in the mud." At his glittering coronation on May 22, 1881, marked by lavish receptions and costly pageantry, Romanians were able to see for themselves how their country had prospered.

In 1883, King Carol I signed a secret treaty with Germany and Austria-Hungary that was to have traumatic consequences: The German and Austro-Hungarian signatories pledged to support Romania against any form of aggression, while Romania promised to come to their aid if they were threatened by Russia or Serbia.

Because Romania was such a new country, succession problems mattered more than in most monarchies. Elizabeth de Wied had given Carol no heir, for her only child, a girl, had died in infancy in 1874. Owing to its troubled past, and the prevalence of intrigue and in-fighting among the descendants of the *hospodars,* the Romanian constitution expressly forbade the king's heirs to marry Romanians. Should they do so, they would forfeit their rights to the throne. Having provided the Romanians with a king, the Hohenzollern-Sigmaringens were expected to provide them with a successor as well: The attitude of the Romanians was that theirs was a form of "service warranty" responsibility. The family cast around for a likely candidate and came up with King Carol's nephew, Ferdinand. He was a jug-eared, painfully shy, worthy young man, whose interests included religion, reading, botany—and uncomplicated sex. He was, as Hannah Pakula pointed out, hardly the ideal person to rule such a complex, contradictory Latin country, but "conducting his life largely by default," he was too passive, or too shy, to refuse and duly became heir apparent, moving to Bucharest, where, hideously bored, he lived in awe of *der Onkel.*

Casting around for a bride for Ferdinand, the royal marriage brokers selected Princess Marie of Edinburgh, the half-British, half-Russian granddaughter of Queen Victoria, then seventeen, who had already expressed a preference for "cousin George," later King George V. At first, Ferdinand was not particularly anxious to marry her. He had been romantically in love with one of the Romanian court's ladies-in-waiting, but it was pointed out to him that if he married her, he would not succeed his uncle. However, Princess Marie, whom he encountered at a number of minutely planned, chaperoned occasions, charmed him, and he urged a quick marriage, "for I have few pleasures enjoyed by my peers."

Queen Victoria was not at all pleased. "We have been much startled lately to hear of Missy's engagement to Ferdinand of Romania," she wrote in her inimitable style. "He is nice I believe and the parents are charming—but the country is very insecure and the immorality of the Society at Bucharest *quite awful.*" Even before her marriage, Princess Marie, or Missy, as she had been known since childhood, began having doubts about its wisdom. "There were occasional moments," she wrote while still engaged to him, "when it suddenly came to me that Nando and I had not perhaps exactly the same tastes about everything." She was a beautiful, spirited, unconventional girl with no intellectual pretensions. After her marriage, she would gain fame at first for her superb horsemanship and later for the open way she took on lovers and for her many eccentricities. She became, however, a much-loved queen, and would put a forceful personal imprint on Romanian policy in the years to come. This period in Romanian history has been deliberately ignored by official Romanian historians. The anonymous authors of the Maxwell/Pergamon Press biography of Ceaușescu deal with this crucial period in Romania's past without once mentioning either King Carol I or the establishment of the monarchy. In time-honored Marxist jargon, the Russo-Turkish war that led to Romanian independence is referred to as the achievement of "the South Danubian peoples [which] had already started on the anti-Ottoman struggle . . ."

Ferdinand was Marie's complete opposite: a hopelessly bad horseman, a totally humorless intellectual, convinced of the superiority of German culture, who hated parties, dancing, or any kind of fun. Sexually, their relationship was a classic example of incompatibility. Because of his shyness and awkwardness with his social equals of the opposite sex, he found solace and ease only with lower-class courtesans and prostitutes, who were no threat to him. A British diplomat noted his "taste for somewhat indiscriminate fornication." Princess Marie, in her memoirs, was to write surprisingly frankly about the crude nature of his physical advances—for he remained physically attracted to his wife even after her affairs had become the talk of Europe—and the impossibility of having any real relationship with him other than sexual. Even in this field, she hinted in letters to friends, the pleasure was all his.

Though she was to be homesick for years, the country that she was to defend with dedicated, newfound patriotism was very different from the one King Carol had first seen. King Carol had an obsession for palaces—a "royal" fixation Nicolae Ceaușescu would later share—and there had been an orgy of building under his reign. A lack of good taste was another shared characteristic: Castle Peleș, where Princess Marie and Ferdinand first lived, was a 150-room structure built in the German renaissance, neo-Gothic, Byzantine, and Transylvanian styles. "Turreted, pinnacled and ornamented down to the last square meter,"[4] it had taken Carol ten years to complete, and he had fiddled with every minor ornamental detail very much as Ceaușescu himself would dither over the decoration of his infamous House of the Republic. Princess Marie, too, proved herself a confident, if not always tasteful, builder and decorator. She embarked on the refurbishing of Cotroceni Palace, near Bucharest, without questioning the cost, and the results were embarrassing, even to her friends, who described her bedroom there as resembling "both a church and a Turkish bath."

On October 15, 1893, in considerable pain (Romanian doctors would not allow her chloroform) she gave birth to a son, Carol. Romanians rejoiced. No one, at the time, could possibly foresee how disastrously he would conduct himself. Three other children—Elisabeta, Marie, and Nicholas—followed in fairly quick succession. Two more children were born later—Ileana in 1909, and Mircea in 1913. There was to be much gossip about their paternity.

Princess Marie's serious lovers were certainly, over the years, at least as numerous as her children. Some of her affairs were so public they enraged *der Onkel*, though Ferdinand by this time had found solace elsewhere, with a string of undemanding, ephemeral women. Princess Marie was outspoken, aggressively English in many ways, and surprisingly free for the age, which fettered women and denied them any of the freedom their husbands enjoyed by right. Inevitably, she antagonized cohorts of stuffy aides, snobbish French-speaking Romanians, German governesses, and Swiss tutors. Misjudging her completely, King Carol felt she was too flighty to look after her eldest son's education. She was, in fact, extraordinarily modern: She chose her lovers and companions for their horsemanship, their talent to amuse, their looks and—in the case of Prince Barbu Ştirbey—other statesmanlike qualities as well. Her last child, Mircea, who died of typhoid fever in infancy, was almost certainly fathered by Prince Barbu Ştirbey.

Marie and Barbu met in unusual circumstances. The year 1906 had been a triumphal one for King Carol I: Romania's first international exhibition had been staged to mark the first forty years of his reign, and it had been an unexpected success. The outside world now knew that Romania was no longer a Ruritanian backwater but a kingdom with a navigable Danube, steelworks, bridges, railways, and roads galore, as well as a fledgling oil industry. It was still an overwhelmingly agricultural country, but for all the enduring poverty of its peasants, it was no longer bankrupt. The Romania of the 1900s was a good credit risk, in the eyes of the foreign banking community. But its reputation was shattered a year later, by the "peasants' revolt," which Ceauşescu's historians, later, were to see exclusively in Marxist terms. "The big peasant revolt of 1907," one of them wrote, "turned into a bloodbath by the rich classes, stirred [Ceauşescu's] childlike imagination and contributed to the molding of his character."[5]

The truth was rather different. In a society that limited access of Jews to certain professions, moneylending had become, especially in the countryside, a largely Jewish preserve. No Romanian banks were interested in acquiring a clientele of poor peasants borrowing pathetically small sums and offering no collateral of any kind. As in present-day rural India, the moneylender was often their only recourse. Inevitably, this bred a crude form of anti-Semitism. Similarly, many Jews, seeking ways out of ghetto poverty to respectability and whatever social promotion *was* available to them, took on jobs as stewards, administering the large estates of mostly absentee landlords. All over rural Romania, Jews had been hired to watch over the interests of landowners, to such an extent that certain parts of Moldavia were called Fischerland, after the name of the zealous Jewish steward administering the huge estates of a Moldavian landowning family there.

The 1907 peasants' revolt began as a protest against the inhuman conditions that prevailed at the time. Almost inevitably, it took the form of an initial pogrom before escalating into a generalized attack on the landowners themselves, with the peasants invading the towns and attacking the landlords in their luxurious mansions, in an orgy of arson and destruction. The revolt spread, a state of siege was declared in Bucharest, the army was mobilized, and a brutal repression followed. For months, wealthy Romanians feared for their lives, and the climate was so uncertain that many wives and families of aristocratic Romanians were sent to the safety of mountain resorts like those in Sinaia, high in the Carpathian Mountains. Here, at the Posada home of Marthe Bibesco, then only nineteen years old, who enjoyed at the time a precocious-writer status rather similar to that later assumed by Françoise Sagan in France, Princess Marie met Barbu and Nadejda Ştirbey. The meeting changed her life.

It so happened that Ştirbey's sister, Elise, was married to Ion Brătianu Jr., son of the kingmaker and now King Carol's trusted prime minister. Elise and Marie became firm friends and in due course Marie fell in love with Prince Ştirbey. The king, reconciled to the separate private lives of Ferdinand and Marie, at first regarded this liaison with disapproval but made no effort to banish Ştirbey from the court. Ştirbey was appointed superintendent of the crown estates, which afforded him even greater legitimate daily contact with Marie. For the first time, she was brought into direct contact with the old king to discuss matters of state. Ştirbey, aware of Princess Marie's sharp mind, for all her anti-intellectualism, became her political mentor and lifelong adviser, and now, for the first time, King Carol began to be aware of Marie's qualities of decisiveness and common sense. Had it not been for the Marie-Ştirbey relationship, it is likely that the course of Romanian history would have been even more disastrous.

It was a testing time for the old, ailing king. In 1912 a coalition of Bulgarians, Serbs, and Greeks had gone to war

against Turkey, giving this moribund empire its virtual coup
de grace. Then Bulgaria, flexing its muscles, had turned on its
former allies and, in 1913, attacked *them*. Romania joined in
against Bulgaria, too late to fight but not too late for its army
to suffer large casualties as a result of a cholera epidemic.
Princess Marie made her mark as a hospital organizer, taking
enormous health risks, and this, more than anything else, restored her tarnished image and endeared her to King Carol I.

Then, a year later, came the Sarajevo murder of Austrian
crown prince Franz Ferdinand, plunging the whole of Europe
into war. Germany, allied to the Austro-Hungarians, attacked
France in the west and Russia in the east. The German-Austro-
Hungarian Central Powers confidently expected Romania to
side with them and mobilize against Russia, arguing not only
the existence of the secret treaty of 1883 but King Carol I's
own German origins and predilections. His wife, Queen Elizabeth, was, if anything, more hawkish than her husband.

But if the Romanian king and queen were sentimentally
pro-German (and, moreover, believed that the overwhelming
superiority of the Austro-Hungarian and German forces
would lead to a quick victory), the rest of the country was not.
To most Romanians, the enemy was the Austro-Hungarian
Empire, that long-standing oppressor of the Romanian ethnic
minority in Transylvania. What made the Sarajevo murder so
tragic for many was the fact that the late Franz Ferdinand had
been in favor of a Transylvanian settlement and had spoken
out in the past many times against the Romanian minority's
persecution. It was simply not in the cards for Romanians to
accept an alliance with a country that was a hereditary enemy
as an oppressor of ethnic Romanians under alien rule. Moreover, Romania had for decades regarded France as its cultural
mentor. The lingua franca of educated Romanians was
French; Paris, their spiritual home.

There was also the Marie-Ştirbey factor. Sentimentally,
Princess Marie was firmly on the side of the Allies, but she was
also convinced Germany would be defeated and that Romania
had everything to gain by siding with the Allies from the start
of the war. At Castle Peleş, there was a heated discussion with
King Carol and his wife, Queen Elizabeth, who were all in

favor of an intervention on Germany's side. Marie stood firm. A leading conservative politician, Take Jonescu, just back from London, had been called in to give his assessment of the situation, and said, in no uncertain terms, that England would enter the war "with her last man and her last shilling." Marie turned to Queen Elizabeth. "You hear what he says, aunt," she said. To Jonescu, she added: "That is what I tell them all the time, and they refuse to understand it. They understand nothing in this house."[6]

King Carol was not deterred: At a royal council meeting on the following day, August 4, 1914, he explained that public opinion would never condone a Romanian-Russian alliance after what the tsar had done to Bessarabia. Neutrality would be interpreted as impotence. The only alternative, combining honor and self-interest, compelled Romania to side with the Central Powers.

Almost all those present were horrified, and expressed themselves with unusual frankness. Some questioned the very existence of the 1883 treaty, denying it any validity; others said such a course would lead to civil war. Crown prince Ferdinand, asked to express his own view, disappointed Romania's ministers by his indecisive, deliberately ambiguous remarks. King Carol allowed his frustrations to overcome his usual reserve. "You cannot imagine," he said after the meeting, "how bitter it is to find oneself isolated in a country of which one is not a native." Aware of the dilemma, he continued to weigh a possible Romanian course acceptable to him and to his countrymen. It was never resolved, for two months later, on October 9, 1914, he died in his sleep. Ferdinand was now king and, more important for Romania's future, Marie was queen. The Romanians, aware of her sympathies, which coincided with theirs, cheered themselves hoarse.

From the moment Ferdinand became king, it was clear to most Romanians that the perennially indecisive new monarch, under the influence of his pro-Entente politicians and of his wife, would eventually be persuaded to bring Romania into the war on the Allied side. Romania's neutrality lasted for two years, longer than most observers expected, and the haggling involved upset not only Germany but the Allies as well. Queen

Marie was used as a discreet conduit to sound out both Britain
and Russia on the price to be extracted. As a first cousin to
both Tsar Nicolas and King George V, she was in an admirable position to write personal letters to both royal families,
which were then passed on to their respective governments
and policy makers. The price was high: Romania expected a
return to the fold not only of Transylvania but also of Bucovina, the territory northwest of Moldavia, and Banat, the province in the southwest, and here its historical claims were shaky,
to say the least. It also hoped that in return for its support of
Russia, the province of Bessarabia would be returned to Romania. To all parties, such terms seemed exorbitant, the haggling undignified. Meanwhile, neutrality suited Romania, for
both warring camps were short of food and bought what Romania had to sell at inflated prices, in order to deny the other
the opportunity of doing so. Fortunes were made, nouveaux
riches abounded, and even the peasantry benefited to some
extent from the unexpected prosperity. Finally, in August
1916, Romanian demands were met in full. Romania declared
war, and promptly invaded Transylvania. King Ferdinand
could not forget his German roots, and his emotional an-
nouncement of impending hostilities reflected his gloom and
foreboding. As the Count de Saint-Aulaire, French ambassador in Bucharest at the time, recorded, he seemed "ravaged by
an interior struggle, his voice cut with sobs, his hands trem-
bling."

   To hard-eyed realpolitik experts in both the Allied and the
Central Powers camps, the Romanian decision appeared to be
not only opportune but opportunistic, for it coincided both
with the Allies' Somme offensive in the west and a major Russian push on Germany's eastern front. With hindsight, however, it became clear that Romania had entered the war both
too late and with insufficient preparation. Within months, the
situation had become calamitous.

   The reasons for the debacle were numerous: a lack of
modern weapons and equipment in the hastily trained Romanian army, previously dependent on German materiel; broken promises of support by both the French and British
governments, which were too hard-pressed to open up an-

other front with long lines of communications; superior German generalship; and the halfheartedness of the Russian troops, which moved into northeastern Romania but left the Romanian armies to do the fighting. Last but not least, Bulgaria's decision, along with Turkey's, to enter the war on Germany's side, attacking Romania on her southeastern flank, made the odds against a successful Romanian campaign almost insurmountable. By October 1916, Romania had not only lost the territory hastily occupied in Transylvania at the outset of hostilities but was in retreat everywhere. A combined Bulgarian, Turkish, and German force occupied Constanța, Romania's only major port, in October 1916. By November Queen Marie, along with the wives and families of all those who could afford to do so, had left threatened Bucharest for Iași, the provincial capital of Moldavia, only ten miles south of the Russian border. King Ferdinand left Bucharest on December 2, 1916. Four days later, the Germans moved in. The humiliation was complete.

Worse was to come: The winter of 1916–17 was the most severe in fifty years, the Germans requisitioned everything in sight, the Romanian people starved, both in the occupied and unoccupied areas, and even Marie found herself feeding her family beans.

Miraculously, her personal popularity remained intact, but that was due to her numerous visits to units and hospitals. The twenty-three-year-old crown prince, Carol, though a serving officer, was beginning to display the emotional weakness that was to make him, later, the laughingstock of his countrymen. Though his mother repeatedly urged him to visit the front, he stayed in Iași, following Zizi Lambrino, his *inamorata,* around like a lapdog.

Then, after persistent warning signals, Russia entered revolutionary anarchy. On March 15, 1917, Tsar Nicholas abdicated, and the provisional government that followed very quickly showed it had the backing neither of its people nor of its army. Relations between Romanian and Russian units, never good, deteriorated still further. Romanian officers, with good reason, accused the Russians, well equipped compared to their own troops, of limiting their armed forays to depre-

dations on Romanian warehouses and assaults on Romanian
women. Revolutionary ideas rapidly swept through Russian
army ranks, and a Bolshevik Russian unit swept through Iaşi,
calling on its citizens to rise up against the Romanian monarchy. Fearing quick contagion, King Ferdinand and his government promised sweeping reforms after the war. Two
adventurous individuals did what they could to restore morale. General Henri Berthelot, the French military mission
commander (he was so fat a small crane had to be operated to
drop him in his saddle) set about retraining the Romanian
army with an elite group of French officers and NCOs, making considerable impact. As wily as he was obese, Berthelot set
up a pipeline of French weapons, equipment, and supplies to
Romania through Russia, now in turmoil. In Ploeşti, Colonel
Sir John Norton-Griffiths, an engineer on a British secret service mission, succeeded in blowing up the Ploeşti oil fields in
the face of the invading Germans.

By July 1917, Berthelot's efforts had paid off sufficiently
for the Romanians to attempt a counteroffensive, and Queen
Marie managed to pry Prince Carol away from Zizi long
enough for him to visit the front to contribute to morale. But
once again the Russians proved that with allies like them, enemies were superfluous: They failed to provide adequate support for the brave, dogged Romanian infantry, whose advance
turned into a series of desperate rearguard actions. The retreating Romanian troops were left trying to prevent the Germans from reaching Iaşi itself. There was to be one more
glorious, quixotic Romanian feat of arms at Mărăşeşti, in August 1917. Here the French-trained remnants of the Romanian army defeated the Austrians and the Germans, staving
off a German occupation of Odessa. "In spite of the bad example of the Russians, who had mostly turned Bolshevik and
were daily abandoning their positions by the thousand, our
soldiers, underfed, insufficiently armed and hardly ever relieved, remained staunch to a man, unshaken among the *debacle* of their erstwhile allies," Queen Marie wrote.

It was a swan song: By September, the Romanian forces
were unable to mount even a minor offensive and were fully
occupied with defending their positions. On November 6,

1917, Lenin, the uncontested leader of the Russian revolution, overthrew the Kerensky government and called for a cease-fire, including negotiations with Germany. Overnight, the Russian so-called allies became not just neutral but officially hostile. Ferdinand and Marie had contemplated fleeing Iași for Russia should the Germans overrun the whole of Romania. Now that escape route was impracticable. Queen Marie was also desperately concerned by the news of the disappearance of the Russian royal family. She was, after all, directly related to the tsar through her mother, a Russian grand-duchess and sister to Nicholas.

Among the Russian troops stationed on the Russo-Romanian border, chaos reigned. Thousands deserted. Pro-tsarist officers were murdered by Bolsheviks, and revolutionary officers took command in unit after unit. Revolutionary Russian troops even threatened to turn against Romania and overthrow the regime, exporting the Bolshevik revolution. What was left of the Romanian army now closed ranks to protect Romania against such an invasion. Once more, the Romanian army, almost entirely drawn from the peasantry, displayed its dogged courage, and the Bolshevik troops very quickly abandoned all plans for an invasion. But the situation was untenable: A cease-fire was proclaimed on December 6, 1917, and a separate armistice signed with Germany three days later. As a result, both Britain and America decided that the Romanian conditions exacted from the Allies as a price for entering the war were now null and void.

The German terms of victory were harsh, leading to immediate famine and what was intended to be long-term economic subjugation. Romania lost Dobruja and most of Transylvania; Romanian oil was to be run by an Austro-German consortium for ninety years, and all agricultural produce earmarked for Germany for the next decade, while bankrupt Romania was to pay for a German army of occupation on its soil. The only bright side to the debacle was that the Germans allowed Romania to retain Bessarabia, which had not, at this stage, taken the Bolshevik route and whose moderate National Democratic Party opted for autonomy and links with Romania. Distraught, Queen Marie urged her husband to abdicate rather than have anything to do with conquerors, but he refused, appointing a pro-German cabinet from the ranks of some of the politicians, mostly conservatives, who had always shown a slight pro-German streak.

On January 26, 1918, in the village of Scornicești, in German-occupied Walachia, a third son, Nicolae, was born to Alexandra Ceaușescu, a small-time farmer's wife, and Andruța, her husband. Five days later, Bolshevik Russia declared war on Romania and announced that it had expropriated all the gold bullion and crown jewels the Romanian king had sent there earlier in the war for safekeeping.

# CHAPTER THREE

# MARXISTS AND KINGS

**Q**UEEN MARIE'S GRIEF DID NOT LAST LONG. Nine months later, it was the turn of the defeated Germans and the Austro-Hungarians to sue for peace. Ferdinand and Marie returned to Bucharest to an emotional welcome, but the problems left in the wake of the disastrous war remained. The American ambassador reported that of all the Allied nations, Romania had suffered most. Ceaușescu's official biographers have made much of the dire poverty of Nicolae's early years, but it should be remembered that rich or poor, all Romanians suffered horribly long after November 11, 1918, the official end of the war. Not only had the occupying Germans plundered the country as strutting conquerors. They had also stripped it bare on departure. For once, the peasants were probably marginally better off than townspeople, for famine, typhus, and cholera took an enormous toll on the country's urban population. In any event, Romania's wartime partners, especially President Woodrow Wilson, who hated all the Romanian politicians and personalities he ever met (including even Queen Marie), did not seem overly concerned about its plight.

Romania could not afford the luxury of reconstruction. While the other Allies demobilized, Romanian troops were called up to fight again, this time in Hungary. Romania wanted to make certain that its allies' pledges (involving the return to Romania of Hungarian-speaking provinces) would not be forgotten. So immediately after the war, Romanian troops moved into Transylvania, where on December 1, 1918, at a huge mass meeting, Transylvanians declared their union with Romania— commemorated in the post-Ceauşescu era by the adoption of December 1 as Romania's National Day. There was an additional motive for the Romanian troop move: with Germany's defeat, the Bolshevik Revolution had made converts elsewhere. In Hungary, a revolutionary movement headed by Béla Kun, a disciple of Lenin, had made considerable headway—and Romania was determined to crush this Marxist uprising on her western flank. The Allies, with other more immediate problems, believed Béla Kun's revolution was doomed, but he surprised the world by moving into Czechoslovakia as well. The "powers," assembling in Versailles to carve up the world, made their disapproval of Romania clear. But Queen Marie, dispatched to Paris and London to plead Romania's cause, proved an outstanding public relations advocate, and in the end, after a series of complicated negotiations, Romania obtained all it had demanded on going to war in 1916—and more.

With no international mandate, Romania fought and defeated Béla Kun, its armies behaving, perhaps understandably, as brutally as had the Hungarian and German troops in occupied Romania. The victory over Béla Kun was later to embarrass Ceauşescu's historians. The Romanian armies that crushed him were anticommunist. Their action, however, resulted in the return of Transylvania to Romania—an event glorified in Ceauşescu's history books. This kind of ambiguity toward the past extended to the Romanian revolutionary movement as a whole. It was compounded by an overnight increase in population: Suddenly Romania, as a result of its postwar spoils, had 8.5 million more people to deal with. Inevitably, among the new Romanians were revolutionaries and Marxists the established order could have done without.

It so happens that in order to pay off old scores among his former mentors, Ceauşescu, shortly after coming to power, put historians to work at writing the unvarnished story of the period leading up to the end of the Second World War. The project was never completed, and the series of books planned was not published. Many of the findings remained secret in Romania, but a number of brilliant historians, among them Michael Shafir and Mary Ellen Fischer, have gained access to the material and were able to anatomize the early days of Romanian socialism and communism. Distinguished Romanian historians engaged in the project, like professor Ion Ardeleanu, have also written about this period and were kind enough to talk to me at great length.

The most striking aspect of the findings is that practically all of the early leading leftist leaders were not, strictly speaking, Romanian at all. Constantin Dobrogeanu-Gherea was born Solomon Katz in the Ukraine; Christian Rakowsky was a Bulgarian. The fact that many of these revolutionaries were Jewish branded them as foreigners in the eyes of the proverbially anti-Semitic Romanians. A later study of the RCP membership[1] would reveal that in the 1930s, 26 percent were Hungarian, 22 percent Romanian, 18 percent Jewish, 10 percent Russian and Ukrainian, 8 percent Bulgarian, and 10 percent "other nationalities." Such a cosmopolitan "mix" was bound to result in rival groups and differing ideological shades within the Romanian Communist party itself. There were also graver consequences. The existence of so many "foreigners" fostered the myth of Judeo-Bolshevism and encouraged Romanians to believe that alien forces, especially from Hungary and the Soviet Union, were constantly plotting against them. The reaction to all this was a crude, often inarticulate form of nationalism, which would be exploited by many future Romanian leaders and politicians, not least by Nicolae Ceaușescu.

More important still, the overt number of leftists was tiny. Though socialist ideas spread throughout Romanian cities at the turn of the twentieth century (the socialist paper *Adevărul*—Truth—was established in 1903), it is essential to remember that the very concept of socialism in Romania at the beginning of the twentieth century was enthusiastically endorsed only by a very small minority. In any case, the left-wing organizations, including the later RCP, were not so much political parties as congregations of dedicated men and women operating in almost total isolation amidst the general indifference of the population and the well-established Liberal, Conservative, and Peasant parties. As George Schöpflin, another expert, put it in a BBC radio talk on the RCP's fiftieth anniversary, "the early days of Romanian communism were a rather haphazard affair. Marxist ideas remained confined to small groups of intellectuals. This failure to establish links of any kind with the people remained a fatal weakness in the Romanian communist movement throughout the period before the RCP takeover of 1944."

"Between 1917 and 1921," says Schöpflin, "the left wing in Romania remained in a state of confusion." The Béla Kun phenomenon accounted for part of the disarray, for some of the earliest Romanian communists had served his cause, becoming traitors in the eyes of other left-wingers, for whom the return of Transylvania to Romania was more important than any ideology. The idealism of some of these communist activists was highly suspect. In December 1918, a left-wing mob demonstrated outside the royal palace in Bucharest, demanding the end of the dynasty and the setting up of a republic. Among those arrested were Soviet "agitators" and even German agents—the same German agents who, just before the end of the war in 1918, had distributed communist tracts and even financed the establishment of communist schools as a means of destabilization and disinformation. However, as one former secret policeman revealed decades later,[2] many of the so-called communist agitators were informers in the pay of the Romanian police.

The confusion was compounded, once the Marxist-Leninist Soviet regime became more self-assured, by the short-sightedness of Lenin and Stalin, for whom all communist parties, especially those in sensitive neighboring countries, had the sacred mission of furthering the interests of the Soviet Union—if necessary, at their own countries' expense. The Romanian communists were split between moderates and "maximalists," the latter responding unquestioningly to Soviet demands. The maximalists staged general strikes in 1920, blew up the senate building in Bucharest, and generally alienated all but a hard core of fanatical pro-Soviet revolutionaries. Soon, the maximalists found it necessary to operate outside Romania, becoming known as the Odessa group (Rakowsky was their leader; Marcel Pauker, their foremost ideologue). Needless to say, many ended up before Stalin's firing squads (Marcel Pauker, Rakowsky) or in gulags. They became progressively alienated from their colleagues inside Romania, their jobs and responsibilities reflecting Stalin's total indifference to the conditions then prevailing within Romania. Thus, Rakowsky became head of Soviet Ukraine, tried to steer it into war with Romania in support of Béla Kun, and later headed the exiled communist Bessarabian "government" at a time when, overwhelmingly, Romanians of almost all convictions and creeds believed that Bessarabia's Romanian link was one of the few positive results of the war. Rakowsky showed that his Romanian label was one of convenience only, for he later became Soviet ambassador to Paris (1926–27) before his trial and execution, in 1938, in Moscow—one of Stalin's many loyal servants and supporters who ended up as a victim.

Stalin was to show equal contempt for the needs and preferences of the RCP as such. Zinoviev and Bukharin, in those early days still Stalin's loyal, unquestioning partners, rebuked the Romanian communists for not throwing their weight behind Béla Kun more forcibly. They were not true activists but only "weekend communists," imbued with "legalist delusions." Ignoring the Romanian climate, which was conservative and totally out of tune with revolutionary Marxism, they kept urging the handful of bewildered Romanian communists to set up a workers' and peasants' state, refusing to listen to the unfortunate RCP members' explanations that conditions were certainly not ripe for this kind of experiment. The RCP was urged to work for the secession of Bessarabia, or rather the "Moldavian Soviet Autonomous Republic," as a "cradle of Soviet Romania." Bukharin crudely explained to the RCP that this was a cold-blooded destabilization tactic "which had worked so well in undermining the Kerensky government in 1917." The first RCP leaders were not even Romanian. Alexandru Ştefanski, the earliest "first secretary" of the RCP, appointed directly by Stalin, was a Pole; his successor, Boris Ştefanov, was Bulgarian; *his* successor, Ştefan Foriş, an ethnic Hungarian.

Such was the climate of the tiny RCP when Nicolae Ceauşescu, apprenticed to a shoemaker in Bucharest at the age of eleven, started taking an interest in politics. But the rewriting of history reached such excessive lengths during his lifetime that the official biographies are of no real help in reconstructing his past. The truth lies elsewhere, in the eyewitness accounts of contemporaries who, half a century or more after the events, were kind enough to reminisce about their own youth and Nicolae Ceauşescu's role in their lives. I am also grateful to former official historians, once forced to accommodate the facts to serve a legend they knew was a complete fabrication, now free to speak the truth.

With Ceauşescu's downfall, the old constraints vanished. Ironically, the immediate consequence was that all those who in the past had eulogized him now promptly outdid one another in an attempt to blacken his reputation. I have tried to steer as impartial a course as possible, through careful cross-checking.

The first myth that Scorniceşti villagers and contemporaries of Nicolae Ceauşescu destroyed was that of the family's abject poverty. They were not well off. Nicolae was not, like Mao, the son of a wealthy farmer turned grain dealer. But they were by no means among the poorest members of their community, and Nicolae's contemporaries also cast doubt on the legend of the barefoot little boy working the fields by day and reading borrowed books by night to further his political education. All confirm that the Ceaușescu family finances would have been healthier had Nicolae's father, Andruța, been less addicted to drink. The long-suppressed stories, revealed after Nicolae Ceaușescu's death by his cousin Florea Ceaușescu, in Scornicești, tell of bouts of drunkenness and violence, and of Alexandra's admirable patience in coping with her growing brood at the hands of such a disreputable, unstable, notorious drunk. "Andruța would disappear for days at a time, getting drunk and whoring away in Bucharest, spending what little money the family had," he told me. The reason why, along with Nicolae, two other brothers were given the same name was simply that on both occasions Andruța was so drunk when he went to register the birth of his newly born son that Nicolae was the only name he could come up with. "The Ceaușescu children didn't like working in the fields any more than their father," said a former neighbor who remembers those early days.

The village schoolmaster who taught young Nicolae neither remembers the boy's brilliance nor confirms the legend of a "radical" schoolmaster who, in the official biographies, is supposed to have made him socially conscious at an early age. In fact, Nicolae's formal education, apart from a couple of later spells in communist seminars, was confined to elementary school. The eventual exodus of most of his brothers and sisters to Bucharest resulted less from the dire poverty he claimed than from a need to escape a home ruled by a raging, drunken father and the poor prospects of a better future at hand: Under Romanian law, property was shared out equally among male heirs. The small holding would have been wholly uneconomic after Andruța's death if all the sons had stayed on the land. As Mary Ellen Fischer points out, this may have been one of the factors that led Ceaușescu, in his later years, to prefer large communal farms to small privately owned ones, for his had hardly been a bucolic existence, and rural life as he remembered it can have held few positive memories.

Despite the Great Depression of 1929, the exodus of many people from the countryside to the towns was not exclusively the consequence of poverty: It also embodied the quest for opportunity. The Ceaușescu brothers and sisters who went to Bucharest as adolescents all, except for Nicolae, found reasonably comfortable "niches" in the economy. Bucharest in the 1930s afforded hope to the landless young, provided they had a modicum of education. One of Nicolae's sisters became a schoolteacher; another worked in a department store. On Elena Ceaușescu's family's side, a sister cadged a part-time job as a barmaid in a quite well known café called the Bodega Lui Iancu, at 214 Ghencea Street, and ended up running it. She became quite rich. The place would become a hangout for both the Petrescu and the Ceaușescu young.

In Bucharest, Nicolae lived with his sister, Niculina, whose husband, Ion Rusescu, was a cobbler. Adela, the sister-in-law of Elena Petrescu, whom Nicolae was later to meet, court and then (in 1946) marry, was Jewish and indeed a fervent Marxist. But all of Nicolae's contemporaries reject the notion that Adela was in any way responsible for his converson to communism. They also reject the mythologized version of his early prominence in the Young Communists' League, as does the eminent historian Ion Ardeleanu, former director of the Museum of the History of the Romanian Communist Party which is now closed. Over the years, as an antidote to the propaganda exercise he was compelled to fuel, Ardeleanu kept his own file on Nicolae Ceaușescu, including all of the facts about the later Conducător it was unwise, or illicit, to reveal during Ceaușescu's lifetime. Among the file's fascinating contents, which Ardeleanu kept locked in a desk drawer, is the police-blotter photostat of Ceaușescu's earliest arrest, on November 23, 1933. Hailed in all the histories and biographies as an example of his ardent early conversion to communism, the photostat (which spells his name Necolae Ciaușescu) reveals that the arrest was for street brawling rather than political activity. There was a strike of the Mihăilescu workshops at the time, but as Professor Ardeleanu put it, "Nicolae got involved for the violence rather than for the ideology." What Nicolae's contemporaries recall about those early days in Bucharest was his penchant for violence and his unfocused rage.

Professor Ardeleanu says the likelihood that Nicolae worked sufficiently diligently to actually learn how to make or mend shoes is improbable, for he was constantly on the streets. In 1966, Ceaușescu's sister told Ardeleanu[3] that after an escapade that had lasted several days, her husband slapped the fifteen-year-old's face and said, "Whatever will we do with you if you fail to learn a trade?" "Nene," (Uncle) Nicolae replied. "I won't need a trade. I'm going to be Romania's Stalin." This, Ardeleanu says, was proof of his "will to power" rather than of his ideology. "He was very eager to be where the action was on the streets," says Ardeleanu, "and he didn't mind what kind of action it was." His membership in the Young Communists' League, he adds, came after flirtations with other political youth movements, including the socialists, the Peasant party, and even, perhaps, the fascist Iron Guard.

The most eloquent, reliable eyewitness to those early Ceaușescu years is Mihai Popescu, a contemporary of Nicolae's who had been an early communist convert and had been sentenced to fourteen months' detention in a remand home for minors in Cluj for spreading communist propaganda at the age of fourteen. "I was released before Christmas 1934, and realized that both my school and university career were over before they had even begun, and that I had no choice but to become a worker. I got a job in a leather-processing factory, and became a trade union member in the shoemakers' union."

There, says Popescu, now a retired executive of a foreign-trade promotion firm and (in 1937–39) personal secretary to Ion Gheorghe Maurer, a leading lawyer who would later become a communist convert and Ceaușescu's prime minister, "I met a youngster whom everyone despised. I really don't want to speak badly of him, but that was the truth. Nicolae Ceaușescu was officious, always pretending to be more important than he really was, immersed in trade-union gossip, and completely uninteresting. He was dull, physically unprepossessing, on the small side, and afflicted with a risible stammer, which was so bad that people avoided him—they didn't want to laugh in his face. His stammering spasms were sometimes so violent that his leg would twitch uncontrollably to the rhythm of the stammer, and this got on people's nerves." Popescu says that as a fifteen-year-old with a jail record for communist activity, he looked down on this unimpressive "par-

venu" but feared his unpredictable rages. Popescu is adamant
that at this stage in his life, Nicolae Ceauşescu neither studied
nor read anything. "I doubt whether he even looked at chil-
drens' comic books," he told me. Ceauşescu's official biography mentions the conference of antifascist campaigners of
Romania that Ceauşescu is supposed to have attended as a
"representative of the democratic youth of Romania," and
virtually all of the authorized biographies mention that Nicolae Ceauşescu, at the unusually tender age of fifteen, was
elected a member of Romania's national antifascist committee.
Nonsense, says Professor Ardeleanu. The Ceauşescu involved
was not Nicolae but his elder brother Marin, also a shoemaker's apprentice. To prevent him ever contradicting the official
version of Nicolae's precocious record as a youth leader,
Marin, who was widely believed to have been in charge of
Nicolae Ceauşescu's financial holdings abroad, was in later
years deliberately kept out of the limelight. Shortly after Nicolae Ceauşescu's death, Marin was found hanged in the Romanian embassy in Vienna, an official suicide.

The early 1930s, with young Nicolae Ceauşescu roaming
the streets, picking fights, and sampling the relative advantages of the young liberals' and young peasants' organizations
before opting for the Young Communists' League, were de-
pressing for those Romanians who had hoped that the unexpectedly fortunate outcome of the First World War settlement
would lead to a morally regenerated, as well as physically
greater, Romania. In Bessarabia, there were serious complaints of mismanagement and corruption. In Transylvania,
Romanians displaced successful Hungarians in a vindictive
show of revenge, evicting Hungarian landlords and taking
over local banks and businesses. The seemingly inter-
changeable—almost equally corrupt and ineffectual—Liberal
and Peasant parties continued to dominate Romanian politics.
The 1929 Great Depression took its toll. Inevitably, in Romania as indeed in Germany, financial hardship was blamed on
the Jews.

The Iron Guard phenomenon was, like all ultraright
movements, in part a reaction against conventional right-wing
parties that had failed to deliver the goods. It came to prom-

inence in the late 1920s, becoming a power to be reckoned with in 1930. Its mystic leader, Corneliu Zelea Codreanu, founder of the League of the Archangel Michael, as the Iron Guard movement was officially called, used to ride around on horseback brandishing an icon, encouraging peasants to believe he was actually a reincarnation of the archangel Gabriel. The movement, backed first by Mussolini's Fascists and later by the Nazi party, pandered to Romanian anti-Semitism, called for industrialization and entrepreneurial action, vilified all political parties, and was subsidized by large numbers of industrialists.

The mainstream political parties were certainly open to all kinds of criticism, but it was the gossip about crown prince Carol that turned Romania, in the 1930s, into the world's laughingstock. Had the prince been a swashbuckling rake, there would have been less scandal. The irony was that Carol's "affairs"—though risible—became serious affairs of state because of his weakness and emotional dependence on the series of women he fell in love with. There had been Zizi Lambrino, whom he had eloped to Odessa with in the darkest days of the First World War, becoming, technically, a deserter. Zizi remained his "official" friend, but he also had a much publicized affair with a milliner's daughter, whom Queen Marie paid off and protected. Then Zizi gave birth to his baby in 1920, and Carol, aware of the consequences involved, not only failed to recognize the child but never even visited. Shortly afterward, Zizi and her unfortunate baby faded from public view, having extracted a suitable financial settlement from the royal family.

Carol then appeared to turn over a new leaf, and married Princess Helen of Greece with great pomp, shortly after his sister Elisabeta married the Greek crown prince, George, and on October 25, 1921, Helen gave birth to Mihai (Michael). Almost immediately afterward the marriage floundered. Recuperating from a difficult childbirth, Princess Helen went to Greece, and while she was away Prince Carol met Elena (Magda) Lupescu, the attractive young divorcée of an army officer, who consciously threw herself at him. Once more, he fell head over heels in love. As he had in 1917, Carol behaved impulsively, secretly leaving the country to meet up with Lupescu in

Milan and then moving to Paris with her, holing up in a hotel suite. There was no talk of marriage at this stage. Queen Helen was still Carol's legal wife—and would not obtain a divorce until 1928.

Carol's extramarital adventures inevitably made front-page news all over the world. British tabloids, especially, had a field day. Refusing to give up Lupescu (née Wolff, and Jewish; her name had been romanized), Carol settled with her in Paris, and he renounced all rights to the throne—but not for long.

On July 19, 1927, King Ferdinand died, and Michael, aged five years and nine months, was appointed king under a regency council. He was almost as young as the ill-fated Pu Yi, the last emperor of China. By this time Carol was bored with exile, with Paris, with money problems, and with Lupescu's wheedling, crying fits, and constant complaining. He was determined to get his throne back.

He behaved with a characteristic lack of scruple. He had entered Britain normally, as a private citizen, but his first attempt to fly back to Bucharest failed: A newspaper stunt underwritten by Lord Rothermere, it collapsed when the British government denied him the right to take off by plane from British soil, and expelled him. The British Foreign Office had no desire to encourage allegations (that would doubtless have been made in the popular British press) that it was aiding and abetting him in his attempt to recover the throne. But Carol was typically Romanian in his skill at intrigue and double-dealing. To the upright new prime minister, the Peasant party leader Iuliu Maniu, he pledged that if allowed to return, he would not reclaim the throne but would accept the post of co-regent, ditch Lupescu for good, and stage a reconciliation with Princess Helen. Maniu was trusting and foolish enough to believe him. Returning to Bucharest in June 1930, to the delight of every tabloid newspaper in the world, Carol promptly broke every one of his promises. He proclaimed himself king and installed Lupescu in not one but two discreet houses, which he visited constantly. A disgusted Maniu promptly resigned. "I cannot help thinking he is mad. . . . One wonders what he will do next," King George V wrote to Carol's brokenhearted mother.

Had King Carol II confined himself to looking after la Lupescu, the newspapers, and his Romanian subjects, might have tired of the story and eventually forgotten about it. But the new king underwent a personality change in his new role, not unlike that observed in Ceauşescu after he had accumulated all party and presidential titles. Carol surrounded himself with sycophants who pandered to his vanity, people like Princess Marthe Bibesco, who addressed Lupescu as Ma Souveraine. Princess Bibesco, a social climber and turncoat, never could resist mingling with important people, as she was to prove during the German occupation of Paris during World War II. A maverick backbench Conservative British MP, Hector Bolitho, was a great fan of Carol's, and after a tour of Romania he would write an obsequious biography of the king almost as nauseatingly servile as those penned by Ceauşescu's later biographers. Many unscrupulous business deals were carried out under Carol's tolerant eye, involving shady financiers who showed their gratitude by remitting large sums abroad in Carol's name.

More ominously, King Carol began an ambiguous relationship with Codreanu and contributed to the Iron Guard finances. In November 1933, Jean Duca, an unusually upright politician and Peasant party leader, became prime minister, ending a long period of Liberal party rule. He promptly cracked down on the Iron Guard, arresting thousands of its members on December 9, 1933. Three weeks later, Duca was murdered at the Sinaia railway station after visiting the king. His murderers openly boasted about their crime, and one of them was hidden in a house belonging to a relative of Lupescu's. King Carol's subsidies to the Iron Guard continued.

Carol displayed a vindictive streak toward all those who had offended him in the past. At the top of the list was Barbu Ştirbey, who knew him too well—through Queen Marie—to trust him. He was forced into exile. Carol terminated his mother's civil list pension, expropriating it for himself. He kept his ex-wife, Princess Helen (who had divorced him in 1928), a

virtual prisoner, banning from the court all those brave
enough to visit her, until she could take it no longer and fled
the country. Queen Marie was among the handful who saw
her off at Bucharest's Gare du Nord. (Princess Helen retali-
ated later with a vicious article about Carol's misdeeds in the
*Daily Mail.*) "If you did not fawn on Carol," wrote Hannah
Pakula, "you were his enemy." It was one of several traits
Ceauşescu, in his later years, would share with the controversial, unstable king.

Carol went one step further than Ceauşescu at his most
megalomaniacal, decorating those who had commiserated
with him during his exile with the "Order of Suffering" (*La
Décoration de la Souffrance*), a white enamel medallion with two
interlocking *C*s under a royal crown encircled by thorns.[4] In
such an unhealthy, absurdly baroque political climate, it was
no wonder that tiny communist cells sprang up in Romania in
the early thirties. Ceauşescu, the angry young man with a chip
on his shoulder and a determination to make his mark, became a small-scale communist youth activist in 1933.

It was a year of unrest, culminating in a series of communist strikes and demonstrations. The Youth League of the
RCP had nothing to do with their organization. The man who
inspired and led the outbreaks was a burly railway worker,
Gheorghe Gheorghiu-Dej, who had just been elected
secretary-general of the railwaymen's union. Born in 1901,
Gheorghiu-Dej did not actually join the RCP until he was
thirty, but long before that he had been active in various
unions, as a worker in a timber mill and a textile factory. He
became an electrician for the railways shortly before he became a party member. Railway workers were among the few
solidly unionized groups in the country, and they had a major
grievance: As nominal civil servants, they were not allowed to
strike. Gheorghiu-Dej organized a strike anyway on February
2, 1934, and was promptly arrested. The following day, workers stormed the railway workshops at Griviţa, a suburb of
Bucharest, and remained in occupation there until eleven days
later, when the army was called in and reoccupied the buildings. Shots were fired, workers were killed, and the Griviţa
legend was born. It marked the arrival of Gheorghiu-Dej as a

"coming man" on the RCP scene, especially since *real* working-class leaders were few. The RCP of the thirties was dominated by intellectuals, many of them Jews, which had not helped its cause with average anti-Semitic Romanians.

Gheorghiu-Dej immediately became one of Nicolae Ceaușescu's two heros. There were obvious affinities between them: Both were from authentic working-class backgrounds, neither was Jewish, both had started their working-class lives as shoemakers' apprentices. Ceaușescu's other hero was Stalin, against whom he could not hear a word of criticism without an angry, stuttering rejoinder, sometimes followed by physical violence. His outlook at this time, according to Professor Arde-leanu, who debriefed several contemporaries, was "very limited," and his inarticulate anger mirrored that of the equally "limited" Iron Guards. He had no "intellectual" doubts about Stalin, his contemporaries said, and those among them who voiced concern at Stalin's brutal methods were treated scornfully. The "moral" concept of right or wrong meant nothing to him, one contemporary said. What mattered in Nicolae's eyes was that Stalin was changing the face of the Soviet Union. The end justified the means, and the methods used were not only justified but necessary. When the time came, the RCP should treat the "decadent, cosmopolitan" Romanians in the same way.

In 1934 Gheorghiu-Dej's trial took place, and Ceaușescu was arrested for distributing tracts calling for the accused workers' acquittal, given a light sentence, and ordered back to Scornicești. He soon returned to Bucharest.

He was held very briefly once, shortly afterward, with a batch of young communists, among them Mihai Popescu, who takes up the story. "The police had an anticommunist department and they were in the habit of picking up people, holding them without charges for a short time, and then letting them go. No one was interrogated and there was no police violence. It usually happened just before May first, the aim being to prevent us from organizing demonstrations or rallies. We knew we only had to wait till after May first and we would get out. It was no big deal. We were kept together. Nicolae Ceaușescu was among those picked up, and I remember those seven days chiefly because of the fuss he caused. He would put a wall between himself and others, but occasionally he would blow up in a very provocative manner. He was very hot-tempered, always in a rage. We wanted to calm him down because we knew we would be released almost immediately and didn't want anything to happen that would prevent this. On the other hand, we didn't dare interfere, because we were afraid we would only aggravate his fits of temper." After one such arrest (involving not Ceauşescu himself but another member of the Young Communists' League, called David Constantin), a party was held and a group photograph was taken. Sitting in the front row is Alexandru Iliescu (father of the current president). Popescu is on the extreme right of the last row. Ceauşescu is on the left, standing. Even in the picture, his inner rage is visible.

In 1936 he was arrested again, probably as the result of a Party informer tipping off the police. He had already been forbidden to enter Bucharest, and in any case all RCP members could be arrested without formal charges against them on the grounds of belonging to a banned organization. Since 1924, the RCP had been declared an illegal organization for advocating the return of Bessarabia to the Soviet Union. After Ceauşescu's arrest, a trial of communists was held, not in Bucharest, but in Braşov.

An exaggerated account of this trial, too, has been incorporated into the Ceauşescu legend, with Nicolae the central figure of a historic court scene. Here too his official historians were somewhat economical with the truth. The fact was that the principal figure at the trial was a young communist called Tarnowsky. Ceauşescu was included in the same trial almost as an afterthought and, since the charges against him were minor, was expected to be freed. But Ceauşescu was determined to upstage Tarnowsky. When Tarnowsky and his co-accused walked out of the court in protest, Ceauşescu joined them, going one stage further by hurling insults at the judge as he did so. His conduct, Professor Ardeleanu noted later, was "not appreciated" by his fellow communists. Tarnowsky, Ardeleanu adds, later returned to his native province, Bessarabia, and after it had once more come under Soviet rule, he became a security officer in the service of the Moldavian republic. He repeatedly requested to be allowed to visit Romania but was constantly denied a visa. Here again, says Ardeleanu, the orders from on high were to keep him out of the country, to forestall any crumbling of the legend, which might afford anyone other than Ceauşescu a place in the Young Communists' pantheon.

A Braşov poet and journalist, Eugen Jebeleanu, had a daily column in the local paper, *Cuvîntul Liber*, at the time of the trial. "Ceauşescu is a child," he wrote, "but an intelligent child of surprising maturity. He is short, thin, with small lively eyes like peppercorns. He speaks clearly, a little too fast, wanting to say everything he knows at once. He is nineteen but his eyes have the look of someone who is ninety years old." The piece is interesting as proof that Ceauşescu had already, by this time, taken steps to control his stammer.

In jail, Ceauşescu met some senior RCP leaders (Gheorghe Apostol, Emil Bodnăraş, Vasile Luca, Miron Constantinescu) who, says Ardeleanu, "treated him like a child, protecting him and finding him teachers to instruct him not only in Marxist doctrine but in French, geography, and history." "Ceauşescu was a willing pupil but let things slide," according to Ardeleanu's sources. He made little progress in French, history, or geography but proved an assiduous pupil of Marxism.

Another detainee in Braşov was Ştefan Kostyal, who later rose to the rank of major-general. Two years younger than Ceauşescu, Kostyal was serving a two-year sentence for membership in the officially banned RCP. He remembers Nicolae well. "He wanted to be the center of attention," Kostyal said, and he was "very active in the running of the prison." For all the grim reputation of Romanian jails, its guards were susceptible to bribes, and allowed the prisoners, especially those able to pay, considerable latitude. At this time, the Soviet Union was providing the RCP with substantial funds, "so almost everyone received food parcels and cigarettes," said Kostyal, "and Nicolae would be the one who would divide everything up equally, under the supervision of the more senior party members. He was a prison trusty. The first time I saw him was when he was making the rounds of the cells to distribute food." Kostyal recalled that at the time Nicolae "had great difficulty expressing himself," and displayed an almost pathetic desire to "raise his ideological level." "Locked up with senior RCP members, he latched on to them, becoming their majordomo, their lackey. He behaved like a servant toward them. He was particularly in awe of Emil Bodnăraş and Vasile Luca." Bodnăraş, a former army cadet, had become a communist convert and Soviet spy and was serving a sentence for espionage. "Ceauşescu was very eager, very blinkered, and very sectarian in his half-baked communist beliefs." Kostyal added that "for his age, Ceauşescu behaved rather weirdly. People avoided him because he was such a bore, with absolutely no sense of humor."

After his release, in 1938, Ceauşescu returned to Bucharest, and his courtship of Elena Petrescu, or Lenuţa, as her friends called her, began. They had met earlier. In the tiny, confined Bucharest circle of working-class communists and Marxist sympathizers, it was inevitable that their paths should cross.

In many respects their family backgrounds were similar. Elena's village, Petreşti, was almost exactly like a smaller Scorniceşti. Her parents were perhaps a shade higher up on the social scale. Her father was a small farmer on rented land and also ran a hole-in-the-wall general-goods store out of their whitewashed house with black metal roofing where they sold candles and penknives. Her father's nickname was Penknife.

She was a quiet, solitary child, the village priest recalled. She would spend hours alone in the church tower, birdwatching, and days in the woods, looking for birds' and squirrels' nests. She was lithe and quite pretty, and everyone called her *Păsărica*—little bird—though in Romanian the word also has sexual connotations. One local Petreşti resident believes that the nickname came from Elena's habit of not wearing any panties, thus affording others a glimpse of her *păsărica*.

She hated school. After Elena Ceauşescu's death, a retired schoolteacher produced a school report she had kept hidden for over half a century, for fear of provoking Elena's terrible wrath or that of her flunkies, who, in the last ten years of her "reign," constantly praised her intellectual achievements. The requisite public formula, found again and again in the Ceauşescu-era press, referred to her "prodigious political activity and decisive role in the assertion of Romanian science, education and culture." The report showed that fourteen-year-old Elena had flunked practically all the subjects taught (writing, grammar, mathematics, history, social culture, geography), achieving a passing grade only in singing, gymnastics, and needlework. The schoolteacher's scrawled comment was: "Must stay in the same form a second year" (in French, *doit redoubler*). Instead, Elena quit and, after a season or two of working in the fields, came to Bucharest.

There was something almost inevitable about the coming together, in Bucharest, of Elena Petrescu and Nicholae Ceauşescu. Elena, when she first arrived there, lived with Adela, the Marxist, who was married to Elena's elder brother Gheorgha. They called him Gogu, and he was supposed to have had some education, since he had been to agricultural college. But he was, said Mihai Popescu, who knew them both in the early thirties, "unimaginably stupid." "I don't think I ever heard anyone call him Gogu," Popescu told me. "His nickname was *Cap de Lemn*—blockhead [in Romanian, literally, wood-head]. Everyone called him that, and he accepted it. 'Hey, blockhead,' someone would shout, and he'd come running."

Popescu first met Gogu at Young Communists' League meetings. "Then she started coming, too. She didn't seem too keen on the ideology, but she enjoyed the company." At the time, Popescu said, Elena was working as a hired hand in a tiny, somewhat shady patent-medicine factory. "It wasn't really a factory, just a couple of rooms in an apartment block in a low-rent area," Popescu recalled. "There was virtually no legislation on patent medicines then, and shady doctors and pharmacists would get together and start up a small company, marketing vitamin pills, painkillers, or slimming pills and selling them locally. Elena hated the job."

Many years later, Elena Ceauşescu would run ICECHIM, the principal chemistry research laboratory in Romania, and masquerade as a "world-renowned scientist and chemist," with the complicity of the cowed Romanian scientific establishment.

She could have chosen any branch of science to appear proficient in, but a doctorate in chemistry must have been her way of exorcising those early days of drudgery and poverty in the Bucharest medicine factory.

"One day Cap de Lemn [blockhead] came to see me and asked me if I couldn't find his sister a better job," Popescu recalled. "I approached a friend of mine, Vasile Cristescu, also in the Young Communists' League. He found her a well-paid job in the Jacquard textile factory, where he himself worked as a maintenance foreman." Cristescu was a kind of saint, Popescu added, the sort of person who was always doing people a good turn, never expecting anything in return. In 1985 Cristescu and Popescu met, quite by chance, on a street in Bucharest. Cristescu told him things were grim: He was losing his sight, and doctors had told him that he would soon go blind if he did not have a major operation, which could not be performed in Romania, because facilities existed only abroad. "So the next time we meet," Cristescu said wanly, "I'll recognize you by your voice, but I won't be able to see you." Popescu was furious. "You helped *her* when she needed help, surely *she* can arrange for your eye operation," he said. (Romanians avoided pronouncing the Ceaușescus' real names, even in private. It was always *him* and *her*.) "What about Cap de Lemn?" Popescu asked.

"Oh, I saw *him*," Cristescu said. "He absolutely refused to help. I must have shown how angry I was. He said, 'You know what happened to me? My son got married the other day, and of course, I invited *her*. Do you know what I was told? Protocol absolutely forbids the first lady from attending such a reception.' "

Official Ceaușescu-era history books were to mythologize Elena's past almost as much as Nicolae's, but there was even less basic material available in her case. One of the highlights of her early biography was her coronation as Queen of the Ball at a Young Communists' celebration held at a Sunday picnic in the "Park of Joy" on August 13, 1939.

"That day," Popescu told me, "I organized our annual outing, a combined picnic and small fair, for all my friends of the Young Communists' League. There was to be the election of Queen of the Ball, and all the girls were dressed up to the nines. It was on that occasion that I first spotted Nicolae and Elena sitting side by side and talking earnestly to each other." Each girl was given a number, and the girl who inspired the purchase of the most tickets bearing that number was elected. Elena won, despite the fact, as Popescu pointed out, that "there were lots of much prettier girls around. She was kind of pallid, and lacked personality." In the "official" histories of the couple, this event was magnified into the election of a Miss Working Class at a huge rally. In fact, Popescu said, Elena won because Ceaușescu bullied his friends and fellow youth-league workers into buying tickets for her as part of a campaign to free one of their Young Communist friends. This was Eftimie Iliescu, brother of Alexandru and uncle of Ion Iliescu, Romania's first president in the post-Ceaușescu era.

But Popescu felt far more outrage over the Ceaușescu version of the famous 1939 May Day parade, another piece of fictionalized myth-making. As one official history put it:

On May 1, 1939, King Carol II wanted to organize an official "worker demonstration" to coincide with a kind of congress of all guilds. This was a scheme intended to demobilize the workers, to weaken, disunite and defeat them. Agreeing to the "demonstration," the workers, led by the communists, decided to turn it into an anti-fascist demonstration. Those instructed to carry through that task included Nicolae Ceaușescu, whose participation in the organizational preparations was most important. Although he was followed permanently and had to change his address every few days, he, together with other prominent activists of the party, arranged the preparation of the demonstration . . .
On the same May Day afternoon a traditional open-air feast was organized, and Nicolae Ceaușescu managed to lend to that feast an obvious political character. . . . The day of May 1, 1939, marked an important success in communist Nicolae Ceaușescu's revolutionary activity: he had actively participated in the preparation and unfolding of the strong manifestation organized by the party, which had turned into a luminous page in the history of the Romanian People's struggle for national and social freedom.

Popescu remembers the occasion vividly. "I was among those who mobilized the Young Communists' League, got them to make posters, and made sure they were properly camouflaged so the police would not confiscate them as we stepped off the trains. For purposes like these, the RCP divided Bucharest into several zones. I was looking after zone three. Ceaușescu was conspicuous by his absence. I never saw either Nicolae or Elena that day. They may have been part of the crowd, but they certainly didn't take part in any of the preparations, or I would have spotted them."

Romania's political climate, during the period of Nicolae's courtship of "Lenuța," Elena's nickname at the time, was fast deteriorating. One of the king's few responsible, internationally recognized politicians of the day was Nicolae Titulescu, twice president of the League of Nations, who became foreign affairs minister in 1934. Titulescu did his best to reassure France and Britain that the new royal regime was worthy of their confidence and support. Realistically, he resumed diplomatic relations with the Soviet Union and tried to exert his influence on King Carol to get him to break totally with the Iron Guard. He failed, and the Guards, never formally constituted into a political party (for they despised the parliamentary process) but immensely powerful nevertheless as a maverick fascist organization, became a law unto themselves. Two years later, in 1936, under pressure from the "lunatic-fringe" rightists, which included the Iron Guard and its sympathizers, the king dismissed Titulescu, and with his departure the government's credibility plummeted. Codreanu's Iron Guards rampaged through ghettos, terrorizing ordinary people, and generally using their vigilante status to intimidate critics and inhibit any opposition. The tactics were strangely similar to those used decades later, in June 1990, by President Ion Iliescu's vigilante coal miners to smash noncommunist opponents, sadly emphasizing the lasting characteristics of Romanian political patterns regardless of time frames and ideologies.

King Carol had always displayed an unpredictable, almost lunatic streak in his personal life. Now it extended to all other aspects of his life as well. He surprised the public by appearing in a new uniform of his own design, with a flowing white cape; in his family affairs, he developed paranoid suspicions of his mother, Queen Marie, whom he surrounded with his own house spies. Her mail was read, and her son deliberately isolated her from all contact with diplomats and politicians, ordering that her appointments be vetted by officials of the royal household, all of whom reported her activities to the king. He also tightened the purse strings, making it impossible for her to travel without his express permission.

The Iron Guard, disillusioned with Carol, began publicly attacking him in its press. So powerful had the movement become that even an upright politician like Maniu, the Peasant party leader, was compelled to come to an electoral pact with the Guard before the elections of November 1937. After the elections, unpredictable as ever, King Carol appointed a virulently nationalist anti-Semite, Octavian Goga, leader of a fringe party that had obtained only 9 percent of the vote, as prime minister.

In 1938, Hector Bolitho, the British MP and King Carol's gushing apologist, was told by Goga, a former Romanian poet laureate, that no outsider could possibly understand Romania's Jewish problem. Over 14 percent of the urban population was Jewish, he asserted blandly; 50 percent of all doctors, and 25 percent of all journalists, were Jews; likewise, over half Romania's "commercial employees" and 80 percent of all bank clerks. Jews, he said, controlled 65 percent of Romania's financial assets and occupied 85 percent of all senior management posts. After 1921, he told Bolitho, the Jewish minority had risen from 550,000 to over 1 million, and their motto was *ubi bene ubi patria* ("where the profit is, there is the home"). In actual fact, Jews in Romania made up 4 percent of the population, or roughly 757,000, with over 40 percent of Jews of working age engaged in industry and commerce and 3 percent in the professions and civil service.[5]

Bolitho's comment was that "there is a slight Oriental twist to the Jewish problem which we do not understand," adding that while he didn't approve of Goga's views, "en masse, Jews are terrifying to me."[6] During his brief prime ministership, Goga suppressed Jewish-owned papers, also indulging in ridiculous pinpricks, such as withdrawing free railway passes from Jewish journalists. Such anti-Semitism explains, to a large extent, why so many Jewish intellectuals in the thirties committed themselves to the tiny RCP and became Soviet sympathizers. As Romania's chief rabbi, Moses Rosen, was to write, somewhat naïvely, "I saw the Soviet Union as the one great power which could hold back the evil march of fascism and Nazism and which would save the Jewish people from Hitler. We did not believe the propaganda of right-wing Romanian governments against the Soviet Union, as we knew nothing of the excesses that Stalin was committing."[7]

A few weeks after appointing him, King Carol sacked Goga, scrapped the constitution, dissolved all political parties, closed the National Assembly, and in February 1938 proclaimed himself "Royal Dictator." He also cracked down on the Iron Guard, arresting thousands of its members. A court sentenced its charismatic leader, Codreanu, to ten years' hard labor. Though welcomed at the time by a short sighted Neville Chamberlain, Carol's actions would, in the long run, help the Germans win indirect control of Romania, through a skillful combination of fifth-column-type activity and economic pressure. For all his turbulent private life and many personal flaws, Carol was a lucid, and intermittently shrewd, leader of a country that had been a buffer state for hundreds of years. On a visit to Britain, he desperately tried to impose the view that as far as Romania was concerned, purchases of oil and wheat by Britain (both were priced higher than the current world prices) represented a political commitment. He was unsuccessful, and Romania had no alternative but to increase its exports to Germany.

Hitler's scenario for the control of Romania was made easier by King Carol's "dictatorship," which had little support among the proverbially cynical Romanians. Hitler wanted above all to lay his hands on the Romanian oil reserves in Ploești, without which his entire plan for the subjugation of Europe would have failed. Fearing sabotage, he wanted to take over the country without bloodshed. Tragically, neither France nor Britain effectively committed to Romania's self-defense, except with words and hollow treaties that could not be implemented if war broke out.

Yet in those few months before the actual outbreak of the Second World War, King Carol did his best to steer a neutral course. Upon returning from his trip to London and Berlin, where he had listened to Hitler's brazenly false assurances that Romania had nothing to worry about insofar as her Transylvanian and Bessarabian acquisitions were concerned, Carol unexpectedly ordered the executions of fourteen leading Iron Guard figures currently in jail. Codreanu was "shot while attempting to escape." It was a typically impulsive royal gesture, but it failed to stem the Iron Guard tide. Codreanu's so-called Green Shirt followers went on a rampage throughout Romania, killing Jews and "leftists." Hitler did not react to the Codreanu execution: He was playing for higher stakes and knew that for all the king's sudden onslaught, many Romanians in high places were secret Iron Guard sympathizers and would, in time, make their pro-German bias felt.

Though Romanian public opinion was still overwhelmingly pro-British and pro-French, many Romanians now started to believe that given Romania's geographical position and the pro-German sentiments of neighboring Hungary and Bulgaria, self-interest dictated that they should work out an accommodation with Hitler's Germany. This sentiment was to be reinforced by the Ribbentrop-Molotov pact. Then came Hitler's invasion of Poland, and with the outbreak of war, and especially the debacle of May–June 1940, Romania's fate was sealed.

Clare Hollingworth, a young foreign correspondent then working for the *Daily Express*, arrived in Bucharest after witnessing the German invasion of Poland. She crossed the border along with large numbers of Polish refugees. Later, she wrote a lively account of those uneasy days, consistently downplaying the very considerable dangers involved.[8] She found that while the war was the prime topic of conversation, King Carol's failings and idiosyncrasies were an almost equally obsessive preoccupation. Like the first king, he had a mania for building. In several respects, King Carol's expensive architectural undertakings anticipated Nicolae Ceauşescu's later excesses. Dissatisfied with the old palace, Carol had set about building a new one. "He wanted his palace to be larger than

Buckingham Palace, and had he remained king it would undoubtedly have ended by being bigger than Windsor castle," wrote Hollingworth.[9] It included "a theater to hold 1000 people and a church to hold 400," and, to Bucharestis, "it had long been a stale joke."

"This palace," Hollingworth added, "probably did him more harm than the political hatred of the left, right and center combined. Any peasant who returned to his village from Bucharest told his cronies all about the palace and the houses that were being pulled down around it, in order that the king might have a vista. The peasant could not be expected to realize that the vista was really a good sweep for machineguns . . . he would boast to his friends on his return to his village of the lavish way the king was spending money in the capital."

Gossip also focused on the king's financial dealings. "Under Carol," wrote Hollingworth, "Romania had become a business with the king as managing director." The Romanian leu had plummeted on the free market, but the king was the only person in Romania who could order the national-bank president to provide him with foreign currency at the official rate; he used some of the proceeds to invest in a textile factory and to import cloth too expensive for ordinary businessmen, who were forced to pay the market price for it. This factory produced uniforms for the king's newly formed paramilitary organization, the National Reconstruction Front, and Carol inaugurated a scam, later copied on a large scale by a series of African dictators, which made the purchase of the uniform compulsory for whole groups of civil servants. Then, when they had paid for it, the king changed the uniform's design and they had to buy new ones.

The still-favored Elena Lupescu fascinated Romanians too, and accounts of her life-style paralleled those of Elena Ceaușescu in her later years. "Her house was full of treasures; she had beautiful clothes and bought a great deal of jewelry. . . . On a patch of land (near the airport) she was building herself a large and beautiful country house. . . . Pillars for the courtyard were imported from an old chateau in Italy, doors which opened and closed by electricity, sunken baths and beautiful terraces, all in good taste, were already built, the kitchen equipped to cook for at least two hundred people. There was a secret path from the house to the airport, where King Carol's plane was always in readiness to take off at a moment's notice."[10] There were other curious parallels between the royal dictatorship and the Ceaușescu regime: Both men were unaware of the extent of the hostility around them, surrounded, as they were, by yes-men, whose vested interest was that their master's rule last as long as possible.

For all the political unrest, and the sense Romanians had of living on the edge of a volcano as they watched events in Nazi Germany, Austria, and Czechoslovakia leading up to war, life in Bucharest, the "Paris of the Balkans," in the late thirties could be singularly pleasant. Food was cheap, abundant, and of high quality, and many of Bucharest's restaurants boasted international reputations. Ivor Porter, on a British Council lectureship there, noted the charm of the horse-drawn cabs, the *trăsuri*, the profusion of garden restaurants and cafés, and the beauty of the women, the excellence of grocers' shops like that of Dragomir Niculescu ("one of the best in Europe, selling wonderful hot meat and mushroom patties"), and the gypsy flower stalls on the Piața Brătianu. It was a city of contrasts: "Lagondas and Hispano-Suizas swerving to avoid ox carts" or braking suddenly at night before a ring of gypsies cooking over the burning tar.[11]

In light of Romania's near-famine conditions in the last decade of Ceaușescu's rule, such accounts, as well as the first volume of Olivia Manning's *Fortunes of War*, set in Bucharest at the outbreak of the war, make fascinating reading. In real life, Porter, later a member of Special Operations Executive (SOE), the ultrasecret British organization that parachuted volunteers into occupied Europe to liaise with resistance groups, had the lecturing job ascribed in Olivia Manning's trilogy to Guy Pringle, the exasperating hero and husband of Harriet. Here is Harriet Pringle talking to Bella, an Anglo-Romanian friend. "I have to keep all the food locked up," Bella says. "Why bother," Harriet asks. "Food is so cheap here. It's less trouble to trust them." At Pavel's, a well-known restaurant, "the heart of the display was a rosy bouquet of cauliflowers. Heaped

extravagantly about the centre were aubergines as big as mel-
ons, baskets of artichokes, small coral carrots, mushrooms,
mountain raspberries, apricots, peaches, apples and grapes.
On one side there were French cheeses; on the other tins of
caviar, grey river fish in powdered ice, and lobsters and cray-
fish groping in dark waters. The poultry and game lay un-
sorted on the ground." Throughout Bucharest, the tantalizing
aroma of food was inescapable, and Porter recalls "the hungry
smell of corn-on-the-cob cooking over street braziers," and
construction workers "eating slices of garlic and white cheese
on a cold corn polenta called *mămăligă*." The contemporaries
of Nicolae Ceaușescu I talked to all remembered Bucharest
during this period as "the breadbasket of the Balkans" and a
cornucopia of cheap, high-quality food. Not only did no one
starve in Bucharest, they said, but the profusion of cheap,
tasty street vendors' food was probably unequaled anywhere
else in Europe. Despite what Porter described as its "ostentatious, almost oriental, disregard for the poor," Bucharest was,
in that immediate prewar period, something of an earthly
paradise, and despite an unstable monarch and political unrest and extremism, Romanians "liked to think of themselves
as part of democratic Europe."[12]

In 1938, Ceaușescu was still in jail (he would be released in
December). The RCP was less shocked by news of the Russo-
German pact than were other communist parties in Europe:
So strong were the Stalinist convictions of RCP leaders, both in
the Odessa group and within Romania itself, that there was
little heart searching. Whatever Stalin did must have an effective purpose.

Paris fell to the Germans on June 14, 1940, and Romanians wept in the streets. It was not just the collapse of the only
consistently friendly power they mourned but their own anticipated fate. They didn't have to wait long: Exploiting his
advantage, Hitler now demanded the return to Hungary of
Transylvania, while Stalin demanded Bessarabia and Bucovina, which Hitler was prepared to let him have. Young
Ceaușescu, along with nearly all of Romania's Stalinist Communist party, was delighted. This was what the Party had been
advocating for years.

*Sărută mîna pe care nu o poţi muşca*: "Kiss the hand you cannot bite," according to the old Romanian proverb of Turkish origin. Many Romanians began to feel they had been wrong to put their faith in such weak, feckless allies as France and Britain now that Nazi Germany so clearly held Romania in a life-or-death thrall, and self-interest demanded that they ignore their pro-Allied emotions. The remnants of the Iron Guard once more became an active, then a determining, force. German infiltration was stepped up, with Bucharest now awash in German agents, "businessmen," and "journalists."

The failure of King Carol's policies, combined with his personal unpopularity, led to a plot against him. Marshal Ion Antonescu, a highly ambitious soldier who had long wanted to get rid of Carol, conspired with the respected Peasant party leader Ion Maniu, and together they challenged the king. Antonescu demanded that most royal prerogatives be surrendered to him. Carol had no alternative but to accept, and Antonescu, with the support of the Conservative, Peasant, and Liberal parties, and the wholehearted backing of the army, became the Conducător.

Though temperamentally pro-British, Antonescu now accepted the inevitable consequences of the Allies' defeats in Western Europe and set about mending Romania's fences with Hitler. The maverick king was still unpredictable enough to get in Antonescu's way, so in September 1940, he forced Carol to abdicate in favor of his son Michael, now aged nineteen. With his mistress, Carol left Bucharest aboard a royal train consisting of nine carriages crammed with their most valuable possessions. He had asked for asylum in Germany, but Hitler, because of Lupescu's Jewish origins, refused to have them. Crossing the Atlantic, they settled first in Mexico, then in Brazil. There they remained throughout the war, eventually marrying in 1946.

Three months after their departure (December 1940), again acting on a tip-off, the Romanian police's anticommunist squad picked up Nicolae Ceauşescu (already sentenced in his absence to a short prison term) in Bucharest and sent him to jail for the third time.

# CHAPTER FOUR
# WARS WITHIN WARS

**H**OWEVER REPREHENSIBLE THE BEHAVIOR OF King Carol, until his forced abdication and exile, and that of Ion Antonescu, the arrogant Conducător with royal prerogatives who succeeded him as a virtual king, it is difficult not to feel some sympathy for them, caught as they were between the Nazi rock and the Soviet hard place. Written off by their traditional allies once the going got tough, unable to face up to either neighbor's military strength, and with virtually no strong diplomatic cards to play, Romania's leaders lacked valid options. Their indecisive, inglorious behavior until August 1944 was in many ways foreordained. Only recently have historians revised their attitudes toward them.

Marshal Ion Antonescu, so reviled during and after the war, is now seen as a misguided patriot and a man of honor, albeit a stubborn, reactionary, and unimaginative one. Unlike in the countries under German occupation, Romanian Jews were not forced to wear the yellow Star of David, and there was no officially organized holocaust. Antonescu, according to a number of substantiated accounts, did oppose the systematic persecution of Jews, as did young King Michael, who lacked any direct powers of intervention. The casualty rate among Romanian Jews was eventually to reach horrifying proportions, though it fell short of the kind of annihilation that took place in Poland, and even compared favorably, statistically speaking, with the deportations of the Jews in France. Mainly as the result of German action in "liberated" Bessarabia and Bucovina, some 300,000 Jews there were deported. Those in the prewar provinces of Moldavia and Walachia fared better, though here too there were instances of savage massacres at the hands of the Iron Guards.

After forty-five years of communist rule and a distorted, deliberately partisan interpretation of the past, opinions have changed: In May 1990, a Bucharest municipality committee even considered naming a street after Antonescu. But this new awareness of Romania's past, among the post-Ceausescu-era National Salvation Front junta, did not extend to ex-king Michael. The NSF leaders, who were the real beneficiaries of the "revolution" after Ceaușescu's death, showed that some ingrained prejudices inculcated in schoolbooks and Party manuals for the past forty years remained alive among these supposedly "new look" ex-communists. By refusing to allow ex-king Michael to return to Romania for a brief visit during the election campaign of April–May 1990, and expelling him when he showed up on a private visit at the end of December, they missed a valuable opportunity to acknowledge that the ex-king, for all his youth during the war years, had played a far more important part in Romania's liberation than any of its communist "liberators." Instead, they behaved like their communist forebears.

Though he was king in name only during the early years

of the war (for Antonescu ran the country on dictatorial lines), King Michael used what influence he had to try and restrain Antonescu from committing Romanian troops alongside Nazi Germany's on the Russian front, once Bessarabia had been recovered. Throughout the war, he consistently refrained from doing or saying anything that might have been interpreted as an endorsement of Romania's reluctant but vigorous pro-German policy. Toward the end, he was to overcome the reticence of the politicians and engineer a "coup" that would help shorten the war and restore Romania's badly tarnished image as a German collaborator.

Among Romania's supposedly inactive but still vigorous noncommunist parties, there was some covert pro-Allied activity throughout the war, for Antonescu never enforced a token ban on them and was in close touch with the staunchly democratic Peasant party leader Iuliu Maniu, even flirting, from 1943 onward, with both his British and Russian enemies.

Nicolae Ceauşescu spent these crucial war years in jail. He was never alone, and the prison environment became an essential ideological training ground. In jails, as inside concentration camps, the communists enforced their own discipline and kept themselves apart from other prisoners. Ceauşescu was in constant contact with senior RCP leaders like Gheorghiu-Dej, who was promoted to be a Central Committee member while already in jail in 1935. Those who shared his prison experience later compared it to life in a boring but harsh monastic order, with Marxism-Leninism replacing the Bible as a constant source of preoccupation and study. During his earlier jail spell, Ceauşescu had been an assiduous student of Marxism at Doftana prison, which the Romanian police authorities described as a "communist university," such were the indoctrination powers of the communist inmates there. Now—first in Jilava, and then in Tîrgu Jiu camp—he became, if not a bookish RCP member, at any rate an extraordinarily keen and doctrinaire one, for the first time acquiring, if not at first entirely mastering, the indigestible Marxist-Leninist vocabulary he would spout at such interminable lengths later in his career. Marxist-Leninist thought became a bedrock for

Ceauşescu. As an uneducated, eager young man "lacking the tools of thinking," the Romanian-born historian Ghiţă Ionescu later wrote, "he swallowed the Marxist ideology whole."[1]

Inside jail, Ceauşescu was relatively safe. Underground RCP leaders like Ştefan Foriş and Lucreţiu Pătrăşcanu on the outside lived more dangerously, and the vague, sometimes contradictory, directives received from Stalin through Comintern agents made their task even more hazardous. For the clandestine remnants of the Party at large—or at least those leaders who had not found refuge in the Soviet Union (as Ana Pauker, widow of the executed Marcel Pauker, had done)—were finding it almost impossible to determine, let alone implement, an ideologically "correct" line. The Romanian communists underground were an infinitely small group, politically insignificant except for the close proximity of their powerful Soviet neighbor, isolated and incapable of any "direct action" and sabotage. It was only in the closing stages of the war that the RCP would display any kind of clandestine combativity, and then it would be either in areas already under Soviet control or else extraordinarily short-lived. The RCP would, at a later stage of the war, receive considerable funds from the Soviet Union, but these funds were largely spent on bettering the material conditions of communist notables in jail.

From 1940 to April 1944, there was no sabotage and no overt "resistance" activity of the kind displayed by the French CP from 1941 onward. There were, however, countless plots and intrigues, and bitterly pursued feuds.

Stalin, unscrupulous as ever, and with the Soviet Union's sole interests at stake, had urged the RCP to play a dangerous game, asking it to infiltrate, and in the last resort even collaborate with, both King Carol's National Reconstruction Front and Antonescu. With the same disregard for practical possibilities, the RCP had even been told to "infiltrate" the Iron Guard, despite a relentless witch-hunt against "Bolsheviks" carried out against the RCP ever since the early thirties by both the Iron Guard and the Siguranţa, the pre-1945 secret-police equivalent of the later Securitate. How methodically, and how crudely, the Siguranţa and the army tracked down all those suspected of pro-Soviet sentiments has been described by Chief Rabbi Rosen, no communist himself but a prime suspect because of his Bessarabian origins.[2] How specific the Siguranţa's knowledge was concerning the activities of the tiny RCP and its affiliated groups is proved by detailed police reports, still extant, concerning the activities of even small fry like Elena and Nicolae Ceauşescu from 1934 onward.[3]

The Romanian communists, eager as they were to see Bessarabia become part of the Soviet Union, protested vigorously at the start of the war against the annexation of northern Transylvania, which became part of Hungary by the so-called Vienna Diktat of August 30, 1940. This was followed soon after, on September 2, 1940, by Hitler's dispatch of a huge military mission to Romania, complete with tanks and anti-aircraft batteries, to "secure" Romania's now hideously shrunk borders, and of course to prevent the Ploeşti oil fields from being sabotaged as they had been in World War I. The British Secret Service did its amateurish best to act in Ploeşti, and to wreck the "iron gates" on the Danube, but failed to do any damage to either installation.

On November 27–28, 1940, the Iron Guards, without Hitler's encouragement, and with a misguided sense of timing (for Antonescu had just met the Führer in Berlin five days earlier), staged a coup of their own, going on a rampage and butchering not only suspected communists and leftists but also several hundred Jews and a number of Romanian officials held in Jilava jail for their part in the murder of Corneliu Codreanu, the late Iron Guard leader. Ironically, the Jilava prison guards made no attempt to prevent the Iron Guards from executing those held responsible for Codreanu's murder but did protect the communist prisoners from the same fate. Among the inmates of Jilava jail at the time was Ceauşescu.

The Iron Guard uprising was put down with considerable brutality by Antonescu's loyal army, and Hitler made no move whatsoever to protect the Romanian Green Shirts from the consequences of their actions. He did, however, agree to transfer to Germany a small number of their top men, including Horia Sima, the fanatical ex-schoolteacher who had succeeded Codreanu. They were taken under the Gestapo's wing and kept in a camp throughout the war, an ultimate weapon to be unleashed against Antonescu should he fail to toe the German line.

For all sorts of reasons, the Iron Guard threat proved unnecessary, for Antonescu, despite his genuine pro-British bias, was even more viscerally anticommunist, and this led him to "collaborate" with Germany more enthusiastically than the Allies (and many Romanians) deemed necessary. On June 22, 1941, the Romanian government proclaimed a "holy war" with Germany against the Soviet Union for the recuperation of its lost provinces. King Michael was to learn of this decision through radio bulletins and newspapers. That Romania should join Hitler against the Soviet Union for the recuperation of Bessarabia and northern Bucovina was understandable, and even anti-German politicians like Maniu accepted the fact that it was both justified and popular in most Romanian eyes—though of course the RCP denounced the unprovoked "attack by German and Romanian fascists on the peace-loving Soviet Union."

Bessarabia and northern Bucovina were safely in Romanian hands by July–August 1941, and there, many Romanians hoped, the German involvement would end. King Michael, in one of his rare addresses to the nation, congratulated the Romanian armed forces on their victories, but urged that having achieved their objective, they should now cease joint operations with Germany against Russia and withdraw behind Romania's frontiers. The British government hinted that it understood Romania's predicament, for it did not formally declare war on Romania until December 1941. By this time, Marshal Antonescu had made the fatal error of committing Romanian troops on the Russian front proper, sending them across the Dniester. Romanian troops found themselves fighting alongside Hitler's troops, occupying Tiraspol and Odessa, where their conduct, according to later historians, compared favorably with that of the Germans. Romanian troops also took part in the advance on Stalingrad, and a whole division would eventually be captured there. Six more divisions were to remain in the Crimea more or less for the duration of the war.

In 1943 almost all "politicals," including all the communists in detention, were regrouped in Tîrgu Jiu. In the official postwar history books, Tîrgu Jiu is described as a "concentration camp." This is a misnomer, for it was, one former inmate recalled, a typical POW camp, a collection of Nissen huts and barracks originally destined for the fleeing Polish army and air force officers and men who crossed the border into Romania in 1939 whom the Germans wanted interned. To its credit, the Romanian government at the time helped those Poles escape in their tens of thousands, rather than fall into either Russian or German hands, and make their way, with covert British assistance, to Allied-held territory.

Among the Romanian Tîrgu Jiu detainees, from 1941 onward, were social democrats, Jews, and anyone thought to serve the Allied cause, such as the openly pro-British general Nicolae Rădescu. The testimony of several former Tîrgu Jiu inmates all concurs: Though conditions were harsh, especially in winter, and the food indifferent to bad, the Romanian officers in charge of Tîrgu Jiu behaved on the whole not only humanely but with considerable ambiguity, considering Romania's formal alliance with Nazi Germany.

Among the Tîrgu Jiu detainees was Eugen Rusu, a social democrat interned since 1941 because of his militant pro-Allied activities. Apart from a year spent working as a slave laborer on a railroad line, Rusu was a permanent inmate of Tîrgu Jiu and remembers it vividly. When the war was going well for the Germans, he recalled, the guards could be quite tough and the atmosphere oppressive. But as soon as things started going badly for both the Germans and the Romanians on the Russian front, "they became nicer." There was no concentration camp atmosphere and no compulsory labor, though small workshops had been set up and those who worked there could earn some money. As an example of the ambiguous relations between those running the camp and its communist inmates, Rusu cited the fact that the daughter of the camp commandant joined the RCP immediately after the war and became a lifelong Party member, working in the RCP's Central Committee as a secretary—a post of considerable sensitivity.

Rusu recalled that the class differences among the interned communist prisoners caused them to split at first into two separate, self-contained units, one comprising the "intellectuals" (including Ceaușescu's later premier and foreign minister, Gheorghe Maurer), the other, the workers. On his return from working on the railway-construction gang in April 1944, Rusu found that the communist and social democrat internees had been regrouped into one barracks, the "number-seven group."

The man in charge was the senior-most communist detainee in Romanian hands, Gheorghiu-Dej. His twelve-year prison sentence had come to an end, but he remained under "administrative detention" for the duration of the war. "Gheorghiu-Dej didn't live in a communal barracks like the rest of us," Rusu recalled. "He had lodgings of his own. The Romanian camp authorities treated him with kid gloves. He was a powerful figure in the camp." As a token of his new importance within the camp, Gheorghiu-Dej had a trusted servant-bodyguard who brought him his meals, shined his shoes, slept outside his bedroom door, and in general acted as a Cerberus, an obedient, silent watchdog totally devoted to his master. This, Rusu remembers, was none other than Nicolae Ceaușescu.

"He was humble, he was silent, he was enormously hard working, an admirable butler-manservant," said Rusu. "I found him full of complexes, impossible to talk to, not only because of his stutter, which was still severe, but also because he had no real conversation, no ideas of his own. He would spout Marxist-Leninist jargon like an automaton. I remember once trying to convince him that for all the contrary propaganda, the Soviet military machine had not behaved too well in the initial stages of the German invasion of 1941. 'Not at all.' he said. 'What could they have done against the surprise effect?' His culture was limited to Stalinism, his vision of the world extraordinarily narrow. We were allowed to read Romanian newspapers, which of course all toed the pro-German line, but we were able to gauge the real state of the war from the official communiqués. Here too, because of his unquestioning Stalinism, it was clear that Ceaușescu was both sectarian and immensely naive." His views were those officially held by the RCP as a whole, but he did not entertain the private doubts expressed by some of the communist intellectuals. Rusu also recalls that Ceaușescu seemed most at home with fellow communists in Tîrgu Jiu who had originally started out as members of the Iron Guard. Other inmates recall that Elena Petrescu visited Ceaușescu regularly, but that none of Nicolae's relatives ever came to see him.

At the time of Rusu's return to Tîrgu Jiu, the pro-Allied detainees, irrespective of their political labels, had formed a "National Patriotic Front"—and *România Liberă* was their clandestine newspaper. Though the Romanian communists formally adhered to the view that such a "united front" put them on a par with the other political parties (and they were, of course, far less numerous than the other established parties within the country as a whole), the communists inside Tîrgu Jiu reflected the attitude that "everything will come out all right in the end, thanks to the Soviet Union. They'll look after us and tell us what to do." The communists, Rusu said, not only had no blueprint of their own for a postwar Romania but felt no need for one. In their eyes (and Ceaușescu, Rusu recalled, was particularly dogmatic in this respect), Romania's future was entirely in the hands of the Soviet Union, which could do no wrong. The internees made no attempt to conceal the fact that insofar as they had a plan, it was to implement, under Russian control and supervision, a Russian-type October 1917 revolution, including the elimination of landlords and the bourgeoisie. The idea that Ceaușescu—as the official hagiographers later implied—had a policy-making role in those early days was doubly risible, Rusu said. In the first place there *was* no policy, apart from blind obedience to Stalin. In the second place, Ceaușescu's self-appointed role as bodyguard-valet to Gheorghiu-Dej, while it brought him considerable material advantages (for by this time, Rusu recalled, RCP funds were flowing into the camp and this enabled the communists not only to buy choicer food but to conduct their own affairs with little interference from heavily bribed guards), made him a somewhat despised figure. He was the one Gheorghiu-Dej used to

pass on commands and camp rulings and, Rusu says,
Ceauşescu seemed to revel in this small fragment of
authority—as he had reveled in his earlier trusty role, in
Doftana jail, allocating the numbers of cigarettes each detainee was entitled to on orders from his superiors.

Throughout the war, desultory British efforts had been
made to win over the one "respectable" democratic statesman
the Allies felt they could count on—Iuliu Maniu. The former
Peasant party leader had never hidden his pro-Allied sentiments and remained in touch with the Allies throughout the
war. In 1943, he decided to fly out of Romania to head a
government-in-exile, his last-minute change of mind stemming from an honorable feeling that he was more useful inside the country than outside it. He was an infuriating,
obstinate person to deal with, however. As Sir Reginald Hoare,
the former British minister in Bucharest, wrote in a Foreign
Office report, his very qualities made him a difficult, prickly
interlocutor, for he "preserved a rugged and obstinate adherence to principle in a land where expediency reigns supreme."

What neither Maniu nor Antonescu fully realized was the
fact that Romania, as the war progressed, had become a low
priority for the British and Americans alike. It was unrealistic
to expect Franklin D. Roosevelt, whose black-and-white vision
of the world precluded any sympathetic understanding of Romania's predicament, to be swayed by any arguments in Romania's favor after her entry into the war on Germany's side.
To him, Romanians were all fascist pro-German puppets, on
a par with the pro-Nazi Ustachis in Yugoslavia. Churchill knew
how wrong Roosevelt was, but he had other, more urgent
priorities to deal with. As Ivor Porter pointed out in his remarkable *Operation Autonomous*,[4] Maniu never was able to understand that Romania had become a Soviet preserve with
Churchill's reluctant, passive consent. To the end, he preserved "the illusion that his commitment to democracy gave
him a special relationship with the Allies."

As early as 1942, Maniu had entertained the notion of a
pro-Allied coup, but his distrust of the Soviet Union was such
that he wanted assurances that the Allies would guarantee
Romania's postwar political independence and that there

would be no Soviet invasion of Romania. But after the January 1944 Casablanca conference, Churchill's hands were tied: Roosevelt had—without consulting Churchill—announced that "unconditional surrender" would be "forced on all our enemies." This gave the Soviet Union a virtual whip hand over Romania, with the result that Churchill, as Ivor Porter wrote, "had no Romanian policy" after Casablanca.

In retrospect, Britain's handling of Maniu was shamefully duplicitous, for not only was he never told that Britain had virtually given up on Romania, but he was also kept in ignorance of the fact that all his secret messages (through SOE) to Britain were automatically passed on to Moscow. Not only that, but in his secret correspondence with Britain, much had been made of a possible Baltic landing of an Allied expeditionary force. Churchill finally was to shelve his plans for a drive on "the soft underbelly of Europe," and they were definitively abandoned at the Teheran summit of November 1943. Neither Maniu nor Antonescu was ever informed of this, and indeed—in order to mislead Hitler and tie up German divisions on Romanian soil—an elaborate piece of disinformation was concocted: Rumors were deliberately leaked that the eventuality of such a landing had indeed been discussed, and approved, at the Teheran Summit. Here too, the reality was kept from Maniu, as was the tacit Churchill-Stalin bargain sealed at the Potsdam Conference in July 1945.

Winston Churchill, in his *Memoirs*, would describe how at Potsdam he scribbled a few words on a piece of paper indicating that Stalin was to have 90 percent predominance in Romania in exchange for Britain being allowed a 90 percent predominance in Greece, and that Stalin had grunted his approval.

There were many reasons for Churchill to propose such a deal. Greece was a gallant ally and had fought heroically. Strategically, diplomatically, and historically, at the time, it was far more important than Romania. The Stalin-Churchill deal over Romania was, however, only the first of many concessions that would place the captive East Europeans behind an Iron Curtain for nearly half a century. In the long run, as Porter noted, Maniu, who had put his faith in the Allies, and Antonescu, who had put his faith in Germany, were both equally betrayed.

Though the Soviets knew from reading his dispatches to the British Secret Service that, unlike some Romanian politicians, Maniu would never "collaborate" with them, they were prepared to make a deal with him, for the simple reason that—as Ivor Porter points out[5]—he, and not the RCP, represented "the only effective anti-German opposition in Romania." Porter was, in 1944, in a unique position to observe Maniu's—and Antonescu's—reactions to the changing war situation. This former British Council lecturer in Bucharest had been parachuted into Romania in December 1943 as part of an SOE team which was immediately captured. Porter and his companions had reason to fear the worst, but their captors—including the obese Eugen Cristescu, the head of the Romanian secret police and counterespionage and a German agent to boot—treated them more like guests than like prisoners, refusing to hand them over to the Germans, and using them as conduits to communicate with British government representatives in Istanbul and Cairo. Antonescu, despite repeated requests from the Germans, also unyieldingly replied that the SOE team were Romania's prisoners of war and would remain in Romanian hands. In *Operation Autonomous*, Porter afforded numerous glimpses of the real sentiments of Romanian police, gendarmerie, and army personnel, who brought them wine, flowers, țuică (fiery Romanian plum brandy), took them to restaurants, arranged for them to have efficient and expensive dental treatment, and generally looked after them with considerable graciousness and hospitality. Porter and his team leader, Colonel Gardyne (Chas) de Chastelain, became privileged observers, and eventually participants, in the unfolding Romanian drama.

The week the Soviet forces edged close to the Romanian border at Iași (March 10, 1944), Porter, in his diary, outlined Romania's options: It could fight on until its total occupation by Russia or capitulate to the Russians or else turn against Germany "and reap the profits." Not only Maniu but also Antonescu himself realized these were the only bleak choices. But faced with the formal demand of unconditional surrender—made, probably thoughtlessly enough, by Roosevelt in Casablanca but shamelessly exploited by Stalin—Antonescu could not bring himself to accept these terms. In a message to the British commander in chief in the Middle East, General Maitland Wilson, Antonescu begged him: "Do not ask an old man and honest soldier to end his days in humility. . . . We are friends not enemies. . . . No country with its forces almost intact could capitulate without some serious guarantee of her future." Porter noted that Antonescu's "maudlin tone" irritated the British. In light of later events, it did not lack pathos.

The Russians, in the spring of 1944, made a determined effort to woo Maniu and get him to commit himself to an anti-German coup. On April 2, Molotov, in a broadcast, assured Romanians that the Soviet government did not intend to change the political or social order in postwar Romania. Just how hollow such a pledge was could be gauged from the fact that at the time, the Russians were devoting considerable resources to the "Tudor Vladimirescu Division," a unit of Romanian POWs enrolled in a Soviet-controlled force and specially trained in internal security duties.[6] Shortly afterward, the Russians forwarded to Maniu their terms in the event of an anti-German coup. These included the return of Bessarabia and northern Bukovina to the USSR, Romanian "war reparations," and the demand for "freedom of movement" of Soviet troops—but no permanent occupation. On the plus side, Russia would support Romania's claim, at war's end, to the Transylvanian territories annexed by Hitler and handed over to Hungary.

At face value, these Russian terms seemed moderate and highly favorable. The British could not understand why Maniu did not immediately react positively. In retrospect, Maniu's reservations were understandable: A longtime observer of Stalin, he doubted—as it turned out, with good reason—that Stalin would ever keep his word on anything. Though Maniu's pro-Allied stance was well known, Antonescu by this time was in touch with him, and he too was dealing with the Russians as well as the British: The venue was the Soviet embassy in Stockholm, whose ambassador was Madame Kollontay, the veteran revolutionary. Maniu's emissary to the Allies (and occasionally Antonescu's as well) was none other than Prince Barbu Știrbey, the faithful friend of the late Queen Marie of Romania. Știrbey's nephew, Alexandru Cretzianu, the Romanian minister in Ankara, became, for the duration of the war, the unofficial representative of Romania's noncommunist, pro-Allied democratic parties.

In the event, both Antonescu and Maniu turned down the Soviet proposals. The bottom line was that they distrusted the Soviets. Maniu's argument, which infuriated the British at the time, was the not unreasonable one that—since Stalin's word could hardly be considered his bond—the United States and Britain as well as the USSR should act as guarantors that there would be no interference in Romania's postwar internal affairs and that free elections would take place under the supervision of the Allies as a whole, and not just the Russians. As Porter noted, "Such lack of faith in Russia's word exasperated both London and Washington." It was, in light of what was to happen later, a reasonable enough request.

Stalin's plans for Romania provided the classic example of the three-stage move toward totalitarian domination he would eventually apply to the whole of Eastern Europe. First would come the period of genuine coalition, with the Romanian communists accepting a minority role among the "majority" noncommunist parties, all enjoying freedom of organization, freedom of speech, and their own political platforms and policies. This would be replaced, as soon as possible, by a "bogus coalition" composed of noncommunist political leaders, selected by the communists, who were naive or cowed enough to do the Communist party's bidding. Opposition views at this stage would still be voiced, but from outside the government, by those noncommunist political leaders removed from office but not yet fully "purged." The third stage would come with the abolition of all noncommunist political parties other than docile "front organizations" masquerading as forces nominally independent from the Party's own line.

There can be little doubt that at least some of Romania's communist leaders were aware of the broad lines of such a policy. But in Romania's case, the circumstances were somewhat special, for the RCP was far from homogeneous. There were, in effect, three groups in this party that had almost as many leaders as members. There was the "hard core" of jailed communists, headed by Gheorghiu-Dej and including Gheorghe Apostol, Alexandru Drăghici, Chivu Stoica, Miron Constantinescu, Teohari Georgescu, Iosif Chişinevschi, and, much lower down in the hierarchical scale, Ceauşescu. Then there was the latter-day equivalent of the prewar Odessa group, the exiled Romanian communists who had spent the war years on Russian soil. The acknowledged leader of this group was Ana Pauker, and she was flanked by Vasile Luca, Constantin Pîrvulescu, Silviu Brucan, Chivu Stoica, and—a latecomer after the war began—Emil Bodnăraş. Finally, there were the leaders of the RCP who had neither been arrested nor fled the country, the most prominent of these being Lucreţiu Pătrăşcanu and Ştefan Foriş.

The labels were slightly deceptive. Among the Tîrgu Jiu internees there was at least one hard-core Soviet agent, Iosif Chişinevschi, who was later to become, almost certainly, the NKVD's man in Romania as well as the great and good friend of Beria, its sinister boss. Within the new-style Odessa group exiles, Bodnăraş, for all his dedicated Soviet past, was to reveal a certain independence of mind. The conflicts within the RCP had less to do with ideology than with old-fashioned rivalry and a naked will to power. There was no doubt that Ana Pauker believed herself uniquely qualified to be the real leader of the RCP. Gheorghiu-Dej was equally convinced that his leadership credentials were undisputed. All his working-class prejudices conditioned him to regard Ana Pauker (née Rabinsohn) as his most dangerous, and distasteful, rival. The daughter of a Jewish kosher butcher in Iaşi (though she later encouraged the myth that her father had been a rabbi), Ana Pauker had herself been highly Orthodox in her youth, teaching Hebrew in a Jewish school before going to Paris, where she became an atheist communist after mingling with French intellectuals and, reportedly, having an affair with the French communist leader Maurice Thorez.

Given the master-servant relationship of Gheorghiu-Dej and Ceauşescu in Tîrgu Jiu in 1943–44, it was inevitable that

Gheorghiu-Dej's views should become Ceauşescu's, though he was secretive enough at the time to give no hint of this in his talks with Rusu.

In April 1944, a strange meeting took place inside the Tîrgu Jiu camp infirmary, attended, but only in his "butler" capacity, by Ceauşescu. The RCP leaders there met with a certain "engineer Ceauşu," having bribed the guards to let him in. By this time, the Russians were advancing on all fronts, and the Romanian guards at Tîrgu Jiu, like their compatriots all over the country, were increasingly aware that Germany was going to lose the war. This made them amenable to most RCP requests, and though the internees were still confined to the camp, visitors of all kinds now had untrammeled access. Ceauşescu knew engineer Ceauşu well: He was Emil Bodnăraş, his onetime cellmate and one of the most mysterious, enigmatic figures in the history of the RCP.

Bodnăraş, from a well-to-do "bourgeois" family of Ukrainian origin, had graduated at the top of his class from the Romanian army's cavalry school in Timişoara and promptly become a Marxist-Leninist convert and—thanks to an able Soviet recruiter—Soviet agent. Deserting from the army almost immediately after being commissioned, he spent some months in the Soviet Union, almost certainly in an espionage-training school, and returned to Romania under an alias in 1935. By chance, while his train was in Ploeşti station, he was spotted by a former army colleague and ignominiously arrested at Bucharest's Gara de Nord on arrival there. It was in Doftana prison, while serving a sentence for desertion and espionage, that he became an official card-carrying RCP member. The young Nicolae Ceauşescu hero-worshiped him almost as much as he worshiped Gheorghiu-Dej.

Despite their earlier prison intimacy, one communist source claimed, Bodnăraş snubbed Ceauşescu at the time of the Tîrgu Jiu infirmary meeting and was embarrassed when Ceauşescu attempted to parlay their earlier prison experience into a show of intimacy. It was another one of the many important lessons during those years that Ceauşescu would never forget.[7]

After his prison sentence expired, in 1943, Bodnăraş had

set up shop as an innocuous wood salesman in Braila, where his brother Manole also had a photographic studio. It was an ideal front for his clandestine RCP activities. During his detention in Tîrgu Jiu, before release, he had been given extremely favored treatment by one of the camp's senior officers, Colonel Radu Ionescu. One of Bodnăraş's first decisions, in 1945, once he was in a position of authority, would be to have Colonel Ionescu shot.

At the Tîrgu Jiu infirmary meeting, Bodnăraş, the NKVD emissary, brought harsh words from Stalin. The message was that the RCP had better start proving its existence by taking part in anti-German sabotage. Bodnăraş then had to listen to a furious Gheorghiu-Dej, who claimed that the RCP's passivity was not his fault. The RCP's wartime stance toward the Germans was already a sensitive issue. Shortly after his release from prison, Bodnăraş had sought out the still at large titular head of the RCP, Foriş, and urged him to initiate a series of armed "resistance" activities against the Germans. Foriş had refused, and Bodnăraş was determined to get even with him.

It was in Tîrgu Jiu, at the meeting between engineer Ceauşu and Gheorghiu-Dej that Ceauşescu, listening in the wings, got his first lesson in the realities of power politics and the bitterness of communist-style in-fighting. Gheorghiu-Dej spent most of his time denouncing, to Bodnăraş, Foriş's inadequacies and timorousness as a leader, and Bodnăraş heartily agreed with him, for he had in fact already secretly met Foriş twice, urging a start to communist guerilla activity, and Foriş had demurred. After the well-known French principle of *les absents ont toujours tort* (absentees are invariably in the wrong), Gheorghiu-Dej was intent on discrediting not only the Soviet refugees of the latter-day Odessa group but especially Foriş, alleging to Bodnăraş that Foriş was a police informer and traitor and should be eliminated from the leadership. He was on fairly safe ground, given the extraordinary infiltration of the RCP by an anticommunist division of the secret police. One of its members later described how—in the late 1930s and early 1940s—the inner workings of the RCP had become something of a joke to them. The tiny Party, the ex-policeman said, received funds from the Soviet Union to publish tracts and clandestine newspapers and then more funds from Siguranța, the pre-communist-era secret police organization, to hand them over.

In light of the investigations of later Romanian historians, it became clear that Foriş was no police informer. His only crime was in attempting to follow Stalin's impossible instructions, including the directive to "collaborate" with Antonescu. He did, however, become one of the RCP's earliest sacrificial victims: Arrested by Gheorghiu-Dej henchmen and kept under wraps until well after the pro-Allied "coup" of August 23, 1944, he was then rearrested and held, in appalling conditions, in the cellar of an RCP "locale" in Bucharest that later became the Polish embassy building. An RCP thug, Vasile Posteucă, battered him to death with an iron bar in 1946 and was rewarded by promotion to deputy interior minister. Many years later, in 1968, Nicolae Ceaușescu awarded Posteucă the "Tudor Vladimirescu Order (second-class)."

The example of Gheorghiu-Dej denouncing a comrade unable to defend himself was not lost on Ceaușescu. It was a technique he himself was to use repeatedly later, posthumously blackening not only Gheorghiu-Dej's reputation but that of almost all his predecessors.

One RCP leader at large whose authority even Gheorghiu-Dej could not impugn was Lucrețiu Pătrășcanu. The son of a well-heeled Moldavian landowner, Pătrășcanu was a lawyer and unashamed intellectual. His wife was a well-known interior decorator. This "salon" communist, who was inclined to place Romanian national interests above those of the Soviet Union, had considerable social standing, an entrée among politicians like Maniu, and was even in touch with King Michael through his confidential private secretary, Mircea Ionițiu, who met him several times from January 1944 onward. Pătrășcanu, perhaps genuinely, believed in the so-called united front. He had secret meetings not only with the palace but also with senior officers in the army. "Pătrășcanu was an intellectual," ex-king Michael recalled. "Some form of dialogue was possible with him." He was the RCP's "respectable" face, and Ionitiu noted how when he first met with Bodnăraș on June 13, 1944, he realized the enormous difference that existed between a

Romanian "salon" communist intellectual and the real thing. Pătrășcanu may have been oblivious of the latent hostility toward him that existed among the incarcerated Tîrgu Jiu communists, but he cannot have been unaware of the sectarian disapproval of the Odessa group. Ana Pauker and Vasile Luca never tired of saying that Pătrășcanu's antics were unnecessary. Why bother to go through the pretense of cooperating with "bourgeois" parties when it was possible for the working class to seize power immediately, with the help of the Soviet Union's armed forces?

In June 1944, Gheorghiu-Dej "escaped" from Tîrgu Jiu, with the tacit complicity of the guards. That same month, Ceaușescu was formally freed—a sure sign, according to Rusu, that he was not regarded as an important figure in the RCP hierarchy.

That summer, as the Soviets intensified their offensive against the Germans, Antonescu was summoned to Berlin by Hitler on August 4, and left with considerable foreboding. With his crumbling empire and retreating forces, Hitler, still bandaged from injuries sustained during the attempt on his life a month before, wanted to extract from Antonescu a pledge that Romania would remain on the side of the Axis come what may. It was a pledge Antonescu refused to give, though he replied with understandable ambiguity, aware that he might pay with his life if he said the wrong thing. Such was the mistrust between Germans and Romanians at the time that before leaving for Germany, he had ordered thousands of Romanian troops into the city, to forestall a possible German coup. No sooner did he return to Bucharest on August 6 than a new Soviet offensive began.

Now King Michael, having prepared the ground carefully, decided it was time to act. Later, he was to tell Colonel de Chastelain that he himself had been in readiness since February 1944 but had waited in vain for either Maniu or Antonescu to take the initiative. With Maniu's encouragement, and having sounded out the opinions of a number of other politicians and army officers he felt he could trust, King Michael summoned Antonescu to the royal palace in Bucharest. Antonescu, who had in the past treated the king with scant courtesy, almost failed to show up, pretexting the need to visit the crumbling front.

On August 23, 1944, they met in the Casa Nouă, a small house inside the palace grounds that King Carol II and Elena Lupescu had used for their amorous assignations. The king asked Antonescu to break with the Germans and negotiate a surrender with the Soviet Union. Antonescu refused. He was more angry at the usurpation of his authority than anything else, for he too had been secretly negotiating a possible end to Romania's war. He would never put the country in the hands of a child, he told him. Twenty-three-year-old King Michael promptly announced his dismissal and arrest. Previously warned officers loyal to the king stepped forward to carry out his order. "You'll live to regret this. Tomorrow you will all hang on Palace Square," the outraged Antonescu told the king and his advisers. Inside the Casa Nouă was a huge safe, the size of a small room, used in the past by King Carol to hoard his valuable stamp collection. Here the disgraced Conducător, and his prime minister, were taken. In the contingency plans made before August 23, King Michael and Maniu had agreed to turn Ion Antonescu over to the handful of communist mi-litia set up earlier in the month by Bodnăraş, and Pătrăşcanu had pledged the king that his detention by the communists would be "dignified and humane." In the event, they were spirited away by Bodnăraş's hastily armed "patriot workers," hidden in a small village, and, eventually, handed over to the Russians.

Maniu, to the irritation of all pro-Allied personalities, from King Michael downward, had refused to accept the post of premier in the new, pro-Allied regime. A figurehead general was appointed instead, with representatives of all political parties as ministers of state, including Pătrăşcanu, who was later to become justice minister. The coup had been meticulously planned: Even as the king was meeting with Antonescu, German telephone lines were being cut, and for the next few hours the considerable German military and diplomatic establishment in Bucharest was in total disarray. As Porter pointed out, not a single army officer disobeyed the king's new command. The only Romanian to side with the Germans was fat

Colonel Cristescu, the head of the secret police, who promptly sought asylum inside the German embassy.

Romanians learned of the coup that night. Broadcasting on Romanian radio, King Michael announced that

> in this most difficult hour of our history I have decided, in full understanding with my people, that there is only one way to save the country from total catastrophe; our withdrawal from the alliance with the Axis powers and the immediate cessation of the war with the United Nations.
>
> A new Government of National Unity has been formed. The United Nations have guaranteed the country's independence, and non-interference in our internal affairs. The new Government means the beginning of a new era in which the rights and liberties of all citizens of the country are guaranteed and will be respected.

In the heady hours that followed, Porter and his SOE team were formally freed and rushed to the palace, where they began operating as an impromptu transmissions unit. King Michael told Colonel de Chastelain quietly, "I hope I have done the right thing."[8]

That night, a huge crowd gathered in front of the palace. Cries of "Long live the king," "Long live England," and "Long live America" predominated, while in a corner of the crowd, a small communist enclave shouted, "Long live the Soviet Union." The following day, the Germans began their murderous bombing of Bucharest, destroying the palace and causing considerable civilian casualties. Porter and the SOE transmission team moved to the national bank vault. United States Air Force raids began on German units in the Bucharest area, and Hitler's enraged orders to crush the insurrection, capture the king, and appoint a pro-German Romanian general in Antonescu's place were ignored. The German ambassador, Von Killinger, committed suicide.

It had been Bodnăraş's intention to stage an "armed uprising of patriotic workers," but this didn't happen. There were far too few "patriotic guards," and in any case, Ana Pauker, Vasile Luca, and other members of the exiled Odessa group wanted them kept handy for "internal security" purposes—to fight recalcitrant Romanian anticommunists, not the Germans. The Romanian administrative "establishment" as well as the Romanian army, implementing the king's new pro-Allied policy, took over the direction of the new war against the Germans, with considerable enthusiasm and efficiency.

On August 26, the RCP issued a communiqué. Without once mentioning the role of King Michael, Maniu, or the Romanian army, it announced that the Party alone had united the "patriotic, anti-Hitlerite" forces. "It maintains its ideological, political and organizational independence and complete freedom of action in the solution of all problems of a social, economic and political nature in Romania." The rewriting of history had begun.

# CHAPTER FIVE

# CEAUȘESCU COMES OF AGE

**D**URING ALL THIS PERIOD, CEAUȘESCU HIM-self was conspicuous by his absence, surfacing in Bucharest only on August 30, 1944. His "absence" from the scene on August 23 was never revealed in any of the historical monographs compiled by official historians during Ceaușescu's lifetime, and remains mysterious. One high communist source suggested that he was simply scared and sat out those few weeks in the safety of a village in the company of a Young Communist called Andrei Neagu. The same Neagu, despite his incompetence, was later promoted to general by Ceaușescu, enjoying an almost unlimited paid vacation and a privileged status for most of his army service. His extraordinarily privileged status, it was said, was the result of his knowledge of Ceaușescu's behavior and whereabouts on and around August 23, 1944. There were also rumors that Ceaușescu took advantage of his release from Tîrgu Jiu to enjoy an idyllic two months with Elena Petrescu, whose whereabouts and behavior during part of the war also remain unclear. A Petrescu relative, in the immediate post-Ceaușescu era, claimed that Elena—far from pining for Nicolae—had occupied herself in Bucharest with a succession of German soldiers. Mihai Popescu doubts this. "She wasn't the type," he says. "It wasn't a question of morality. She didn't have the right personality for that sort of thing. She was not the kind of girl the Germans fell for."

Whether Elena had whored with German soldiers or not (an allegation made by Adela, her sister-in-law, shortly before her death in August 1990), all Ceaușescu's early contemporaries agree that she was far more sexually experienced than he. "He never knew a woman except for Elena," said Professor Ardeleanu, "and he never seems to have wanted to stray." Indeed, he regarded sex as relatively unimportant. When, in 1974, one of his early cronies, Chivu Stoica, killed himself as the result of an unhappy love affair, Ceaușescu expressed only contempt for such conduct. "That's what comes from allowing oneself to be seduced by outsiders," he said—leading his cronies to believe that Ceaușescu believed Stoica had been "entrapped" by a Soviet spy. By this time, his behavior had become increasingly paranoid.

Inevitably, the hagiographers and official Ceaușescu-era historians place Ceaușescu at Gheorghiu-Dej's side from June onward, before, during, and immediately after the August 23 coup engineered by King Michael. The truth is that not only was Ceaușescu—at that time, a communist of only middling importance—not present but that Gheorghiu-Dej was certainly not present, either. As ex-king Michael was to recall, the only two communists in the palace on August 23 were Pătrășcanu and his aide Bodnăraș, still using the alias "engineer Ceaușu."

Nicolae Ceaușescu's first appearance after his release from Tîrgu Jiu, according to the historians in his employ, was on

August 30, 1944, when he organized a parade of the Young Communists' League, as its newly appointed head. Rusu remembers the day well, for by this time he too had been sprung from Tîrgu Jiu (along with all other political prisoners) and was in charge of the Social Democratic Youth League, taking part in the same united-front parade. Nicolae was, Rusu recalled, more of a Stalinist than ever. According to Professor Mihnea Gheorghiu, a later academician, young Nicolae was selective in his public appearances. In the heady days following the coup, youth groups from the Liberal, Peasant, Social Democrat, and Communist parties held several joint rallies in the Bucharest streets. This was during the time the Germans were savagely bombing the capital of their former allies. "When the bombings threatened," said Professor Gheorghiu, "Ceaușescu invariably failed to show up."

Ceaușescu's role in the events of August 23 was only a minor element in a gruesome, fluctuating hagiographic exercise that reflected internal RCP leadership rivalries and policy shifts exclusively—with no concern for what had really happened. Above all else, the still tiny RCP's main priority was to magnify its role in the August 23 coup while downplaying its dismal anti-German-resistance record. In fact, its only function, during the events of August 23, had been to act as a sort of cleanup detail: Emil Bodnăraş's hastily created Patriotic Guards had whisked Antonescu away to a secret hiding place, later turning him over to the advancing Soviet troops. Mythology soon overtook reality, and by 1946 the RCP newspaper, *Scînteia* (The Spark), while reviewing the events of August 1944, would admit the role of King Michael but exaggerate that of Pătrăşcanu, noting that "the evolution of the political situation and the secret audience of comrade Lucrețiu Pătrăşcanu with His Majesty the King created favorable political conditions." Other reports further embroidered upon reality by claiming that Soviet army officers assisted with the coup (there had been none, unless by extension Bodnăraş could be considered as such) and hinting that it was the determination and the courageous example of the RCP "patriots" that had "spurred the king to take action" in the first place. Pătrăşcanu himself, of course, knew better and, being an honest man, said so. He was later admonished for not making more of the RCP's role. Later still, after Gheorghiu-Dej had clawed his way to power, the new RCP version was that *he* had masterminded the coup, whereas Pătrășcanu and, to a lesser extent, Bodnăraș had been the only communists directly involved.

Gheorghiu-Dej's supposed responsibility for the coup was not only part of a burgeoning Gheorghiu-Dej "personality cult" but a deliberate attempt to cut down to size the Odessa group of Romanian communists like Vasile Luca and Ana Pauker. It is essential to remember that in the 1944–45 period, the Romanian communists were all outdoing each other in their fulsome praise of the Soviet Union, which could do no wrong, and it was impossible for them to ignore King Michael's role altogether, since Stalin had awarded him the Order of Victory, the highest Soviet military decoration (the only other non-Russian so honored was General Eisenhower). Later, when Romanian communist and Soviet leaders started falling out, it would be acceptable to remove all references to Soviet participation not only in the coup itself but in its immediate repercussions. The final version of the August 23 coup, once Ceaușescu had come to the fore, dealt only in generalities. In suitably vague terms, August 23 was to be referred to as "a day of social and national, antifascist and anti-imperialist liberation." Nowadays, very few young Romanians are aware of the truth—namely, that the overthrow of Antonescu was the work, first and foremost, of King Michael and of Iuliu Maniu, with the RCP playing a very minor role.

The August 23 coup did of course provide Ceaușescu with immediate promotion—and a formidable springboard, now that Gheorghiu-Dej, his mentor, was among the ranking top three members of the RCP. On September 22, 1944, Ceaușescu's byline first appeared in the communist newspaper, *Scînteia*, over a suitably pro-Soviet piece of prose headlined "The United Front of Youth." The article praised young Romanians fighting side by side with the "liberating Soviet forces" in the struggle to free northern Transylvania from fascism. His byline appeared again in *Scînteia* three times in quick succession—on October 3, 4, and 14. Communist veterans who remember Ceaușescu then affirm that he was incapable at the time—and, indeed, later—of writing even a simple report without horrendous spelling and grammatical mistakes. Silviu Brucan, the veteran communist and later dissident, was *Scînteia*'s first postwar editor and recalls that his prose "had to be translated into Romanian." He maintained that Ceaușescu's near illiteracy was to last well into the fifties. Constantin Mitea, an early *Scînteia* writer, became, from 1947 onward, Ceaușescu's discreet rewrite man, turning his master's clumsy, illiterate prose into more polished Romanian.

The first article Ceaușescu signed dwelt on the substantial Romanian military contribution to the war against Germany, but again the truth was somewhat at variance with the legend being spread by the RCP. The troops that attacked the retreating Germans, capturing 100,000 of them, were the very same units that had fought alongside them against the Soviets earlier in the war. The Romanian army, in 1944–45, was hierarchically and socially an army whose allegiance was to its king, not to the communists and not to the Soviet Union. The purges would come later. Similarly, the united front was a misnomer as far as the Romanian trade unions were concerned. From the start, under the pretense of unity, the RCP had been engaged in a vicious struggle with rival political organizations for the hearts and minds of the Romanian workers. The Romanian communists organized strong-arm squads (*ciomăgeni*) armed with staves and clubs who marched on the large Malaxa arms and locomotive factory in Bucharest, which would later be renamed the August 23 Factory, and whose workers were overwhelmingly social democrats. The aim was to terrorize the Malaxa factory workers into switching allegiances, but things did not work out that way. There was a bloody battle, in which Gheorghe Apostol, one of the leading members of the Gheorghiu-Dej group heading the operation and the head of the Patriotic Guards, lost an eye. Nicolae Ceaușescu was not present.

In October 1944 Ana Pauker and Vasile Luca, a Transylvanian, returned to Romania from the Soviet Union, and almost imperceptibly at first, the power struggle for the command of the RCP began. By this time, Foriș, the wartime

Romanian communist leader, had simply disappeared, though there was no official news as to his status or whereabouts, and only a handful of people, including of course Gheorghiu-Dej, knew the truth: that he had been arrested in late August 1944 and was being held (by Patriotic Guards) in the basement of an RCP building,.

Soon the struggle between the pro-Russian intellectual faction and Gheorghiu-Dej began in earnest. Pătrăşcanu, who had served his party more altruistically than any other RCP leader during 1944, was not even a contender: His principles, moral sense, and intellectual honesty were, in the end, fatal drawbacks.

What offended Pătrăşcanu most was not the power struggle itself but the means used to turn the small RCP into a determining political force. Largely at Ana Pauker's behest— for she took charge of internal Party affairs almost immediately after leaving the Soviet Union—membership snowballed. A veteran former communist recalled to me a joke circulating at the time: "When you filled in your application form to join the Communist party, did you mention your past Iron Guard affiliation? Yes, I thought it might help." To a certain extent ("kiss the hand you cannot bite"), this reflected the conviction of many Romanians that they should join not only the winning side but the winning party, since the Soviet presence was manifesting itself. But while it was understandable that over 100,000 peasant farmers would receive their RCP membership cards along with grants of snippets of land confiscated from the big, and now dispossessed, landlords, it was certainly unusual to extend Party membership on demand to anyone asking for it, especially when it must have been obvious that many of the new Party members joined only to escape the consequences of their Iron Guard past. In the 1945–47 period, the RCP would expand a hundredfold. Pătrăşcanu found such opportunism repugnant and was unwise enough to say so, but the recruitment practices approved by Ana Pauker and Vasile Luca prevailed. Vyshinsky, the Soviet deputy foreign minister, who made frequent visits to Romania in his capacity as Stalin's personal troubleshooter as far as Romanian affairs were concerned, was well pleased. At a banquet on November

14, 1944, he toasted "the health of the new democratic government of Romania, which thus enters the great family of democratic countries in the world." The Soviet view was that, as in "liberated" East Germany, individuals' past records counted for little. All that mattered was their degree of collaboration and subservience to Soviet interests and diktats.

Faced with the growing Soviet presence in Romania, as Germany neared collapse and with evasive allies reconciled even before the event to Romania's becoming a puppet state under Stalin's thumb, the noncommunist politicians and King Michael tried to resist the RCP tide, with very little means at their disposal. The king appointed General Rădescu as prime minister, the same general who had been in Tîrgu Jiu camp for his pro-Allied sentiments. Although the king wisely took over the interior ministry, he found himself under pressure to appoint a communist as interior ministry undersecretary, and shortly afterward it became clear where power actually lay. Gheorghiu-Dej and Ana Pauker led an RCP mission to Moscow in January 1945 (there was much juggling at the formal photo session to determine rank and precedence, but Gheorghiu-Dej emerged in the front rank, with Ana Pauker behind him). Ceaușescu, in his youth leader capacity, was not sufficiently senior to attend. "He was nothing but a glorified messenger boy at the time, a *piccolo*,"[1] said Corneliu Coposu, Maniu's personal aide during those months. Shortly afterward, the RCP-dominated National Democratic Front staged a mass meeting in front of the interior ministry. Shots were fired, almost certainly not by the army but by agents provocateurs, and after bitterly attacking Pauker and Luca on the radio, General Rădescu was forced to take refuge inside the British mission building. With Soviet tanks surrounding the palace, Vyshinsky handed the king an ultimatum: He was to accept a National Democratic Front government under Petru Groza, a singularly unprincipled former Transylvanian Peasant party leader who had formed a small crypto-communist party called the Ploughmens' Front. The king had no alternative, and on March 6, 1945, stage two of the communization of Romania began.

In Vasile Luca's own words, March 6 was far more of a

historic occasion than August 23 had been, for this involved "detaching Romania from the imperialist camp." Groza was not the only discredited noncommunist politician to make this process possible: An equally flaky Liberal, George Tătărăscu, accepted the foreign affairs portfolio, and six other cabinet posts went to renegade Liberal and Peasant politicians. Emil Bodnăraş, now a senior aide to Groza, had an office near his. Gheorghiu-Dej became minister of communications. Because the presence of noncommunists in the government ostensibly seemed to guarantee its representative character, both the United States and Britain recognized the Groza government as "legitimate." To his credit, after Churchill's electoral defeat and his replacement as premier by Attlee, the new British foreign secretary, Ernest Bevin, was to describe the Romanian government as totally "unrepresentative of the wishes of the Romanian people."

In May 1945, Antonescu's trial took place in Bucharest. The resulting death sentence was a foregone conclusion, though we now know that during Antonescu's imprisonment in the Soviet Union, the Russians had toyed with the notion of sending him back to Romania as a Soviet-controlled puppet ruler. Antonescu behaved with immense courage, attempting to spell out in court the ambiguities inherent in Romania's policies from 1941 onward. His sincerity and utter lack of fear made a considerable impression. Iuliu Maniu, cited as a witness, appeared in court and, after giving evidence, pointedly shook Antonescu's hand. This gesture probably sealed his own, later, fate. King Michael tried to have Antonescu's sentence commuted, but the Groza government prevented this. Because Groza's men knew that the Romanian army might refuse to provide a firing squad for the execution, communist "shock troops" in Romanian army uniform were brought in. Their first volley failed to kill Antonescu. Rising up on his knees, he had the strength to shout, "You people can't even shoot straight," before a second volley felled him. This was not lethal either, and Antonescu shouted, "Long live Romania" before being given the coup de grace.

King Michael was now experiencing the Soviet "squeeze" in earnest but was determined not to resign. "I had decided I would not make it easy for them," he recalled. Shortly after the Potsdam Big Four meeting, where Churchill and Stalin cynically underwrote their respective responsibilities for Greece and Romania, he tried to force Groza to resign but failed. By this time an administrative "purge" had begun, and arrests were a daily occurrence. Shortly afterward, on October 16, 1945, the first national conference of the RCP took place since it had been forced underground in 1924. The struggle for RCP leadership was reflected in the absence of any single first secretary. Instead, a secretariat, itself the inner core of the Politburo, included both Pauker and Gheorghiu-Dej. Ceaușescu, expectedly, was promoted to the Central Committee, but this proved only temporary. Equally expectedly, Pătrășcanu was not included in the new Politburo: His fall had begun. He would "disappear" in 1948.

Ceaușescu, a junior figure in the RCP "working-class" faction, may have had some qualms now that Ana Pauker's star appeared to be in the ascendant. Their backgrounds were completely different, and he knew she held him in low esteem. He, like many up-and-coming Romanian communists in the immediate postwar months, must have been relieved by the fact that while she dominated the Party at home, the Soviets clearly preferred Gheorghiu-Dej as leader, for all Ana Pauker's unquestioning subservience to Stalin. On the other hand, had she not proved her loyalty in the most uncompromising way, gaining Stalin's confidence and basking in his approval despite the fact that he had had her husband executed? And was she not, as Bodnăraș admitted years later, the "real" leader of the RCP in all but name? Ceaușescu's secretive, suspicious, and security-conscious nature precluded any candid discussions on such themes, even with like-minded comrades, for who could tell where spies and informers lurked?

Ceaușescu's energy and youth, and his closeness to Gheorghiu-Dej, singled him out for lightning promotion, despite Ana Pauker's coldness toward him. During the summer of 1946, he was sent by the Party to Constanța to "arbitrate local problems." A photograph shows him on the beach with Elena. Nicolae looks absurdly young, Elena wistfully appealing—practically the only the photograph of her that does not reflect her shrewishness. It was a photograph whose use she later banned, perhaps because of its very innocence.

In October 1946 he was promoted to regional party secretary of Oltenia, almost certainly to prepare his native province for the elections due the following month. Old men and women in Scornicești still remember Ceaușescu's return to his village. He was imbued with his new sense of authority, and they resented it. When he started touring Oltenia district to monitor "collectivization" in agriculture, angry farmers overturned his chauffeur-driven car.

In the post-Ceaușescu era, no longer fearing reprisals, these same villages also recalled an incident that showed Ceaușescu's violent outbursts and street-fighter instincts still came to the fore when provoked. In Slatina, they said, he got into a violent argument with a local bank manager over the forthcoming elections and the communists' role. Ceaușescu demanded money from the bank to be handed over to the local RCP organization for electioneering. The bank manager refused. They traded insults, then started brawling. The bank manager was stabbed to death—whether by Ceaușescu or by his bodyguard is still uncertain. The whole affair was hushed up, and such was the climate of the time that the bank manager's family never even filed charges against him. In 1946 the newly married Elena Ceaușescu also showed up in *her* village, briefly, to show off her status as the bride of an up-and-coming communist. The inhabitants of Petrești, its elders recall, were not impressed.

The November 1946 elections (which also led to Ceaușescu's first seat in the Grand National Assembly) were perhaps the most gerrymandered elections in the immediate postwar history of Eastern Europe. The methods used by the RCP were typical. Opposition meetings were broken up by bullyboys, and many Liberal and Peasant party candidates were prevented from campaigning at all. The intimidation tactics had little effect, for Western observers estimated that 75 percent of the votes cast were for Liberal and Peasant party candidates. The RCP and the Groza government had other means at their disposal, however. In the five-day period after the election, ballot boxes were systematically switched, and enough prefabricated ballots to give the Communists 70 percent of the vote were substituted for the original ones. As Romanians themselves put it, "Maniu went into the boxes, and Groza came out."

Shortly before the November 1946 elections occurred, a pact was sealed among Gheorghiu-Dej, Ana Pauker, and three senior Iron Guard leaders living in exile in Austria. Under the terms of the secret agreement, both sides settled on a "non-aggression" contract. All Iron Guard members except for those directly accused of murder were to be allowed home and were guaranteed immunity. As part of the bargain, those who *did* return were to help the communists disrupt meetings and otherwise terrorize the noncommunist parties into submission and passivity. The Iron Guards soon returned to Romania in large numbers and faithfully fulfilled their part of the bargain, some of them, in the process, entering the ranks not only of the RCP but also of the police and growing security forces. A number of Iron Guards, however, refused to take part in the deal and attempted to rally to Maniu's Peasant party. The sordid behind-the-scenes deals between Iron Guard leaders, Ana Pauker, and Gheorghiu-Dej, on the one hand, and Maniu on the other, were only divulged years later. Needless to say, there was no reference to them in any of the Romanian postwar official histories.

The predetermined results of the November 1946 elections, masterminded by the RCP, gave the new parliament 348 seats for Groza, his fellow travelers, and the RCP and only 66 for the opposition. Romanians were well aware, of course, that the results had been faked on a truly huge scale, and there were American and British protests. Nevertheless, the fiction was maintained that this travesty of the democratic process had resulted in a "freely elected and representative government," and the Allied protests were soon forgotten. The two "token" Liberal and Peasant party politicians in the previous Groza government resigned, and by February 1947, when a peace treaty was signed between Romania and the U.S., Britain, and the Soviet Union, all was set for the third stage of the communization of the country: The RCP, from a thousand members in August 1944, now had over a million card-carrying members, and the RCP, taking its orders from Moscow, was now in complete control of the government and the country.

Iuliu Maniu, the most revered Romanian politician of his era, was arrested in May 1947 on a series of trumped-up charges, including that of "conspiring with foreign agents." He was seventy-five years old, had repeatedly been urged to flee the country, and, obstinate to the last, had refused to do so.

Maniu's trial, with eighteen other accused, before a military tribunal five months later illustrated both the servility of Romania's institutions and the abjection of its functionaries, as responsive to the wishes of the communist-dominated Petru Groza government as they had been to the fiercely anticommunist Antonescu regime. The tribunal's president, a Colonel Petrescu, had prosecuted Ana Pauker at her trial in 1936. He had a fearsome record as a zealous anticommunist prosecutor at military tribunals in Bessarabia during the war, demanding maximum sentences for communist "traitors." Pauker knew that she owed her life to Maniu, who had intervened behind the scenes in 1936 to prevent her execution. As Ghiță Ionescu pointed out, a further irony was that the justice minister, Pătrășcanu, had successfully lobbied Maniu's Peasant party before the war to provide lawyers and intellectual support for those communists charged—by men like Colonel Petrescu—before military courts with accusations of treasonable activity. Pătrășcanu's private feelings about Maniu's trial can only be imagined, for he and Maniu had been colleagues before, during, and after the August 23 coup, and Pătrășcanu had even urged Maniu to become the first free prime minister after the German occupation.

To charges of smuggling political colleagues out of the country, Maniu, with total composure, replied that he had done so to allow their voices to be heard, since free speech was impossible inside Romania. What about "unlawful channels of secret correspondence"? What was wrong with that, Maniu asked, since all normal channels were closed? Sentenced to life imprisonment, Maniu would die in prison at the age of eighty-two, of neglect and starvation in solitary confinement. Apart from a handful of Western experts who had been aware of his role on the side of the Allies during the war, and the exiled Romanians close to him, few voices were publicly raised to protest his arrest or the verdict. There were, then, few highly publicized "prisoners of conscience." "At this time, indifference to Romania in the West was general," ex-king Michael recalled. "People in the West did not want to know what was going on." He agonized over the Maniu trial without any means at his disposal to prevent its inevitable, monstrous conclusion. By this time, he was himself a virtual prisoner of the Groza government.

In December 1947 King Michael, who had stubbornly refused to abdicate, was confronted with a fait accompli. He had attended the wedding of Prince Philip and Princess Elizabeth in London, and the RCP leadership had expected him to take the opportunity of his visit to stay in permanent exile. "When I left Bucharest for London, the entire government was lined up to see me off with smiles on their faces," said ex-king Michael. "They clearly believed I would not come back." When he *did* return, and the same government officials paraded before him at Bucharest's Gara de Nord, "I got an icy reception, no one would look me in the face." Not only did he return after the royal wedding, but while still abroad, he announced his engagement to Princess Anna Marie of Bourbon-Parma, a member of the Danish royal family he had met, and courted, in London.

The prospect of a still-popular young monarch not only retaining his prestige but also, in time, producing an heir to the throne was too much. First Groza told the king that Romania was far too poor to afford the expense of a ceremonial royal wedding; then Gheorghiu-Dej and the "puppet" premier called on him and told him that he had to resign forthwith and leave the country—or face the prospect of an open clash between his supporters and the new Romanian "establishment," a contest the king knew he could not win. "You are an unsettling influence, and while you are here there will always be trouble," Gheorghiu-Dej told him bluntly. "Every reactionary looks to your person as an inspiration for resistance." The queen mother, Helen of Greece, attended the meeting.

When—in the king's absence—she accused the communists of repeatedly exploiting his popularity, Gheorghiu-Dej cynically replied that she should "not place too much importance on the feelings of the people. Yesterday they were told to love the king, and they loved him. Today they are told to love us, and they will."

While the meeting was taking place inside the royal palace, armed Siguranța and Tudor Vladimirescu militia surrounded it, and both Gheorghiu-Dej and Groza, while hinting that they were only acting at the request of Stalin, implied that should the king refuse to go quietly, he might suffer the same fate as Maniu. Afterward, the queen mother described how "Groza the clown" half jokingly produced a pistol. "I wasn't going to let you do to me what you did to Antonescu," he said.[2] Shortly after the departure of King Michael and his mother, first for Sinaia, then for Switzerland, the communist militia and the security troops indulged in a wholesale looting of the palace. Groza's promise to grant the king a substantial "privy purse" payment was never implemented. The royal party left Romania with only their clothes and personal effects. A government commission was appointed to make an inventory of the crown estates—ironically foreshadowing the procedure followed by the Iliescu-headed National Salvation Front after the death of the Ceaușescus.

The new, "republican" government lineup was one that fully satisfied the Soviet Union, with Ana Pauker as foreign minister, Bodnăraș as defense minister, Vasile Luca as finance minister, and Gheorghiu-Dej minister of national economy. Pătrășcanu was forced out of the justice ministry and arrested a year later.

In the space of little more than two years, Nicolae Ceaușescu had made a number of discoveries concerning the Party that had long been his real family: that past bonds and shared hardships counted for something but not all that much—yesterday's patriot could become tomorrow's traitor with disconcerting ease; and that personal relationships could prove embarrassing if loyalties were extended to the wrong person—i.e., to Foriș and Pătrășcanu, who fell foul of the system. It was therefore inappropriate to lower one's guard.

Discretion, secrecy, impersonal and cold formality were de rigueur.

Another discovery concerned the ease with which, under generalized "state terror," individuals could be manipulated without being overtly threatened. The military prosecutor in the Maniu trial was a case in point. So was the behavior of many Romanian intellectuals under the deceptively impish but hard-lining agitprop boss Chişinevschi. One of the best-known right-wing columnists and fawning courtiers at the time of King Carol I, Cezar Petrescu, became a leading apologist of the Gheorghiu-Dej regime. No wonder Ceauşescu believed that everyone had his price.

A further lesson was that under Marxism-Leninism, all truth was relative. Ceauşescu knew that neither he nor Gheorghiu-Dej had played any part in the August 23 coup, but this did not prevent him from accrediting a "higher truth" provided it advanced his cause, and that of their brand of Romanian communism. The system was also full of pitfalls, as the Pauker-Luca-Georgescu case histories were to show. But there must be key formulas that guaranteed advancement and success. Gheorghiu-Dej had clearly mastered them, so he was the man to watch, and emulate.

In photographs taken during this period (1945–46) showing leading Romanian communists at public functions, Ceauşescu is seen in their ranks for the first time. Unlike Gheorghiu-Dej—huge, bearlike, but full of apparent bonhomie—or Chişinevschi—clowning and playing the fool—Ceauşescu never smiles. Always on the fringe of any group, he invariably directs his gaze at the personalities at the center of the stage. His intensity is frightening. He seems to be saying to himself, When will *I* be center stage? And how do I go about it?

# CHAPTER SIX

# BADGES
# OF
# RANK

**F**ROM JANUARY 1948 ON, UNDER GHEORGHIU-Dej and Ana Pauker, Romania became a full-fledged puppet communist state, utterly subservient to Moscow. The same process, involving nationalizations, centralized planning, collectivization of agriculture, and "social realism" in what passed for the arts, along with repression, deportations, persecution, and constant secret police and Party harassment for all those suspected of only lukewarm support for the new regime was occurring all over Eastern Europe. The state terror may have differed in degree in Poland, Hungary, Czechoslovakia, Bulgaria, and Romania but the Soviet blueprint, faithfully carried out by Stalinist loyalists everywhere, was the same. Accurate figures of those killed during the Romanian state terror are hard to come by. In 1946–47 alone, those executed are believed to have numbered 60,000. Hundreds of thousands more were deported to work on the Danube–Black Sea canal, Gheorghiu-Dej's pet project. Fear was compounded by exceptional hardship. Romania, already plundered twice during the war, first by the Germans and then by Soviet troops, was being robbed blind through Soviet "reparations" and Soviet-run joint corporations that paid no taxes and exported Romanian products to the USSR at rock-bottom prices.

All this was made worse by the exceptionally harsh winter of 1946–47 and drought in 1947 and 1948. The descending Iron Curtain also coincided with a curious indifference on the part of the West as to what was happening behind it, especially in the Balkans. With war memories still vivid, many otherwise responsible Western officials and politicians chose not to believe the horrendous tales of recently arrived Romanians in exile. Apart from the Berlin airlift, the Western media appeared to have given up on Eastern Europe, especially on Romania, with its ambiguous recent past. The Korean War, beginning in 1950, was to focus media interest elsewhere.

Nowhere in Eastern Europe were the communists popular, and nowhere except Czechoslovakia would they have become a majority government through free elections. What singled out Romania, however, was the knowledge, still widespread among the population, that the communist myths being spread were grotesque. The Romanian soldiers who had fought first the Russians, then the Germans, the king's men who had masterminded the August 23 coup, and the politicians and civil servants who had aided and abetted it, the ordinary citizens who had gathered in hundreds of thousands around the palace to shout pro-British and -American slogans that same night all knew that the bombastic prose of the now completely orthodox newspapers was full of lies. It was well known that the only reason the communists had been able to seize power in Romania was that Vyshinsky and a large Soviet army had called the shots, while the West had passively acquiesced to events in this new Russian "sphere of influence." For

all the Romanian peasants' poverty, they had, unlike their
prerevolutionary Russian counterparts, at least played a political role in the recent past, through the National Peasant
party (dissolved, like other noncommunist parties, in August
1945), and their violent reaction to collectivization was pre-
dictable. Ceauşescu, as one of the local enforcers of the new
rules, behaved with fanatical zeal. He had protesting farmers
shot out of hand.

Elena and Nicolae married in 1946, and such is the discretion of Ceauşescu-era hagiographers that nothing is known
of the circumstances of the ceremony, if there was one. A
former communist cadre contemporary of Ceauşescu's believes that neither Nicolae's nor Elena's parents attended what
was almost certainly a perfunctory five-minute registry-office
affair, and he cannot remember any Party bigwigs being aware
of it at the time. Valentin, their eldest son, was born in 1948,
Zoia in 1950, and Nicu, the favorite, in 1951. They now lived,
compared to most Romanians, in considerable luxury in that
leafy part of Bucharest reserved for the budding *nomenklatura*.
Like other up-and-coming cadres, the Ceauşescus were allo-
cated a house on Zdanov Boulevard and had access to all the
privileges of the *nomenklatura*, which included special shops,
restaurants, clubs, medical care, and holiday resorts. In 1948,
Gheorghiu-Dej singled him out for a key task: that of supervising the political indoctrination of the "new" Romanian
army, now in the process of being purged of its traditional
officer class. Though Ceauşescu, in light of his later public
differences with the USSR, never referred to it, contemporaries are adamant that his new job, which came with instant
major-general's rank, involved a military-political "short
course" in the Soviet Union—eight months at the Frunze military academy. Perhaps it was Ceauşescu's growing self-
confidence, or perhaps it was the overt arrogance of the Soviet
instructors toward officers of "satellite" countries, that made
him unresponsive to this form of tutelage. At any rate, says
Kostyal, who served as his deputy for several months (with
colonel's rank), "he couldn't stand the Russians." In 1949,
Soviet military advisers were present at almost every staff ech-
elon. Not only did Ceauşescu refuse to learn Russian, always

dealing with the Soviets through an interpreter, but he also tried to bypass them at every turn.

In the words of Emanuel Valeriu, then a noted rugby player and sports journalist working for army newspapers (in the immediate post-Ceauşescu era, he was to become deputy director-general of Romanian Television), "Ceauşescu reveled in his uniform and his medals. The trappings got to him; he came to believe he really *was* a general." Chameleonlike, in army company he spoke with the gruffness of the professional soldier. Though abstemious by nature, he competed drink for drink with fellow officers. "On the rare occasions he visited army barracks, he inspected bed alignments like a sergeant-major," Valeriu recalled. He also remembered a theatrical performance put on for the army, and Major-General Ceauşescu's "lewd comments" afterward on the physical attributes of some of the actresses. "We were summoned for a drink after the show, and Ceauşescu made a point of speaking crudely about their charms, joining in some coarse banter," he said. "Then, after the women performers had changed and the cast showed up, I saw him switch: He became all of a sudden the remote, austere communist militant, full of hypocritical clichés about the ideological importance of their work. I said to myself at the time: the man's a consummate actor."

Kostyal remembered Ceauşescu as a martinet, first to arrive in the morning, last to leave at night. "He was a glutton for work, and so formal and ferocious that I decided to be formal too and decided not to refer to our spell in jail together as teenagers." It was Ceauşescu, Kostyal recalled, who raised the matter. "It was six months after we had started working together that he said, 'Don't you remember me?' But that was all. There was no sense of camaraderie, no bond between us as a result of that experience." This, apparently, was an aspect of his past life Ceauşescu was trying to forget, perhaps because it brought back not only memories of his inferior status but his many inadequacies, his poor prospects, and his stammer. Kostyal recalled that Major-General Ceauşescu was "still handicapped by his lack of formal education and still found it difficult to write a formal report." He was, in Kostyal's words, "servile to his superiors and awfully tough on his subordinates. All he read was Communist party literature, but on this he spent a great deal of time. He read *Scînteia* [the official CP daily] from cover to cover."

He was not a martinet as a father. Some years later (in the meantime, Ceaușescu had become deputy defense minister), Kostyal found it necessary to discuss some urgent official matters at Ceaușescu's home. It was difficult to concentrate, he recalled, with his two small sons, Valentin and Nicu, running around the house shouting, Nicu in particular "completely out of control, running amok with a bow and arrow, with which he eventually shattered a windowpane." Ceaușescu made no attempt to discipline the child. His only comment, Kostyal recalled, was that of weak, henpecked fathers everywhere: "Wait till your mother comes home."

In 1950, Ceaușescu was back in civilian clothes as deputy minister of agriculture, another key assignment in light of the Romanian peasantry's persistent opposition to collectivization. His own peasant origins seem to have weighed little in his tough attitude toward them. He never went to Scornicești now, perhaps because he was aware of the hostility felt for him there. After this difficult assignment, whose failure no amount of report writing could disguise, he was promoted again, to deputy minister of defense. His direct superior was Emil Bodnăraș, the former Soviet spy. Ironically, the up-and-coming young communist was no longer a member of the Central Committee, though he would become a full member again in 1952, for in 1947 there had been a merger of the RCP and the by now heavily infiltrated social democrats—and room had to be found for them on the Central Committee.

As an insider on the fringes of power and policy making, Ceaușescu was aware of the ongoing crisis within the Romanian Workers' Party (RWP)—as the RCP was now called. He had not been at the Central Committee meeting of June 10–11, 1948, when Gheorghiu-Dej had launched an attack on Pătrășcanu, denouncing him for behavior "in complete contradiction to the Party line." According to Gheorghiu-Dej's rhetoric, Pătrășcanu's criminal past had begun in 1945, when he had started his "collaboration with the bourgeoisie," defending "the thesis of an alliance with the whole peasantry including its exploiting elements," and "falsifying the history of the heroic struggle of the workers in Romania"—i.e., acknowledging the fact that in the August 23 coup, the Romanian communists had played only a minor role. The crucial speech was delivered by Gheorghiu-Dej, but the man leading the attack on Pătrășcanu was one of the staunchest Stalinists in the Central Committee, Vasile Luca. In retrospect, some expert historians (Ghiță Ionescu, Mary Ellen Fischer) suggest that the Pătrășcanu manhunt may have been a possible preemptive move on the part of Gheorghiu-Dej, Luca, and others to forestall a Romanian "Tito phenomenon," for the Soviets were already reeling from Tito's challenge to Stalin. But Pătrășcanu was never the charismatic figure Tito had already become, and his downfall was more likely the result of the RWP leadership's impatience with anyone who had conscience enough to recall embarrassing facts of history at a time when RWP propagandists were inventing, for Gheorghiu-Dej and others, an imaginary role and building up personality cults for the top members of the Secretariat. Integrity and intellectual honesty were precisely the qualities the RWP leadership most feared, for if a Pătrășcanu was bold enough to tell the truth about the recent past, what would deter him, some time in the future, from being equally frank about the abysmal present? There was also the undeniable fact that Pătrășcanu was an intellectual, while Luca and Gheorghiu-Dej were of working-class origin. Intellectuals were still suspect—unless, like Silviu Brucan and Miron Constantinescu, they proved, in word and deed, that they were firmly in the Gheorghiu-Dej camp.

Ironically, the Pătrășcanu accusers were themselves coming under the gun from another quarter. Gheorghiu-Dej had never reconciled himself to joint leadership and the fact that, internationally, Ana Pauker was far better known than he was. He initiated the kind of indirect campaign that politicians, communist or not, indulge in whenever they wish to discredit potential rivals: He began attacking her record. Without mentioning Pauker or Luca by name, at least at first, Gheorghiu-Dej got his henchmen to investigate the past references of newly admitted RWP card-carriers. The way ex-Iron Guards and other "undesirable elements" had flocked to the Party was known to everyone, and they had, of course, in the period leading up to the elections, fulfilled a useful purpose as "enforcers." Now they were a growing liability. Between November 1948, when the verifications began, and 1950, when they were completed, some 300,000 "foreign elements" were removed from the Party. It was not just an affront to Ana Pauker and her closest ally, Vasile Luca, but an indication that they too were in trouble.

The first overt move against these old allies came in 1952, and characteristically, the guns were turned not on Pauker but on Luca. The Chinese have a saying: Kill the chicken to frighten the monkey. For alleged fraud in his recently bungled currency reform, Luca was dismissed from his post as finance minister. Then he and another member of the wartime exiled clique, Teohari Georgescu, the man General Rădescu had been compelled to take aboard as deputy interior minister, were removed from their posts as vice-presidents of the council of ministers. Pauker fell in July that year. Luca went before a tribunal to be duly convicted of fraud and was sentenced to death, which was commuted to life imprisonment. He died shortly afterward. Ana Pauker, too internationally known to be eliminated physically, lived on in retirement till 1960, a bitter but dignified old woman.

Only now did Ceauşescu win back his early promotion and become once again a member of the Central Committee. He deserved it. In his speeches, he had toed the new Party line to Gheorghiu-Dej's entire satisfaction. That he should attack Pauker was expected: She was everything he hated, and she had always treated him with contempt, despising his lack of education and unsophisticated ways. Her Jewishness was especially distasteful to him, imbued as he was with the crude anti-Semitism that affected most of Romania's working class. Ana Pauker, in fact, was ambivalent about her background: She combined atheism and an unshakable faith in Stalin with considerable sympathy for Israel and for the Romanian chief rabbi, Moses Rosen; her brother Solomon, a regular visitor to Bucharest, lived in Israel. But Vasile Luca and Georgescu came, like Ceauşescu, from solid working class backgrounds. To demonstrate his loyalty to Gheorghiu-Dej, Ceauşescu had no compunction in branding them as "deviationists" and "counterrevolutionaries." Pauker, Luca, and Georgescu had "combined a right-wing deviation with a leftist adventurist line."

On June 2, 1952, Gheorghiu-Dej became premier as well as Party secretary-general, emulating other satellite "little Stalins" like Hungary's Rákosi, Bulgaria's Chervenkov and Albania's Enver Hoxha. Three months later, Romania's new constitution abrogated what little was left of formal liberties. For good measure, unspecified "acts dangerous to society" were punishable even if not specifically defined by law as crimes.

In 1953 Ceauşescu, by now a member of the Party's own disciplinary commission, the Orgburo, as well as the Central Committee, was given the kind of recognition that *really* counted with his peers: He was among the small Romanian delegation in Moscow, led by Gheorghiu-Dej, that attended Stalin's funeral.

One further military tribunal helped exorcise the past, leading to a further rewriting of the history of the August 23 coup: Lucreţiu Pătrăşcanu's trial, followed by his execution, took place in April 1954. As with the Maniu precedent, the behavior of his docile military tribunal did nothing to enhance the Communist party's prestige. Defiant to the last, Pătrăşcanu poured scorn on his military judges and those manipulating them, who were trying to prove that throughout his career he had been a police informer and, during the war, an "Anglo-American agent." He was particularly scathing toward one witness, the renegade liberal politician George Tătărăscu, the former foreign minister trotted out to uphold charges of his "conspiracy with foreign powers." As an Athens-based exiled Romanians' paper, *Vocea Libertăţi*, reported, Pătrăşcanu told the court that producing such "scum of history to try and prove that I am not a Communist proves the bankruptcy of the current Romanian Communist party which has to rely on such elements." Resorting to such a witness, he added, showed the "total lack of proof against me" at this "odious trial." Ceauşescu himself would deliberately raise the whole question of Pătrăşcanu's rehabilitation many years later, in a brilliant tactical exercise to discredit his former colleagues. By an accident of history, he was able to divest himself from any responsibility for Pătrășcanu's fate, for he was appointed to the Politburo a few days *after* Pătrășcanu's death sentence had been carried out, and could therefore claim that he had had nothing to do with it. He did, however, write, or at any rate sign, at least one editorial denouncing Pătrășcanu.

The struggle within the Party establishment honed Ceaușescu's political skills: He became aware of the many Machiavellian techniques available to dispose of one's enemies. In the case of Vasile Luca, the charges were clearly unfounded— but the economic plight of Romania was such that scapegoats for the malfunctioning state could easily be found at any time, and pretexts were easy to come by in almost any domain. Ceaușescu must have reflected that but for luck, the same kind of criticism that had led to Luca's trial could well have been leveled at him, for collectivized agriculture was in equally wretched shape.

Ceaușescu must also have reflected on Gheorghiu-Dej's use of military tribunals. Unlike Stalin, Gheorghiu-Dej avoided staging a series of "public" trials, where veteran revolutionaries, tortured, brainwashed, and broken, willingly confessed to being spies, traitors, and counterrevolutionaries. His list of victims was impressive, but his methods were different. Pauker simply became a nonperson; Luca was sentenced not for ideological crimes but for financial malversations; others were quietly disgraced and even allowed to retain lower-grade jobs. Only Maniu and Pătrășcanu came before military tribunals. One reason may have been, as Ghiță Ionescu pointed out, that "the Romanian communists rightly guessed that no ideological or even psychological subtleties of the self-confessed anticommunist criminal could produce either anger or curiosity among the mass of the people, who opposed [sic] a solid front of hostile indifference to all kinds of variations on communist themes." In other words, the RWP was already so discredited, in the eyes of ordinary long-suffering Romanians, that nothing any communist was alleged to have done could possibly shock them. This, too, was a valuable lesson for Ceaușescu: In years to come, he would never

gratuitously use violence when he could achieve the same de-
sired effect through manipulation or corruption. As Emanuel
Valeriu later reflected, "Ceauşescu never wanted to create
martyrs." In this respect he was more astute, at any rate in his
early years, than his immediate successor, President Ion Iliescu.

In February 1956, Khrushchev made his famous speech
denouncing Stalin's crimes, and the impact was inevitable: The
compliant little Stalins in Eastern Europe knew that their relationship with Moscow would never be quite the same. The
Soviet-Romanian relationship suffered less than most, for
Gheorghiu-Dej took steps to deflect Soviet criticism. He gave
up his post of first secretary, making it over to his close friend
and trusted associate Gheorghe Apostol. (Just before the RWP
congress of December 1955, he reinstated himself as first secretary, in order to control it, and had another loyal henchman,
Chivu Stoica, appointed premier.) In a move that was to have
far-reaching consequences, Ceauşescu was given the job of
overseeing Party organization and cadres within the Central
Committee. From 1955 onward, Ceauşescu thus controlled all
promotions within the Party bureaucracy. It was a job after his
own heart and one that virtually guaranteed further advancement for himself. In his new role Ceauşescu was, through
patronage, able to build a personal power base on a nationwide scale.

The elimination of Ana Pauker and her group proved to
be a godsend for Gheorghiu-Dej, for unlike Eastern Europe's
other little Stalins, he could claim that he had anticipated it all.
Had he not already got rid of the "Stalinists" in the Party? He
was to use this argument again and again in Party meetings.
This in no way made him a rebel. When the 1956 Hungarian
uprising took place, Gheorghiu-Dej offered Khrushchev the
services of the Romanian armed forces, which the Soviet
leader wisely turned down. In a crude reference to Romania's
anti-Hungarian past, Khrushchev told Gheorghiu-Dej that the
Romanian army had left its indelible record on Budapest after
the end of the First World War, when it had occupied Hungary and helped crush Béla Kun. Once was enough, Khrushchev implied. This did not deter him from making use of

the Romanian offer in a more subtle manner: After Soviet tanks had put down the Hungarian uprising, the Russians feared that a hard core of Hungarian insurgents might try and free Imre Nagy, the Hungarian communist leader who had sided with the rebels and ended up leading the uprising. Khrushchev asked Gheorghiu-Dej whether it might be possible to arrange for Nagy to be held on Romanian soil. Gheorghiu-Dej readily agreed. A Securitate operation was mounted. Nagy was held under Securitate guard in a safe house until order was sufficiently restored in Hungary for him to be returned, and tried.

Events in Hungary had been closely followed by Romania's Hungarian-speaking minority, and Gheorghiu-Dej found it expedient to make a few cosmetic moves to prevent the Hungarian anticommunist fever from spreading: Compulsory Russian language lessons in Hungarian-speaking areas were abolished. A number of prisoners in Romanian concentration camps were freed. Gheorghiu-Dej also took advantage of Khrushchev's insistence that the satellite states "destalinize" themselves to get rid of further possible rivals or troublemakers: He fired Iosif Chişinevschi, the hard-lining agitprop boss, without, however, bringing him to trial. He also sacked Miron Constantinescu, one of the few intellectuals left at the top. It was difficult to classify Constantinescu as a Stalinist, though he was purged under this label. In actual fact, Constantinescu had given unmistakable signs of shifting toward an unacceptable "liberal" stance. He had recently put an end to the Romanian-Soviet joint stock companies, the Sovroms, which had contributed to Romania's economic disaster. But by this time the Party apparatus was sufficiently lubricated to take any hint from the Secretariat and elaborate on it: Chişinevschi and Constantinescu (the latter once a close friend of Ceauşescu's) were duly branded as Pauker-Luca supporters, Stalinists, and factionalists guilty of "anti-Party activity" since the thirties.

It was another lesson for Ceauşescu: By tarring him with the same Stalinist brush, Gheorghiu-Dej had got rid of Chişinevschi, who *was* an undoubted Stalinist, and Constantinescu, whose views were far more ambiguous. Again, martyrdom was avoided: Chişinevschi died a natural death in 1963, and Constantinescu spent some years in the quiet, luxurious surroundings of the Romanian academy before his eventual reinstatement. On Gheorghiu-Dej's orders, Ceauşescu himself led the purge against his old friend within the RWP bureaucracy.

Khrushchev almost certainly recognized in Gheorghiu-Dej a somewhat kindred spirit. Both skillfully used similar techniques to achieve their own ends, always within the parameters of ostensibly orthodox communism. Khrushchev regarded Gheorghiu-Dej, for all his outspokenness, as an unconditional Marxist-Leninist. As economic affairs minister in the fifties, he had ruthlessly reduced Romanian consumption in order to pay off "reparations" to the USSR, proving himself an obedient "international socialist." He had also proved his ideological orthodoxy in other ways: After the Hungarian uprising, Gheorghiu-Dej ordered the Party to crack down on the students and root out "bourgeois troublemakers." What took place resembled the repression of the Chinese intellectuals that marked the end of the "let a hundred flowers bloom" experiment.

Romanians who were students at that time still talk of this period with awe. Relying on informers, anonymous letters, and the apparatus of the Young Communists' League itself, and above all taking into account the "social origins" of the students whose future was under review, the leaders of the Young Communists' League terrorized the entire student population. One former student recalled the appalling climate of fear that reigned in university student circles following hearings, secret sessions, and repeated Orwellian cross-examinations of those who, by accident of birth (into "bourgeois" or known "anticommunist" families) or by their casual remarks, had focused the attention of the student inquisitors and YCL leaders on themselves. The most feared, the most extreme, of the triumvirate of YCL leaders heading the purge was Ion Iliescu, a young student who gave unmistakable signs of relishing his powers and his task as inquisitor. As a result of his unremitting hunt for student "bourgeois counterrevolutionaries" and of his merciless cross-examination skills, he was singled out for lightning promotion within the RCP, becoming one of the handpicked young men owing their careers to Nicolae Ceaușescu, the Central Committee member in charge of Party organization.

"True, the purge carried out by Iliescu and his colleague Cornel Burtică didn't involve arrest or dispatch to a labor camp," said a former student purged at the time. "Iliescu's powers extended only to the university field. These men decided who should remain a student and who should be expelled. The list of expulsions was pinned up on university noticeboards, and the decision was final." No appeal was possible. One can hardly gauge in the West, the source added, the impact of expulsion on the lives of students. "It was the equivalent of a death sentence."

The writer Paul Goma was already in jail, in 1956–57, when the Iliescu-inspired purges took place. "I was one of the lucky ones," he recalled. "The suicide rate among those expelled was considerable, affecting girls as well as boys. And inevitably, those affected by the purge were the outspoken, free-thinking ones, intellectually the best and the brightest." This episode has never been evoked in articles dealing with Iliescu's career as a communist, and Iliescu himself prefers to deal exclusively with his later (and somewhat "relative") disgrace and demotion within the RCP from 1971 onward. The student purges do, however, explain why, particularly among the middle-aged intellectual community with still-vivid memories of expulsions and broken careers, distrust of Iliescu is ineradicable.

Largely because of the thoroughness of the 1956–58 purges conducted by Iliescu, Khrushchev became convinced that for all Gheorghiu-Dej's muscle flexing, he remained an orthodox communist, clearly in control. He rewarded him by pulling out all Soviet troops in 1958. Iliescu was also rewarded, becoming soon afterward a candidate-member of the Central Committee, which made his status as one of Ceaușescu's promising "new men" official.

Soon afterward, Khrushchev was to face far graver problems, among them the 1962 Cuban missile crisis and his growing rift with Mao, which made him less able to control in detail the behavior of East European satellites. The Soviet Union's long-term relationship with them was slowly changing and the naked colonialism of earlier days clearly had to be replaced by a new associative form of rule. There were no easy options, and Khrushchev chose the obvious one: economic interdependence. It was, for the Romanian Politburo, the beginning of the end of the lengthy Soviet-Romanian honeymoon.

What Khrushchev intended were new economic ties that would keep Eastern Europe firmly in the Soviets' grasp, but under the guise of serving the interests of the satellites themselves. The catchphrase, when the Khrushchev blueprint was "sold" to her Eastern European satellites, was *economic specialization*. Each Comecon (Council for Mutual Economic Assistance) member was to develop its own special skills, thus avoiding duplication and the kind of wasteful plethora of heavy steel mills that had led, everywhere in Eastern Europe, to overproduction and ruinous investments. In the minds of Khrushchev's planners, Romania's role was especially important. It was to exploit its vast natural resources— agriculture, agro-industries, oil, gas, and petrochemicals—and develop *these* economic sectors to the exclusion of everything else.

Had Romania actually accepted this plan, its long-term material benefits would probably have been considerable. But neither Gheorghiu-Dej nor the Romanians saw it that way. For the veteran communist leaders with prewar experience (and Ceauşescu, for all his comparative youth, was in that category), all such directives were suspect: They could not help recalling how Stalin had compelled the Romanian Communist party to agitate for the return of Bessarabia to the Soviet Union at a time when to do so had amounted to political suicide. With Stalin's passing, and despite the crushing of the Hungarian uprising by Soviet tanks in 1956, the Eastern European countries were no longer ready to accept policies that, they knew, were—in all sorts of ways—designed to further Soviet interests rather than their own. A case in point was the plan for specialization, which would also hugely serve the Soviet Union's economic requirements.

Gheorghiu-Dej deftly used the new Soviet policy to appeal

to an element in the Romanian psyche that, he instinctively knew, paid dividends: nationalism. Should Romania go along with the Soviet blueprint for Comecon countries, the argument ran, it would lose control of its destiny. Gheorghiu-Dej knew, being after all an ethnic Romanian himself, how potent this appeal could be, especially when directed against the Soviet Union.

There were other sound reasons for opposing Khrushchev's plan. Romanian agriculture was in a sorry state because of enforced collectivization, but so rich was Romania's agricultural potential that its food exports to the West still represented sizable hard-currency revenue. Should the Soviet blueprint for Comecon countries become reality, Romania might have to sell more for rubles and less for "real money." Also, Romania's gas, oil, and hydroelectric potential made it not only self-sufficient in energy but also a possible supplier of these resources to the West. Here again the lure of hard currency made it imperative to retain control of its lucrative oil and energy assets. The ghost of the failed Sovroms loomed large, and it was natural for Romanians to believe that the Soviet plan was related to an unspoken desire to revive the hated overprivileged "joint stock" companies in another form. There was still another reason for Gheorghiu-Dej's growing distaste for Romania's close, servile "partnership" with the Soviet Union. In 1962 Gheorghiu-Dej had paid an official visit to the Soviet Union (with Maurer) at the height of the Cuban missile crisis. The two men had observed at close quarters Khrushchev's frenzied activity and increasingly erratic behavior. Maurer, in an aside to Gheorghiu-Dej, had whispered to him: "I hope you realize that if war breaks out between the USSR and the USA, we are committed to join in too, on the Soviet side?" Gheorghiu-Dej, never a skilled diplomatist, was appalled by his sudden perception of the consequences of such close Soviet links. He was determined never to be compelled to subordinate Romania's interests again to an exclusively Soviet cause.

Once the decision formed in Gheorghiu-Dej's mind to oppose the Soviet specialization plan with every weapon at his disposal, he was compelled to take a hard look at Soviet-

Romanian relationships in general. He realized that he could now gain something precious that had always eluded the Romanian Communists: popular support for Party policy from ordinary Romanians. There were no dramatic speeches, no insults were traded, and the official language used to characterize Russo-Romanian relations remained as fulsome as ever. But Romanians could not fail to notice that Bucharest's Russian Bookstore became the Universal Bookstore, that the importance of Soviet-Romanian Friendship Month was downgraded, and that the Romanian text of Karl Marx's essay "Notes About the Romanians" suddenly became available in bookshops. And what had Marx said? That the tsar's decision to crush nineteenth-century Romanian revolutionary movements and to enter into an alliance with Turkey to annex Bessarabia had been unacceptable. It also became fashionable to quote another seminal text, long unavailable in Romania, Lenin's own essay "About the National and National-Colonial Problem": "In the national question, the party of the proletarians must work first for the proclamation of the immediate implementation of the right of all nations and people oppressed by tsarism, incorporated by force or kept by force within the frontiers of the state, in other words annexed, to separate themselves from Russia."

Gheorghiu-Dej's new independent line also led to a rethinking in the field of agitprop. Social realism in art and literature—a copycat, quintessentially Soviet import—was quietly allowed to die a natural death. Romania gradually embarked on a completely new cultural policy, allowing Western books, films, and lecturers to enter what had previously been an almost hermetically sealed environment. The truly great prewar Romanian writers and intellectuals were no longer nonpersons and their works were reprinted. Jamming of Western radio stations ended. In February 1964 Gheorghiu-Dej, in a speech, praised the trend toward increasing contacts with Western culture, and shortly afterward Romania joined the PEN Club, which was still anathema to the Soviets. There were exhibits of abstract art and jazz and atonal-music concerts for the first time. Finally, the Central Committee, in a plenum meeting, gave official recognition to what most Romanians already sensed: A page had been turned in the history of Romanian-Soviet relationships, and a new Romania had been born.

The plenum, for the first time, took a hard look at its party's relations with the prewar Soviet Union and declared that the "solution of problems by an international center is no longer suitable." "Interference in our internal affairs" had been "detrimental to the Party's links with the masses." More important still, the plenum issued what later would be referred to as Romania's declaration of independence: "No one can decide what is and is not correct for other countries or parties. It is up to every Marxist-Leninist Party, it is a sovereign right of each socialist state, to work out, choose or change the forms and methods of socialist construction."

For all but a few Stalinists with a vested interest in the status quo, the new independent line was greeted with enthusiasm by Romanians, and 1964 has gone down in the collective memory of survivors of this period as a "golden year." Independence appealed to the latent anti-Russian feeling prevalent in Romania, even after years of official pro-Soviet propaganda. The fact that Romania could with impunity challenge Soviet power was proof, many Romanians believed, that under communism Romania had become a country to be reckoned with—though Gheorghiu-Dej must have known that it was the ongoing Sino-Russian dispute, focusing Moscow's attention elsewhere, that had made this possible.

The "declaration of independence" turned the RWP, almost overnight, from a hated, alien instrument of oppression into an almost popular party. Ceauşescu, at the center of things because of his job supervising Party organization and cadres, was well placed to observe the country's mood and how the new policy had the Romanians' wholehearted approval. It was clear to him that even loyal Party members had longed for just such a change and deplored that it had taken the leadership so long to make up its mind. He himself continued to display a very strong allergy to all things Soviet, as his erstwhile army colleague Major-General Ştefan Kostyal soon found out. Kostyal had been sent on a staff college course to the Soviet Union in 1957, and during his stay he had fallen in love with a Russian woman whom he wanted to marry. On his return to Romania, he met Ceaușescu, "who advised me against it, in very crude terms. There are any number of Romanian girls you can fuck and have children with," Ceaușescu told him, adding that his choice was a simple one: Either give her up or quit the army. "I became," Kostyal told me, "at forty-six the youngest retired Romanian major-general." Kostyal's failure to follow Ceaușescu's advice led to years of harassment, including the withdrawal of his pension, house arrest, and an assigned job in the country in a sawmill. His Russian wife couldn't take it anymore and returned temporarily to Moscow, where she would live, off and on, for the next few years. Much of his torment, he claims, was a direct result of Ceaușescu's vindictiveness, and power to implement it, as he rose in the Party hierarchy.

Nationalism paid, handsomely: This was perhaps *the* key lesson Ceaușescu learned during these apprenticeship years under a master tactician. It would also be the last. By the time the Soviets acknowledged their defeat and abandoned their specialization process in 1964, ousting Khrushchev for his embarrassing failures abroad and at home, Gheorghiu-Dej was a sick man. In early 1965, he was informed that he had inoperable cancer, and only a few more months to live.

# CHAPTER SEVEN CENTER STAGE

THE CAUCUS AROUND GHEORGHIU-DEJ WAS aware of its leader's fatal illness long before the general public was. No mention of his health was made in the media until March 18, 1965, when *Scînteia* reported it to be "alarming." He died the following afternoon.

It would have been difficult for Gheorghiu-Dej to conceal his predicament from his colleagues. Despite the personality cult around him and his splendid, secluded residential palace in Bucharest (for he had acquired, in middle age, a liking for extreme luxury), he remained accessible to his cronies, regardless of their Party hierarchy. Silviu Brucan, a veteran communist and (under Gheorghiu-Dej) an effective Romanian ambassador to the United States, was often called in for a chat and a glass of Gheorghiu-Dej's favorite red wine, and Brucan remembers him as a thoughtful host and surprisingly candid conversationalist. Emanuel Valeriu, the army journalist and far lower down on the Party scale, also saw Gheorghiu-Dej from time to time. The first secretary admired his dash as scrum-half in a leading Romanian rugby team and would have liked to have had him as a son-in-law. Ceauşescu, Apostol, Chivu Stoica, Drăghici, and Maurer were also frequent visitors, and it would have been impossible for Gheorghiu-Dej to hide the gravity of his illness without immediately arousing their suspicions.

Of all Gheorghiu-Dej's cronies, Valeriu recalled, Ceauşescu was the one who probably had the easiest access to him. This was not surprising: Their master-servant relationship went back a long way. For Gheorghiu-Dej, wrote Vladimir Tismăneanu,[1] Nicolae Ceauşescu was the perfect embodiment of the Stalinist apparatchik. He appeared to Gheorghiu-Dej as a modest, dedicated, self-effacing, hard-working, and profoundly loyal lieutenant. But by 1964, Valeriu recalled, Ceauşescu had become more self-assured. He still, in Tismăneanu's words, "found special pleasure in complying with and cultivating the general secretary's passion for secrecy and intrigue," but now, said Valeriu, "he had no compunction about standing up to Gheorghiu-Dej, and Gheorghiu-Dej appreciated this, frequently asking him, 'What do you think, Ceauşescu?' " possibly to test him out. In one respect the former railway-yard electrician had not changed: He remained a surprisingly candid conversationalist and something of a wit. Silviu Brucan recalls that Gheorghiu-Dej, in a good mood, would indulge in a superbly accurate give-and-take in Yiddish with Bodnăraş, a language both were familiar with from growing up alongside Jewish communities, and that Gheorghiu-Dej would even on occasion, but never in his presence, do a devastating takeoff of Ceauşescu's stammer, walk, and mannerisms. "He had us all in stitches with laughter," Brucan recalls.

In communist regimes, succession problems are handled with enormous discretion. A mafialike oath of silence was im-

From left to right, King Carol I of Romania, Queen Carmen Sylva, and the royal family at Sinaia, Romania. COURTESY ROGER-VIOLLET, PARIS, FRANCE

*...ght:* The ex-king Michael of Roma-
...a and his wife the Princess Anna
...arie de Bourbon-Parma leaving the
...rthodox church of Nice, after hav-
...g attended a Christmas service on
...cember 27, 1948. Behind them, the
...ueen Mother Helen, and Major
...rgotti, the king's aide-de-camp.
...OURTESY ROGER-VIOLLET, PARIS,
...ANCE

*...ow:* King Carol II with his mistress,
...ena Lupescu, in France, shortly after
...ving Romania in the 1920s. COUR-
...SY ROGER-VIOLLET, PARIS, FRANCE

Nicolae Ceaușescu, age 27. AUTHOR'S
COLLECTION

The original house in Scornicești where
Ceaușescu was born (before it was "redec-
orated" and turned into a museum).
AUTHOR'S COLLECTION

Ceaușescu (second row, extreme left) in a May 1939 group picture of Young Communists' Leag
members. Seated with his arms folded, second from right in the first row, is Alexandru Iliescu, father
President Ion Iliescu. In the center of the top row, with glasses, is Grigore Preotasa, one of Ceaușescu
closest friends. In the same row as Ceaușescu (third from right, with striped tie) is Teohari Gheorgeso
who became the first communist interior minister (1946–52). Finally, top row, extreme right, is Mih
Popescu, who talked at length to the author about his prewar relationship to Ceaușescu. AUTHOl
COLLECTION

Ceaușescu (standing in front
of truck) in 1939 with a
group of Young Commu-
nists' League activists and
sympathizers about to
embark on a whistle-stop
propaganda tour of
the countryside. AUTHOR'S
COLLECTION

Elena Ceauşescu's favorite picture of Nicolae. He is in his late twenties.
AUTHOR'S COLLECTION

*Below:* "Police blotter" record of Ceauşescu's first arrest (November 23, 1933) for "disturbing the peace in a public place"—note misspelling of his name—together with a record of subsequent arrests, on August 26, 1934, for distributing tracts, and on June 27, 1934, for more public disturbances.
AUTHOR'S COLLECTION

FOAIA MATRICOLĂ

Ciausescu Neculae

The date is February 1945 and the Russians are being welcomed to Bucharest. From the balcony of the RCP's headquarters (now the Tourism Ministry), Ceauşescu is just visible, slightly to the right of the British flag. AUTHOR'S COLLECTION

Marshal Antonescu meets Hitler in Munich in June 1941 after the Romanian Conducător's decision to enter the war on Germany's side against the Soviet Union. COURTESY ROGER-VIOLLET, PARIS, FRANCE

A December 1944 RCP rally i Bucharest. Ceauşescu is at th extreme left, then Vasile Luc then Gheorghe Gheorghiu-D (his hand to his mouth), the Ana Pauker, then Emil Bo năraş, all of whom were lat disgraced, discredited, or rel gated to obscurity by Ceauşesc AUTHOR'S COLLECTION

Major-General Ceauşes addressing a group of offic while in charge of the arm political education, 194 AUTHOR'S COLLECTION

CP members gathered on a balcony near University Square in Bucharest (which became a focal point
anti-Ceaușescu demonstrators in 1989 and for anti–National Salvation Front demonstrators in
90). On the extreme left (profile only) is Gheorghe Apostol, later Ceaușescu's chief rival for the
ccession in 1965. In white is Elena, then Ceaușescu. The others are unidentified. AUTHOR'S
LLECTION

previously unpublished picture of Nicolae and Elena on the beach at Constanța in 1946. The man on
extreme left is unidentified; the center figure is Chivu Stoica, an RCP official who at the time was
nior to Ceaușescu and who committed suicide in 1974. AUTHOR'S COLLECTION

The only existing photograph of Nicolae Ceaușescu in an unabashedly good mood, enjoying himself.
He is celebrating just having been elected First Secretary in 1965. On his immediate right is a Hungarian CP envoy. AUTHOR'S COLLECTION

*Above:* Ceaușescu (right) looks on as Gheorghe Gheorghiu-Dej greets the Soviet ambassador to Bucharest in 1963. In the middle is Alexandru Drăghici, the interior minister, whom Ceaușescu destroyed politically on his climb up the RCP ladder. AUTHOR'S COLLECTION

*Right:* President Nixon and Ceaușescu wave to cheering crowds at Otopeni Airport, Bucharest, following Nixon's official two-day state visit to Romania. UPI CABLEPHOTO/COURTESY THE BETTMANN ARCHIVE

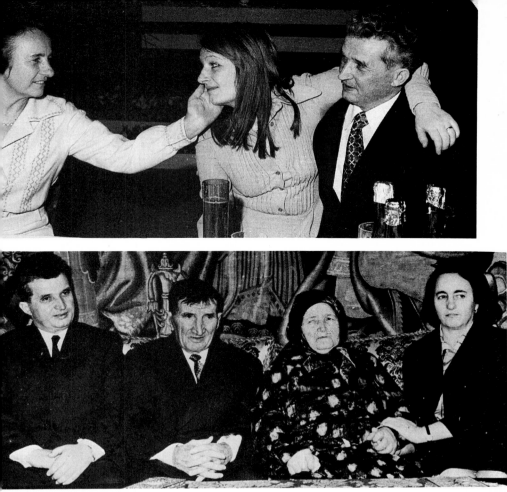

*Top:* A rare informal photo of Ceaușescu celebrating his sixtieth birthday on January 26, 1978, with his wife and daughter, Zoia. For the occasion he organized a banquet for his family and friends of the regime. COURTESY GAMMA LIAISON, NEW YORK, N.Y.

*Center:* Ceaușescu (extreme left), his aged father, Elena's mother, and Elena in 1968. AUTHOR'S COLLECTION

*Left:* The scene outside the Central Committee building in Bucharest on December 21, 1989, when what was to have been an official pro-Ceaușescu rally turned into a spontaneous demonstration against him that led to his flight on December 22 and his subsequent downfall. GEORGES MERILLON; COURTESY GAMMA LIAISON, NEW YORK, N.Y.

*Above:* In this image taken from Romanian television, Ceaușescu stops Elena as she answers the questions of the military during their trial on December 25, 1989. REUTERS/BETTMANN; COURTESY THE BETTMANN ARCHIVE

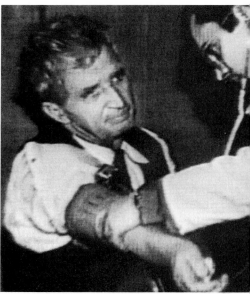

*Right:* December 25, 1989: Image from Romanian television of Ceaușescu having his blood pressure checked by a doctor. Less than two hours later he was dead, shot by a firing squad. REUTERS/BETTMANN; COURTESY THE BETTMANN ARCHIVE

*Below:* Undated Romanian television images showing Elena and Ceaușescu after their execution by firing squad on December 25, 1989, at an undisclosed location. REUTERS/BETTMANN NEWSPHOTOS; COURTESY THE BETTMANN ARCHIVE

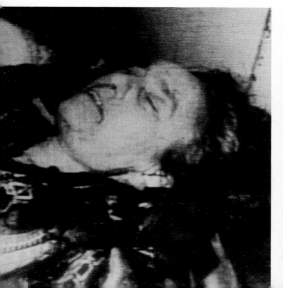

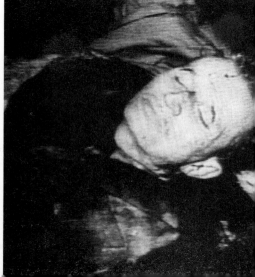

posed both on those who eliminated first deputy premier Beria shortly after Stalin's death in 1953 and those who foiled Chiang Ching's expected bid for power immediately after her husband Mao's death in 1976. We will probably never know the detailed chronological sequence of events that took place inside the Kremlin after the deaths of Brezhnev, Andropov, or Chernenko.

In the case of Gheorghiu-Dej's death and succession, part of the curtain was tantalizingly lifted when, in the immediate post-Ceauşescu era, Emanuel Valeriu interviewed some old-time RCP establishment survivors about the past. Maurer, Apostol, and others were quizzed at length, and while their answers were self-serving and contradictory, they did shed *some* light on what occurred then. According to Gheorghe Apostol, Gheorghiu-Dej not only admitted he was dying but freely discussed the question of succession. "He told me that he had decided that neither Chivu Stoica nor Nicolae Ceauşescu was up to it," Apostol said on Romanian TV in January 1990. "He told me I was the most suitable person to succeed him."

Shortly afterward, he went on, "Maurer asked me to see him. In his office I found him alone with Bodnăraş. 'We must discuss an important issue,' Maurer said. 'Gheorghiu-Dej has asked us to name a successor before he dies. He wants you to be the next first secretary.' "

Apostol replied that it was up to the Central Committee to name a successor, "to decide," as he put it, "what Gheorghiu-Dej had already decided." The three men went to the Central Committee, where they met with Drăghici, Ceauşescu, and Chivu Stoica. But it immediately became clear to him that Ceauşescu was running too. "I then realized that there would be two groups contending for power and that party unity would go down the drain."

In a desperate effort to block Ceauşescu, Apostol then had a heart-to-heart talk with Maurer and proposed that Drăghici be adopted as a compromise candidate. Maurer said he'd think about it. After Gheorghiu-Dej's death there was a meeting of the Politburo. Before the meeting, Maurer told Apostol that "several of the older members had come to the conclusion that the best man for the job was Nicolae Ceaușescu." Maurer said he personally was in favor of this, "for he is young and eager to learn." At the Central Committee session, it was Emil Bodnăraș who officially proposed that "the youngest of us all" should become the next first secretary. "And so," said Apostol, "Ceaușescu won. The person responsible for this was Maurer, ever the opportunist and fractionalist. He cultivated Ceaușescu, pandered to him, backing him to the hilt. Ceaușescu and Maurer were in this together."

Most of the Romanian Communist party establishment, aware of the behind-the-scenes drama played around Gheorghiu-Dej's deathbed, agree that Maurer was the key figure who ensured Ceaușescu's victory. This, Valeriu recalled, was "all the more surprising because Maurer thoroughly despised Ceaușescu." Though a lifelong communist, Maurer was an intellectual, with a cosmopolitan background and a French mother, and he liked to give himself patrician airs. It was the knowledge that he would continue to be foreign affairs minister, a post for which he rightly believed he was eminently suited, that made him behave as he did, and his reward was commensurate with the deed—he eventually became prime minister. "In retrospect," Maurer told me in 1990, "I do feel a great responsibility for having inflicted Ceaușescu on Romania."

Quite apart from the light they threw on the past, the interviews with these old survivors were fascinating because they showed the degree of visceral hatred Maurer, Apostol, and Brucan still harbored for one another after all this time. Even in their twilight years, they still seemed more intent on destroying one anothers' reputations than in telling the whole truth. Their behavior in turn underlined the climate of suspicion, personal hostility, and backbiting (contrary to the frequent editorials in *Scînteia* extolling the remarkable degree of party unity) that was a durable feature of life at the top within the ranks of the Romanian Communist party. The 1990 TV interviews afforded a rare glimpse into the Orwellian, dog-eat-dog ambience of the Romanian Communist party's top establishment: Without in the least excusing Ceaușescu's behavior, these men were living proof of how, in such a climate, extreme suspicion and paranoia flourished.

Apostol's version of the succession is contradicted in *Red Horizons*, the autobiography of Ion Pacepa, Ceaușescu's head of foreign intelligence, who defected in 1978. Here, picked up by the inevitable Securitate microphone and quoted by Pacepa, was Maurer reading an excerpt of his memoirs[2] to his wife that same year:

> On Monday, March 19, 1965, I paid my daily visit to Gheorghiu-Dej. He could no longer speak, because of his throat cancer, but he jotted down several words on a notepad with his favorite violet pencil and gave the note to me. I read: "It is my final wish that Comrade Maurer be my successor." After reading it, I tried to tell him how I felt. His eyes were closed. Dej was going. . . . The Politburo meeting the next morning was brief. I presented Gheorghiu-Dej's note but I turned down the position of leader. In an effort to avert a violent succession crisis, I proposed that "the youngest man" be appointed temporarily, until the next Party Congress, which had to elect the Party leader. My proposal was seconded by Emil Bodnăraş and was accepted.

Valeriu, for one, believes Apostol's version. "Everything Maurer did or said was an exercise in self-vindication," he commented. The likeliest interpretation is that Party elders like Maurer and Bodnăraş were in favor of Ceaușescu because, on the basis of his past record, they believed they would be able to manipulate him, using him as a convenient figurehead or transitional first secretary.

Elena Ceaușescu was not idle during this vital period in her husband's career. Proof that Ceaușescu was seriously in the running to succeed Gheorghiu-Dej came in the weeks preceding his actual death. One veteran communist recalled that Elena Ceaușescu was "exceptionally charming" to the wives of the senior-most leaders during this period, congratulating them on their looks, deferring to them in every way, and telling the Maurer, Bodnăraş, and Drăghici wives that "the four of them will make a terrific team." Such conduct was unusual, for Elena was already acquiring a reputation as a shrew and purveyor of scurrilous, denigrating gossip concerning all her husband's colleagues, their wives, and their girlfriends.

While Ceauşescu was beginning his rise in the Party hierarchy, Elena was working as a secretary in the foreign affairs ministry, but her incompetence and lack of skills were such that she was very soon "let go." She then began attending chemistry courses for "mature" students in Bucharest (1955–56). Because she had a family to attend to, she was very often absent, but as the wife of an up-and-coming communist she was afforded considerable leeway. There is no record of her obtaining a chemistry degree in advance of her doctorate (a junior professor supervising a chemistry exam and expelling her from the examination room for cheating lived in fear of his life for decades afterward), but by 1960 she had a full-time job as a researcher at the Bucharest-based Institute of Chemistry (ICECHIM—Institutul de Cercetări Chimice), and by 1965 she had become its director. Mircea Corciovei, a scientist at ICECHIM, recalled that "in her new position, it was very difficult to talk to her. She gave orders; she wanted no arguments." It was impossible for him to discover the extent of her knowledge of chemistry, for she never discussed the scientific aspects of the institute's work, "concerning herself only with political and administrative matters."

By the time Corciovei discussed Elena Ceauşescu's scientific credentials, or lack of them, she had been dead for several months, but such was the fear she continued to inspire that he, like all the other ICECHIM staffers, was extremely reluctant to talk, only by stages gathering up sufficient determination to express his true feelings. He had to be reminded more than once that the microphones in the room were no longer active and that even if they were, *she* was no longer around to listen to our conversation. Even so, he kept glancing worriedly around him, as if convinced that his laboratory was still bugged.

Elena Ceauşescu, he and other laboratory workers eventually admitted, had been a monstrously harsh, mean-spirited boss. In every conceivable way, she had cut down on the institute's expenses, with no regard for its staff's welfare or prospects. Salaries were lower than in other scientific institutes; she scrapped the telephone exchange to save money on operators' wages, linking the institute's phones to the chemistry ministry exchange, which meant it was practically impossible for the ICECHIM staff to receive incoming calls. She personally scrutinized every expense item, assuming that every employee was out to steal from the institute, but she was reluctant to meet with her subordinates, because any technical discussions would have revealed her near-total ignorance of the science of chemistry. For example, Corciovei discovered she didn't know what a chromatograph was, and didn't recognize the formula for sulfuric acid—$SO_4H_2$—taught to first-year chemistry students. Similarly, she would deny researchers applications for ethyl alcohol ("I know you're only using it to make your own home brew," she would say) but put "approved" on the same forms when the ethyl-alcohol applications were formulated in technical terms. She put an end to the practice of the institute's staff receiving payments on patents resulting from their work, substituting tiny salary bonuses instead.

Corciovei recalled that the day Elena Ceaușescu was due to appear before a board of examiners for the oral of her chemistry doctorate, while she was working at the institute, he tried to attend. "It is almost impossible to reach a doctorate level on the basis of adult-education evening classes, so I wanted to see how she reacted to the examiners' questions," he said. The date and time of the examination, open to the public by law and university tradition, was duly posted on the university noticeboard. "But when I showed up, the door was locked. The session had occurred *in camera* that morning."

Six months after Elena Ceaușescu's death, none of the surviving chemistry professors, now retired, who had examined her was willing to talk. A telephone conversation with one of the professors' sons ended abruptly: I was told to "get lost." Nothing much had changed, it seemed. The chemistry institute still lacked its own telephone exchange. Years of financial cheeseparing and enforced cultural isolation gave the institute, when I visited it in 1990, a palpable air of neglect. For lack of funds to pay gardeners, the grounds around the building were a mass of overgrown thickets and weeds.

The Central Committee elected Nicolae Ceaușescu as the
Party's first secretary on March 22, 1965—a mere two days
after Gheorghiu-Dej's death. None of the behind-the-scenes
infighting Apostol referred to twenty-five years later was apparent, for Ceaușescu was elected unanimously. Apostol knew
better than to set himself up as an easy target in a hopeless
confrontation. He told a well-wisher later: "Ceaușescu had
won over the Party organization, the army, Securitate, the
propaganda commission—I was left with nothing at all." With
hindsight, however, some ripples of unease within the ranks
of the elite could be detected. Nicolae Ceaușescu's tactics in
overcoming the latent hostility of his erstwhile rivals were
faultless. Gheorghiu-Dej had accumulated the posts of first
secretary and president of the Council of State. Chivu Stoica,
one of the contenders, was appointed president of the Council
of State, but everyone knew this was a figurehead appointment. In the immediate Party lineup after March 24, Chivu
Stoica's name came first, but in the few months that followed,
until the Ninth Party Congress opening on July 19, the names
of members of the Politburo and Central Committee were
listed in alphabetical order. Ceaușescu knew that only the first
battle had been won.

His course of action, during the March–July period, was a
textbook example of the procedures required to gain the support of fellow bureaucrats within the RWP. Aware that the
most powerful Party figures, Maurer, his kingmaker, and his
two most dangerous rivals—Gheorghe Apostol and Alexandru Drăghici, the man who controlled the security services—
were watching him closely, he was careful not to thrust himself
unduly forward. At Gheorghiu-Dej's funeral, Stoica spoke
first, then Apostol, then Maurer, with Ceaușescu coming last.
All four were in fact engaged in canvassing not only Party
functionaries but also all influential professional groups, in
advance of the July congress. Ceaușescu was tireless in this
respect, but also careful to associate with the others in his
travels and speech making. The group addressed scientists,
intellectuals, security officers. Correctly gauging the country's
mood, they stressed the importance of those measures, already taken in Gheorghiu-Dej's lifetime, that had met with

approval, without however straying too far from the orthodox Marxist-Leninist path. Ceaușescu told the scientists he welcomed "open confrontation of views." His attitude toward writers and artists at this stage was the equivalent of Mao's "let a hundred flowers bloom," but they believed he meant it. To all, the ruling caucus promised more "socialist legality," which meant more emphasis on constitutionality and slightly more regard for individuals' rights. Those arrested had to be charged within twenty-four hours and could no longer be held incommunicado indefinitely. This measure appeared to be more spectacular than was in fact the case, for individual rights still fell far short of an acceptable norm. More important, built-in acknowledgments of the ideological supremacy of the Soviet Union were removed. The popularity of all measures symbolizing the end of the Romanian dependency on the Soviet Union encouraged the new leaders to be bold. They also realized that in the post-Stalin era, the obedience of the people was not enough: Some form of consent was necessary.

Ceaușescu and his team adapted the content of their reform blueprint according to the audience they were addressing. Ceaușescu, in particular, showed unexpected agility in skirting hard issues while giving the impression that momentous changes were ahead. In this spirit, he told Securitate officers that their police powers would not be curtailed and that their vigilance in ferreting out "opportunists and splittists" was as indispensable as ever at the same time he was hinting to the Romanian populace that they might enjoy more latitude than they had in the past.

He displayed the same ambiguity in his statements concerning foreign policy, praising "proletarian internationalism" (which meant, in the Marxist-Leninist shorthand of the time, acknowledging the supremacy of the Soviet Union) while restating the themes of the Gheorghiu-Dej-inspired declaration of independence. In 1966 both Yugoslavia's Tito and China's Chou Enlai were given rapturous welcomes in Bucharest in the communist tradition, with flag-waving schoolgirls lining the streets and blanket media coverage. In stark contrast, ordinary Romanians learned of a visit by Brezhnev to Bucharest only by reading about it in a brief *Scînteia* news report after he had left. All leaders were also careful to reassure Romania's ethnic minorities of their importance.

It was only at the Ninth Congress, in July 1965, that Ceauşescu's tactical dexterity, and the extent of his careful advance planning, became fully evident. Western correspondents covering the event were agreeably surprised by the relative openness and accessibility of its organizers. A personality cult was nowhere in evidence, for there were no pictures of living Romanian leaders. At Ceauşescu's behest, the congress got rid of the workers'-party label and reverted to its old title, the Romanian Communist party. Similarly, the People's Republic became the Romanian Socialist Republic. In small ways like these, the impression was conveyed that sectarian measures handicapping former "bourgeois" families were a thing of the past.

With hindsight, perhaps the most important event at the congress was the report on changes in Party statutes, for it was Apostol, not Ceauşescu, who delivered this key speech, a signal to all that that his days were not over. Apostol announced that Ceauşescu's new title would be that of General Secretary, not First Secretary. This implied that he would be less in command of things than Gheorghiu-Dej, and thus more responsive to collective leadership. But Ceauşescu, in turn, neatly turned the tables on both Apostol and Drăghici. By increasing the size of the Central Committee, where Ceauşescu knew he had most clout, and by reducing the size of the Politburo, which he renamed the Executive Committee, he was able to cut them down to size. Another measure none could formally object to also helped him consolidate his new position: The conference decided not to allow any individual Party leader more than one full-time job. A third innovation proposed by Ceauşescu was the creation of a new body, the Presidium, in addition to the Executive Committee (ex-Politburo). It was difficult for any of his rivals to object to this: On the face of it, such a body, consisting of the seven senior-most RCP leaders, implied a strengthening of the "collegiate" principle. Its members, apart from Ceauşescu and Stoica, were Maurer, Apostol, Alexandru Bîrlădeanu, Bodnăraş and Drăghici.

The latter discovered too late that he had been checkmated. Because of the new rules, he was compelled to give up his post as interior minister, thus losing his only power base, as Ceauşescu had intended he should. The writing was on the wall for Apostol as well. As he was to explain on Romanian television in January 1990, he had—in a private conclave before the formal Ninth Congress—objected to the high rate of industrial investment earmarked for Romania's forthcoming five-year plan. As overseer of all trade-union activities, Apostol knew this would cut into Romanian workers' living standards. "Everyone, including Maurer, ignored me," he said. "The reason was opportunism, and cowardice not only at the top but at the lower level of the Party. Nobody would say anything against Nicolae Ceauşescu. They were like blind people following a one-eyed man." As a result of his remarks, Apostol knew that he too was on Ceauşescu's hit list.

The composition of the newly named Executive Committee was very much the same as before, strengthening Ceauşescu's long-term prospects as uncontested leader of the Party. Of the fifteen members, twelve were old Politburo hands. But nine out of ten of the new candidate-members were stalwart Central Committee members who owed their fledgling careers to Ceauşescu.

The various changes occurring in Romania were seen in a highly favorable light abroad. The Western powers kept the Warsaw Pact countries under constant scrutiny, noting every break, however slight, between the satellites and their Soviet big brother. The policy differences among Poland, Hungary, and, later, Czechoslovakia, on the one hand, and the Soviet Union, on the other, were constantly being analyzed. In the outside world, Ceauşescu was already acquiring a reputation as an interestingly different kind of communist leader. Inside Romania, the impact of the changes was also favorable, especially among intellectuals and the remnants of the middle class. Răzvan Theodorescu, a university professor later to become director-general of Romanian TV in 1990, said, "From 1965 to 1968, I admired Nicolae Ceauşescu." Cătălin Mamali, a Bucharest-based psychologist, described these years as "a period of openness." In the eyes of most Romanians, he added, it was Ceauşescu, and not Gheorghiu-Dej, who was perceived as having made a break with the Russians. "We felt we were being freed from Soviet serfdom," he said. It was probably impossible, Mamali went on, for non-Romanians to grasp what the new intellectual freedom implied. "Imagine a state of affairs where all the traditional values, all great literature, music, and art, whether Shakespeare, Gainsborough, or Handel, were banned or made subordinate to an alien culture and ideology. That was the situation in Romania until the early sixties." Paul Goma, the dissident writer, summed up the Romanians' mood (and their ingrained anti-Semitism) as follows: "The general feeling was, among the vast majority of Romanians, Okay, he's a communist but at least he's against the Russians, the Hungarians, the Jews; he's one of *us*."

The change was welcome because the previous constraints had been so harsh and the Soviet-style agitprop so grotesquely enforced as to be particularly unbearable in a country whose intellectuals and middle class had followed Western fashions in art and literature for decades. For this reason, they were probably less amenable to social realism or to the vocabulary of Marxism-Leninism than any other Eastern European state. French was still the natural second language of educated Romanians, and would remain so. Those Romanians familiar not only with the French language but with the works of Descartes, Molière, Voltaire, and Bergson could never willingly assimilate the prose of hack writers aping Soviet social realists or the Stalinist vocabulary of *Scînteia* editorials.

Even Ceaușescu, whose contempt for intellectuals had been fueled by his jail experiences, realized in the late fifties and early sixties that he needed to acquire a cultural veneer: His remarkable self-improvement, as speaker and writer, dates from this time. The need to marshal his facts coherently, to speak occasionally without notes, to handle himself well not just before an undemanding RCP audience but in the presence of distinguished foreign guests and statesmen, all contributed to the metamorphosis, though he remained, all his life, a below-average performer. The strain must have been considerable: Elena Ceaușescu drilled him, helping to cure his stuttering. Nicolae's stammer now manifested itself only in private, in moments of intense anger or excitement. He remained an indifferent public speaker, his delivery monotonous, his sentences and thought processes molded by the Marxist-Leninist prose he had absorbed since his teens, but he was no longer a total embarrassment on a public platform. There would always be flunkies to correct his grammar—and in any case, his mispronunciations endeared him to some Romanians—they proved he was a man of the people. Elena Ceauşescu molded him in other ways. According to a former close collaborator, "She supervised his diet, and insisted that he become a teetotaler, fearing as she did that the hereditary drinking in his family could jeopardize his career." With his projection on the world stage, he acquired the kind of self-confidence that came from constant public exposure. Soon, he was delighting in it.

Oppression inevitably breeds nostalgia for the past, and it is quite possible that those Romanians who recall 1965–68 as halcyon years may be idealizing them somewhat. It is worth remembering that the restrictive measures concerning divorce and abortions, the ban on contraceptives, the compulsory gynaecological examination of pregnant women to monitor illegal abortion attempts, increased taxation imposed on childless couples, and the extreme difficulties put in the way of would-be emigrants (all of which attracted the belated indignation of the Western world in the eighties) were all introduced as early as October 1966. The new orientation was also very puritanical, with campaigns against miniskirts, beards, long hair, and other "Western decadent" eccentricities, and the new freedom for intellectuals was severely limited. "The common denominator of our socialist art is the Marxist-Leninist ideal," Ceauşescu told a conference in 1968, also condemning "those who only create for a handful of 'elect' people." Similarly, at a meeting in Constanţa in 1968, he told Party workers: "We do not understand democracy in its bourgeois meaning—of babbling, lack of discipline, anarchy. We understand democracy as the active participation of the citizens in formulating and implementing the Party's policy." As Mary Ellen Fischer rightly remarked,[3] it was difficult not to conclude that Ceauşescu was "promising everything to everyone" but refusing to make any really hard decisions that would have broken the Marxist-Leninist mold. And even the new insistence on the need for "socialist legality" could be seen, with hindsight, as a convenient means of destroying the reputation of the former interior minister, Alexandru Drăghici, one of his long-term potential rivals for the leadership, and a formidable one, since he controlled Securitate. Ceaușescu was advocating derussification but not freedom from Party control. Indeed, some of the characteristics that would later assume such caricatural importance in Ceaușescu's later years were already in evidence: In March 1966, a carefully staged conference of the Union of Agricultural Cooperatives included pageants, fulsome praise for Ceaușescu (and other leading communists), and "prolonged spontaneous applause" at key speeches—in other words, the beginning of a personality cult. In December 1967, Ceaușescu was elected president of the State Council, president of the republic in all but name.

Ceaușescu quickly reveled in what under de Gaulle was called *les bains de foule,* "crowd immersion." Mary Ellen Fischer calculated that between July 1965 and January 1973, Ceaușescu would carry out 173 regional tours, each usually involving 48 hours of public meetings, factory and housing tours, after-dinner speeches, and carefully rehearsed *bains de foule.* Not only did he take an instant liking to the business of shaking hands, kissing babies, accepting bouquets, and addressing large audiences ready to cheer every platitude, but he became increasingly self-assured, and something of a know-it-all. He started lecturing factory managers on factory organization, farmers on the correct method of spacing crops, and schoolteachers on the importance of visual aids. He drew heavily on his one "senior-management course" as an up-and-coming communist cadre at the Ștefan Gheorghiu Academy of Social and Political Science, a kind of staff college for senior communists. He had graduated from its Institute of Economic Science with a thesis on "certain questions on the development of Romania's industry in the nineteenth century." Though this piece of research had been highly derivative, it enabled him to pepper his speeches with historical references, all intended to dazzle his audience with a show of economic expertise and historical breadth.

Imperceptibly, and perhaps without his realizing it, the new deference was beginning to alter Ceaușescu's personality. All his life, he had derived ideas from others. His was not an original mind: He was extremely good at absorbing facts, techniques, and gimmicks to use to his special advantage, to suit his tactical ends. There was undoubtedly a peasant shrewdness to him, a capacity to size up a complicated situation and grasp its essentials. But just as he accepted unquestioningly the principles of Marxism-Leninism, so he began to take for granted the deference and the respect his new, exalted rank inspired. From there it was only a short step to believing that he indeed *was* a superior individual, that the homage he was receiving was not due to his new status but stemmed from a deserved if belated recognition of his genius. This was a delusion Elena exploited, encouraging him in his vanity, while at the same time denigrating all those around him, and constantly calling their competence, intelligence, and loyalty into question. Some of the leading members of the RCP establishment sensed danger: Silviu Brucan, from the time of Gheorghiu-Dej's death, became a diplomatic dropout, though he did accept a number of special short assignments from Ceaușescu. Both Maurer and Apostol would later claim that they had detected the growing flaws in Ceaușescu's personality from 1965 onward. After July 1966, Elena Ceaușescu's name invariably appeared in news stories whenever she accompanied her husband.

There was another ominous side to the succession: A leading member of the Ceaușescu entourage in 1965 told me twenty-five years later that it had been Gheorghiu-Dej's conviction, when cancer struck, that he had been the victim of a KGB plot. He believed his illness was the Soviet way of paying him back for his rebellious attitude. He even confided to Ceaușescu, the source said, that the cancer had been induced by radiation beamed into the palace and that it could also have been transmitted through a radioactive doorknob installed in his suite. Whether there was any truth to this wild allegation will probably never be known. It is especially instructive for the light it sheds on Gheorghiu-Dej's state of mind, his paranoid fear of the KGB—and, by extension, of all secret services—and his adherence to the conspiracy theory. In his last years, he had become increasingly subject to fits of persecution mania, believing that even his closest associates were plotting to get rid of him. Political assassination is not a KGB monopoly, nor is it confined to communist countries. But the elimination of Foriş, Pătrăşcanu, and others must have made Gheorghiu-Dej realize that such precedents could be emulated. Romania's precommunist past was more notable than others for its violence: Gheorghiu-Dej remembered the fate of Codreanu, the Iron Guard leader "shot while attempting to escape," and the subsequent Iron Guard retaliations. The source added that Ceauşescu took Gheorghiu-Dej's allegation seriously: Among the many notions Ceauşescu borrowed from his predecessor was that he was in constant personal danger. From the moment he became General Secretary, he displayed a new concern for his own security, which later would reach caricatural proportions, including the screening of visitors to measure radiation changes, and the detailed physical examination, in advance, of those peasant and worker schoolchildren "spontaneously" presenting him with bouquets on his numerous farm and factory visits.

The image Ceauşescu projected abroad between 1965 and 1969 was, however, immensely reassuring. In 1967, Romania became the first Warsaw Pact nation to recognize West Germany diplomatically, and it was the only country that failed to break diplomatically with Israel at the time of the six-day war with Nasser. On the domestic front, Ceauşescu encouraged readers to write in to *Scînteia* and expose abuses by bureaucrats and petty RCP bosses. He called for a detailed, authoritative history of the Romanian Communist party, one that would tell the whole truth about the past. The Museum of the History of the Romanian Communist Party was intended as a reliable record of events, not as a piece of self-serving hagiography. There were of course limits to the kind of freedom intellectuals could expect. The iron rule of all communist parties—that dirty laundry should not be washed in public— was rigidly observed. And many of Ceauşescu's reforms between 1965 and 1968 not only consolidated but also increased his personal powers. The rule banning any leaders from holding down more than one important job was rescinded two years later, once it was no longer useful. In a nationwide administrative shakeup, the sixteen administrative regions were broken up into forty smaller ones, and the intense jockeying for Party and local government jobs that followed gave Ceauşescu further clout among a new generation of up-and-coming Party officials. Among them was the young Ion Iliescu, a former leader of the Young Communists' League and an intellectual whose background was impeccable: His father, his uncle, and Ceauşescu had all been Young Communists together.

The crunch came at the plenum of the Central Committee meeting that began on April 22, 1968. The agenda—a reform of the educational system, foreign policy, and army-procurement methods were the most important items—gave no hint that the plenum was to be a witch-hunt. Under the deceptive title of "Report of the Party Commission on the Rehabilitation of some RCP Activists" Ceauşescu was to get rid of one potential rival, seriously affect the chances and reputations of several more, and "do a Khrushchev" by shattering the posthumous reputation of his late mentor, Gheorghiu-Dej.

The "activists" whose rehabilitation was now sought included Pătrăşcanu, and the report on him read like an accusing Amnesty International document. The historians commissioned to work on the definitive history of the RCP had done their job well. The Central Committee's findings, based on their research, showed that there had been not a shred of evidence to back the charges of counterrevolutionary and spying activities, that Pătrăşcanu had been unsuccessfully interrogated for over two years by leading members of the Politburo, including Gheorghiu-Dej, in an effort to make him confess, that he had almost certainly been tortured, and that Gheorghiu-Dej, from the moment of Pătrăşcanu's arrest, had been aware of this. Ana Pauker and Vasile Luca had had their share of responsibility for Pătrăşcanu's downfall too, but after they had been removed, along with Teohari Georgescu, Alexandru Drăghici had taken over the case "to get at any cost evidence to justify the assertion that he had allegedly been an agent of the Siguranţa and an Anglo-American spy." "On March 18, 1954, based on the information presented by Alexandru Drăghici, the Political Bureau of the CC decided to proceed to the trial of the group of spies headed by Pătrășcanu." This had taken place "in violation of the most elementary procedural guarantees."

The implications were sensational. Not only was Drăghici accused of manipulating evidence, and thereby bringing "false conclusions to the Politburo," but the Politburo (or Executive Committee, as it was known in Romania) members in turn had done nothing to validate his findings and were thus guilty, too. In the same report, but at shorter length, the late Ștefan Foriș was also rehabilitated. He had made "mistakes," the historians showed, but had never been a traitor. Other rehabilitations concerned Marcel Pauker, executed by Stalin in 1938, and Miron Constantinescu, disgraced but never jailed—and still alive at the time.

The day after the Central Committee plenum ended, Ceaușescu showed that he was putting the report to good use. Pătrășcanu's death had been a "dastardly assassination," he told an audience of Party "activists." Drăghici, as organizer and executor, was mainly responsible, but Gheorghiu-Dej, "who had a grudge against Pătrășcanu," had aided and abetted him, been kept informed of the progress of the investigation, and directed the prosecutors' tasks. What infuriated Ceaușescu, apparently, was that Drăghici had attempted to answer back during the Central Committee plenum, saying that similar methods had been used against the Romanian communists prior to 1944—putting previous regimes and the new "socialist Romania" on the same plane. Pătrășcanu, Ceaușescu went on, had been "a man of vast erudition and Marxist-Leninist culture, a remarkable Party leader." No one at the time was bold enough to raise the subject of Ceaușescu's own editorials attacking Pătrășcanu after his arrest, and Ceaușescu in his speech provided evidence of his own integrity and concern for "socialist legality." He had, he said, challenged Drăghici's methods as early as 1956. He quoted himself, at a Politburo meeting at the time, saying: "Comrade Drăghici thinks that he can do anything because he has relations with Gheorghiu-Dej." It was, of course, Ceaușescu's word against Drăghici's, for no minutes of the proceedings of that particular meeting were ever produced.

The Pătrăşcanu affair put paid, as was meant, to Drăghici's career. It also seriously affected the reputations of all those senior figures, like Bodnăraş and Apostol, who had been members of the Politburo at the time of Pătrăşcanu's arrest and trial. Maurer was exempt from such charges, for he had not been in the Politburo then, and neither, by a few days, had Ceauşescu. Apostol had already suffered more than his share of troubles. His car had collided with a motorcyclist who failed to stop. Apostol's wife suffered multiple fractures, his driver a broken leg, and their housekeeper, also in the car, was killed. On Romanian TV, Apostol said in 1990, "I accused the Party leadership of making an attempt on my life." In 1967, he said, there was a second attempt on his life, and after the plenum, "I decided to leave the country," traveling to the Soviet Union. Despite what must have been appalling misgivings, Apostol subsequently accepted the post of Romanian ambassador to Brazil, perhaps to escape from further Securitate-inspired assassination attempts on Romanian soil.

Such intra-Party dirty tricks were, of course, not bruited abroad or generally known inside Romania at the time. Ceauşescu's stand on those responsible for now-ancient crimes appealed to all "liberals" for it showed him in a crusading light, eager to reveal the truth and let the chips fall where they may, defending moral principles and the need to discover the RCP's "objective truth" about its past. The posthumous damage to Gheorghiu-Dej's prestige was considerable. Ceauşescu had dared to impugn the reputation of the one Romanian communist leader who had, in his lifetime, been the object of a personality cult and gained "historic" status. It was a remarkable achievement, even if the inspiration had come from elsewhere, for it was difficult not to link the posthumous attack on Gheorghiu-Dej with Khrushchev's posthumous denunciation of Stalin. It was yet another example of Ceauşescu's skill in adapting a tactic originally conceived by others to his own ends.

Though few of Ceaușescu's contemporaries were aware of it at the time, he was gradually changing his style. There would shortly be no more talk of "collective responsibilities." His earlier luck was holding. Soon, for millions of Romanians, and for many world statesmen, he would become something of a hero.

# CHAPTER EIGHT
# CEAUŞESCU'S FINEST HOUR

**I**N 1968 WORLD ATTENTION WAS FOCUSED ON Czechoslovakia, where a new-style, unorthodox communist leadership, under Alexander Dubček, was steadily dismantling Marxist-Leninist practices, and their attendant rigid controls imposed, ever since 1945, by a succession of Stalinist apparatchiks. It is interesting to speculate what might have occurred had Alexander Dubček's experiment in communism with a human face not been wrecked by Brezhnev's August 1968 invasion of Czechoslovakia. Could Ceauşescu's habit of borrowing from others have led him to follow in Dubček's footsteps, on the grounds that this was the future pattern of communism? His excessive reliance on the ideas of others

■

makes such a hypothesis worth considering at the same time that his incipient megalomania made the eventuality highly unlikely, though he might well, for a short time, have fooled others into believing he was heading in that direction.

It was probably far too late, even as early as 1968, for Ceauşescu to change. Some of the Romanian communists who observed him at close quarters then now claim that, all along, they knew that as far as Dubček was concerned, Ceauşescu was not *truly* supportive of his new liberal reforms. The reason, they argue, that Ceauşescu backed Dubček in 1968 and came out against Soviet intervention was that deep down, he knew that sooner or later his own maverick behavior would tempt the Soviets to intervene in Romania. It was the *principle* of Soviet intervention, rather than (in Dubček's case) the cause of it, that made him speak out. Perhaps understandably, in light of Securitate's continuous monitoring of the Romanian *nomenklatura*, and the fear it inspired, few of its members voiced these reservations until after Ceauşescu's death.

Still, it is a measure of our incomplete understanding of events and personalities at the time that in the West in 1968, many Soviet bloc specialists put Dubček and Ceauşescu more or less on the same plane. Their similarities were stressed, in retrospect unduly, and the differences inherent in both men and methods largely ignored. As we now know, by August 1968 Ceauşescu was embarked on a plan to scrap what was left of the RCP's collective leadership and discredit all those contemporaries of Gheorghiu-Dej, the old guard, who might conceivably challenge his authority and his methods. To the West, what mattered was that both Dubček and Ceauşescu were attempting to break away from their satellite status.

In terms of independence already gained, the Romanian appeared to have stolen a march on the Czech, for by August 1968 he had broken more vigorously, or at any rate more visibly, with the USSR than Dubček had. There had been no Soviet troops on Romanian soil since 1958. Romanian forces had boycotted Warsaw Pact exercises, and within the Warsaw Treaty Organization (WTO) Romania had become something of a pariah, excluded from recent high-level meetings. Romania was also less inclined to follow the Soviet line on interna-

tional issues than was Czechoslovakia, as its voting record at
the United Nations showed, and it been bolder in defying
Soviet wrath by maintaining "normal" relations with the anti-
Moscow Chinese leadership. Relations between Ceauşescu and
Brezhnev, on the surface at least, had reached a crisis pitch:
The two men, clearly, had not only policy differences but
personal differences as well. Brezhnev was aware that
Ceauşescu had ordered a detailed investigation into Brezhnev's postwar behavior as first secretary of the Soviet republic
of Moldavia, as Bessarabia had been renamed since its annexation by Stalin in 1941. The Soviet leader had been a harsh
overlord, and the already powerful Securitate had compiled a
full report on deportations, arrests, and other exactions during Brezhnev's tenure of office. De Gaulle's visit to Romania in
May 1968 and Ceauşescu's much publicized visit to Tito in
Yugoslavia were indications that here was the leader of a Warsaw Treaty country determined to make his own mark and go
his own way.

Brezhnev was far more preoccupied with Dubček than
with Ceauşescu, however, for the latter had shown no intention of destroying the fabric of Marxism-Leninism. Dubček,
on the other hand, threatened everything it stood for. In internal affairs, Romania was just as orthodox as the Soviet
Union, except for one respect: Ceauşescu repeatedly showed
that he supported Czechoslovakia's "new look." At a speech in
Galaţi, he told workers that the Romanian Communist party
"does not share the views of those who are alarmed over what
is happening in Czechoslovakia."

He also indicated in various ways (as Dubček failed to do)
that Romania was determined to resist by force any Soviet
intervention. In speeches both to Party workers and graduat-
ing cadets, he made unequivocally defiant remarks. "There
can be no justification for admitting in any way the use of
armed forces for intervention in the internal affairs of any of
the Warsaw Treaty socialist member countries," he said. Two
days later, on August 16, to make his meaning even clearer, he
flew to Prague and signed a "Friendship, Cooperation and
Mutual Assistance Treaty" with Dubček. The treaty left unanswered one vital, as yet hypothetical, question: Would Ro-

mania intervene militarily should Czechoslovakia be invaded? In Prague, Ceauşescu referred to the treaty as a joint measure taken "against the aggressive policy of imperialist circles"— meaning, of course, the West—which fooled no one. Back in Romania, on the very eve of the Soviet invasion of Czechoslovakia, August 21, he told automobile workers that "the destinies of the Czechoslovak people are in safe hands." In the Czechs, he said, "we have a wonderful friend in the joint struggle for socialism." The next day, along with token Bulgarian, East German, Hungarian, and Polish units, Soviet divisions crossed the border, and Dubček and his colleagues were hijacked by the Soviets, flown to the USSR, and compelled to put an end to their brief experiment in reform from within the communist system.

Ceauşescu must, of course, have anticipated such a move. To his credit, he did not back down. At a huge rally in Palace Square, on August 21, he told an emotional, cheering crowd that the Soviet invasion had been "a great mistake and a grave danger to peace in Europe, to the fate of socialism in the world, and a shameful moment in the history of the revolutionary movement." There was "no justification whatever," he went on, "for military intervention in the affairs of a fraternal socialist state." No outsider, he added, had the right to determine what the road to socialist construction should be. To defend the independence of our "socialist motherland," Ceauşescu announced he was raising a force of "armed patriotic guards, composed of workers, peasants, and intellectuals."

Former members of his staff recall that before making his speech, Ceauşescu strode up and down inside the palace, intensely nervous, as he had every right to be, and sweating profusely. Inevitably, his self-serving foreign policy adviser, Gheorghe Maurer, later claimed that it was *he* who had urged Ceauşescu not only to show his solidarity with Dubček but to stand firm after Soviet intervention. But no amount of second-guessing could alter the fact that as a result of his firm anti-intervention stand, Ceauşescu became, almost overnight, not only a national hero but an international star. Even those who had suffered under the regime, including some who had spent long years in jail and concentration camps for their anticommunism, were moved. There was much tearful applause in Palace Square, and in the country at large, no doubt that Ceauşescu was the man of the hour.

It so happened that shortly after Ceauşescu's speech I myself had firsthand experience of its impact on the Romanian people. As a *Newsweek* correspondent, I had arrived in Prague almost immediately after the Soviet invasion. During my second week of reporting there, my editors, to my silent fury, ordered me to get to Bucharest as soon as possible. The reason was, I later learned, that a senior *Newsweek* editor had been tipped off, by a high-level CIA source, that satellite reconnaissance photographs revealed Soviet forces poised to invade Romania.

I decided to drive along the Romanian-Soviet border. At least, in the event of an invasion, I would have a ringside seat. On the way I stopped briefly in Ploeşti, Cluj, and Braşov, to assess the disposition of the Romanians in the light of Ceauşescu's fighting words.

"For a nation which could be facing an invasion by an overwhelmingly powerful neighbor," I wrote, "Romania remains remarkably unruffled. . . . The only armed figures I saw were a sentry standing with fixed bayonet in front of a small ammunition dump and a wizened farmer on a bicycle out on a day's rabbit shooting with his shotgun slung across his back."[1] There was no trace of any patriotic militia.

I had never been in Romania before, and my first impression was not so very different from Ivor Porter's in 1939: Here were two cultures, ancient and modern, coexisting side by side. The number of churches and ox-drawn carts surprised me, as well as clear evidence, under communism, of a vigorous, traditional village life. In the towns, cinemas showed old Westerns and other Hollywood films. There were lines outside a prewar Johnny Weissmüller *Tarzan* film. The number of Western tourists, West Germans outnumbering the rest, was also unexpected. There were no food shortages: In late-night restaurants, German families guzzled huge portions of stewed pork and put away large quantities of Romanian beer.

Perhaps most surprising of all was the Romanian people's attitude to Ceauşescu. Interviews with a succession of random hitchhikers were highly informative and, I believe, reflected their genuine feelings, for whenever possible, I pretended to be an ordinary tourist, not a reporter. One Romanian Orthodox priest on his way to visit friends in a monastery spoke highly of him ("A very good man . . . he will keep the Russians away") and said that things had never been better in his own church: "Everyone comes to us—the party officials, the people on the collective farms, the young people too. There is no such thing in these parts as a nonbeliever." A Ploeşti oil field worker told me: "We have a good life now, and things are getting slowly better. It could be a very good life if we were certain that the Russians would leave us alone." The "old communism," a foreman in his fifties told me, was "everywhere kaput." What reservations my passengers had involved not Ceauşescu himself but the inequalities of the *nomenklatura* system. Student hitchhikers invariably wanted to travel to the West, and claimed that only those with Party connections were able to do so. Others contrasted their own modest life-styles with those of some of the local Party bigwigs, and wondered how they had managed to acquire their large houses, Mercedes cars, and other luxuries while urging the nation to observe continued austerity.[2] It was clear that here was an unusually popular leader in an uncommon country.

The West quickly reacted to Ceauşescu's stand: Prime Minister Harold Wilson's foreign secretary, Michael Stewart, visited him within days of the Soviet invasion of Czechoslovakia, and though the Foreign Office adamantly maintained that he was there only to discuss Anglo-Romanian economic exchanges, it was clear the British government had wanted to show its respect and encouragement for Ceauşescu's independence of mind.

His real accolade came a year later, when President Richard Nixon visited Romania—his first visit to a communist country as president. He had been to Romania before, on a "private visit" in 1967, had been given the kind of treatment usually accorded to a head of state, and had been favorably disposed to Ceauşescu even before the invasion of Czechoslovakia. The Nixon visit set the tone: Romania, after August 1968, became the fashionable country to visit, as China was to become the "in" place after Nixon's visit there in 1972. Ceauşescu had embarked on a policy of inviting prominent personalities to Romania shortly after becoming general secretary, choosing his guests with care and planning their stay with considerable public-relations skill. Instinctively, he sought out those (like Nixon and Willy Brandt) who might prove useful later on, though he was to show, as time went on, a distinct predilection for royalty of all kinds. It was a shrewd move, for the visits also brought in their wake a small number of prominent journalists, who could be relied upon to present the Romanian case in the most favorable light. Ceauşescu's hospitality not only made him better known abroad—and in the wake of August 1968, there was a growing curiosity about him—but also provided the increasingly deferential Party press with opportunities to show how important he was. The visits of Willy Brandt, de Gaulle, and Nixon were given blanket coverage in the Romanian press.

Even more attention was paid in the Romanian press and on TV to Ceauşescu's visit to Tito in Yugoslavia. In 1968 it was Tito, and not yet Ceauşescu, who was the best known, most acclaimed maverick anti-Soviet communist, having defied Stalin at considerable risk as early as 1947. With his wartime partisan leadership record, flamboyant life-style, and championship of third world nonalignment, Tito was Ceauşescu's envied role model. The impact of Tito's life-style on the Ceauşescu, some former members of their entourage revealed later, was considerable, for both Elena and Nicolae were always on the lookout for traits among the famous to be imitated and adapted to their own life-styles. The extraordinary proliferation of grotesquely ornate chandeliers in all buildings whose decoration Elena would supervise from 1968 onward (the Romanian writers' union mansion was an example) derived from her visits to places like Versailles. One ex-aide recalled that Ceauşescu was ill at ease in his thick suit and heavy shoes aboard Tito's yacht, and shortly afterward started paying greater attention to his appearance, even for a time indulging in Tito's passion for white linen suits and thin-soled white shoes. Likewise, Elena's transformation was complete.

In her youth and early middle age, she had cultivated the

earnest, dowdy look. But she very quickly adapted to her new status as wife of the most powerful man in Romania, seeking out expensive, well-cut suits and indulging in a new passion for expensive jewelry, especially gold. Once svelte, she fought a determined battle to keep her weight down, but could do little about her walk, a graceless, flat-footed, pigeon-toed waddle on thick legs that her more daring colleagues imitated behind her back.

Some of Elena's aspirations as first lady were ludicrous: At the time of the Ceaușescus' first official visit to the United States, in October 1970, former diplomat Mircea Codreanu recalled, she insisted that all the menus for their own private use during their American stay be written out in French—a language neither she nor Nicolae then understood. She also, very quickly in her official life, became extremely predatory. Codreanu recalls that their visit to Detroit, also during October 1970, was almost canceled at the last minute because Elena insisted on receiving expensive gifts the Detroit hosts were reluctant to pay for. "I recall Elena's aide asking, What are they giving her? I said, The freedom of the city, the key to the city of Detroit, that sort of thing. That's not what she wants, the aide said. She wants something in gold—earrings, bracelets, *that* sort of thing. I was on the phone to the advance party in Detroit and the presidential plane was about to leave. I asked the advance party chief, Is there some kind of a present, something in gold? Yes, he answered. They had heard that was what she wanted, so such a gift had been prepared. Elena's man then interrupted me on the phone. 'Ask him how much it weighs,' he said. 'I can't do that,' I said. 'You must,' he said. 'She wants to know.' I got around it by asking him, 'If you hold it in your hand, how does it feel?' He said, 'It feels okay.' "

The gifts, Codreanu acknowledges, were destined for the Ceaușescus' private museum. Greed was not the only factor, he adds. "They wanted, by the size and splendor of the gifts they received, to show the Romanian people how beloved they were, and how highly respected by the foreign community."

Ceaușescu also began to display a special interest in the "third," nonaligned, world. To third world leaders, he downplayed the communist ideology, acting more like the leader of a nonaligned nation. He was already developing the line that Romania understood the difficulties of the third world better than any other East European country because it too faced the same problems of underdevelopment and the same need for industrialization. In this way, Ceaușescu believed, these third world countries would be more amenable to doing business with Romania than with the other countries of the Soviet bloc, and Romanian experts would be more welcome there. This approach was, at least initially, remarkably successful.

Another growing concern of Ceaușescu's, directly stemming from his need to project himself as a leader of international stature, was the Middle East. After 1967, the only Israeli embassy in the communist bloc was in Romania, and this was the rationale for his ambitious role as mediator between the Soviets and the Israelis. Needless to say, this concern—which at first reflected a perfectly natural desire to leave a mark as mediator in an international crisis affecting several continents, became in time a mere vehicle for a very personal ambition indeed: to be awarded the Nobel Peace Prize. To this effect, Romanian institutions would canvass the Oslo-based committee year after year, and Romanians frequently noted that Ceaușescu had been "nominated" for the prize. Ordinary Romanians were not to know that under the Nobel Peace Prize statutes any parliamentary body could nominate a candidate and that the qualification was ludicrously easy to obtain.

After Ceaușescu's stand on Czechoslovakia, and for several years afterward, he could do no wrong as far as most Western countries were concerned. He was "the good communist"—the joker in an otherwise dispiriting Eastern European pack. The insight of Western leaders into his real nature lagged behind that of the Romanians themselves. In 1978, long after Ceaușescu had shown signs of dangerous megalomania (his country by now the most totalitarian of the entire eastern bloc) he was thought worthy of an invitation to Buckingham Palace as a guest of Queen Elizabeth. In 1983, with the Romanian economy in ruins, George Bush, then Reagan's vice-president, would still call him "the good communist."

This pro-Ceauşescu bias on the part of the United States would be immeasurably strengthened by his decision to challenge the Soviet embargo on the 1984 Olympics.

In fact, the most unmistakable signs of Ceauşescu's determination to become Romania's second Conducător came only three days after President Nixon's departure. On August 6, 1969, the Tenth Congress of the Romanian Communist party began, and before it was over, Ceauşescu had changed the rules again. From this time onward, the General Secretary was no longer subject to reelection by a Central Committee vote but by the vote of the congress delegates, a much more malleable body. The interval between congresses was lengthened, from four years to five. The August 1969 congress also marked the end of the Gheorghiu-Dej old guard as a possible threat to Ceauşescu: Neither Apostol nor Stoica was reelected to his seat on the Central Committee.

More ominously, the kind of hero worship that Ceauşescu clearly believed was his due was manifested at the congress for the first time. The several hundred congress members rose as one man to applaud him for minutes at a time, shouting out, "Ceauşescu—the people," interminably. By now he had added a further title to his growing list. He was Chairman of the National Council of the Socialist United Front, a specially created "activist" body. Already, by March 14, 1969, he had acquired two more, as Chairman of the Defense Council and Supreme Commander of the Armed Forces. The personality cult followed a familiar pattern, with detailed accounts in *Scînteia* of the somewhat idealized life of the new Conducător, as told by Ceauşescu himself: "As the son of a peasant," he wrote, "I experienced the landlords' oppression, and after the age of eleven, capitalist exploitation." Listed among *Scînteia*'s paeans of praise for Ceauşescu were his "theoretical and practical contributions to the development and enrichment of political science." He started to believe his sycophants' absurdities all too soon—by 1970 he already showed signs of being out of touch with reality. "A man like me," he told his health minister in the early 1970s, "comes along only once every five hundred years." Under his leadership, another *Scînteia* article said, the

Romanian economy had developed "at a rate that has aroused the admiration of the whole world."

It was certainly rapid, and the figures, on the face of it, were dazzling. As Ceaușescu himself was to hammer home, in speeches of interminable length, from 1950 onward industrial output increased by 12.9 percent per annum, industrial development by 13 percent, and productivity by over 7 percent, while the industrial labor force grew by 5 percent per annum. Investment income reached astronomical figures, from 17.6 percent in 1955 to 34.1 percent in 1971, and 36.3 percent from 1976 onward.[3] From scanning the charts and figures alone, anyone would assume that Romania was enjoying growth rates comparable to those of Taiwan and South Korea and should by rights be embarking on a similar economic takeoff. But while foreign bankers *were* taken in to some extent, rushing in to grant loans on the basis of official reports and Western sympathy for the gallant, maverick leader Ceaușescu, the takeoff never occurred. From 1969 onward, ordinary Romanians experienced increasing hardship with every passing year. The reason, of course, was not only that investments were put to bad use, but that Ceaușescu's insistence on Stalinist economics virtually guaranteed that the loans that poured into Romania would aggravate Romania's predicament and lead to eventual disaster.

Perhaps it was Ceaușescu's absence of intellect, his inability to scrap his own Stalinist baggage, painfully acquired as a barely literate adolescent during his years in prison, that prevented him from adapting himself to the economic realities around him. There was plenty of talent on which to draw, for Romanian universities were still turning out, in the 1960s and 1970s, economics graduate students of high quality and cultural exchanges with the West, including those in the field of history and economics, had not yet been cut off. But Ceaușescu, while constantly teetering on the edge of economic reform, always drew back at the last moment. By the end of 1969, Romania's leading "reformist" economist, Alexandru Bîrlădeanu, had been shunted to a nonjob, and with his departure all hopes of a rational economic policy were shattered.

His successors knew that their job security, and eventual promotion, depended on docile implementation of Ceauşescu's
directives. Since Ceauşescu was, in economic matters, an un-
reconstructed Stalinist, he had an unshakable belief in the
merits of centralized planning, in the precedence of heavy
industry over agriculture, and on economic autarchy regardless of its economic cost. The limits of Ceauşescu's understanding of economics could be gauged from a speech he
made in July 1974:

> To give everyone the freedom of spending our society's
> money on whatever, and however, it might strike one's
> mind—this is not possible. We have a planned economy.
> The slogan of autonomy cannot be used to give everyone the
> right to spend money as he likes. There is full freedom of
> initiative in implementing the plan. Let us understand this
> well: in investments, all growth must be included in the quin-
> quennium or, for things of more minor a nature, occurring
> en route, in the yearly plan. Nobody has the right to build
> what is not provided for by the plan . . .

In other words, there was no room for any kind of real
initiative. Flexibility in implementing the plan was the equivalent of the flexibility enjoyed by a prisoner in determining his
fate. He might have the freedom of deciding on mealtimes
and work schedules but not that of leaving the prison com-
pound. Such grotesque pronouncements abounded and, as in
all dictatorships, decisions were made on the basis not only of
expediency but of whimsy. Ceauşescu was much more likely to
put his signature to a project involving massive expenditure if
the local Party secretary had previously flattered him with
adequate "crowd immersions" and slavish praise, and arranged for a successful bear hunt. For as time went on, local
Party leaders knew that one sure way of finding favor with the
Conducător was to organize lavish hunting trips—and to get
into Elena's good graces. Since, as she grew older, her pet
hatreds and suspicions grew exponentially, this was never easy.
Ceauşescu's limitations as an economist, and his reluctance
to listen to anyone other than sycophants, were sufficient to
ensure disaster. But the consequences of his "independent"
Soviet policy and the oil crisis of the 1970s compounded Ro-

mania's troubles. In the scramble for heavy industrialization, no attention was paid to energy costs, and some Romanian factories were two to four times as costly to run as their Western equivalents. This remained relatively unimportant so long as the world cost of oil was low and Romania's oil production adequate to meet all internal demand. But with the huge rise in oil prices from 1975 onward, Romania's heavy industries became caricaturally uneconomic. The Soviet Union had responded to Ceaușescu's posturings by cutting off cheap supplies of Soviet oil and making Romania pay world prices in hard currency. By 1976 Romania was no longer self-sufficient in oil and, furthermore, had unwisely invested in a huge, and expensive, new refining capacity, which was never used.

Even the Romanian initiative toward the third world countries floundered. Most of the African investments were "joint ventures" that cost Romania more in hard currency than they ever earned in revenue. To maintain its image in the non-aligned world, Romania was compelled to finance many of the ventures in the first place, becoming, after the Soviet Union, the leading communist nation in terms of aid to the developing countries. It was a luxury Romania could ill afford, but for Ceaușescu the cost was a necessary one, for increasingly, what mattered was appearance, not reality, and his personal prestige was literally without price. Imperceptibly, Ceaușescu was moving into a Pirandellian world. As Alexandru (Sasha) Ivasiuc, a dissident writer who was to die in the 1977 earthquake, put it, Romania was a country where "twenty million inhabitants lived inside the imagination of a madman." Like the French tyrant Lucien-Bonaparte (later Napoleon III) described by Karl Marx, Ceaușescu was becoming "a serious buffoon who no longer takes world history for a comedy but his comedy for the world."

# CHAPTER NINE
## KISS THE HAND YOU CANNOT BITE

His Majesty liked to visit the provinces, to give the plain people access to him, to learn of their troubles and console them with promises, to praise the humble and the hardworking and scold the lazy and disobedient.

> —RYSZARD KAPUŚCIŃSKI
> *THE EMPEROR*

O N CEAUȘESCU'S SIXTIETH BIRTHDAY, IN 1978, a huge, 664-page coffee-table book entitled *Omagiu* (Homage) was published, and every right-thinking Romanian communist rushed out to obtain a copy.

It was a tribute to his lifetime achievements, couched in such extravagantly fulsome prose as to provoke embarrassed laughter in any normal society. Ceaușescu's unique genius as family man, leader, and creative thinker was described in endless detail. Each of the forty districts he had graced with official visits was the subject of a lavishly illustrated section, and each one of his childhood and adolescent homes was immortalized in photographs. The book, a birthday present compiled in great secrecy by Dumitru Popescu and other members of his court, placed him firmly in the category of insanely vain dictators like Uganda's Idi Amin Dada, North Korea's Kim Il Sung, Albania's Enver Hoxha, and Mao Tse-tung during and after the cultural revolution.

A later English-language book, anonymously written (and clearly, from its cumbrous style, translated from the Romanian), published in 1983 by the Pergamon Press, brought the Conducător's life story up to date, with the same mawkish reverence. The book listed international titles and distinctions granted him by sixty-one countries, his Knight of the Great Cross of the Bath Order sharing equal pride of place with the Great Girdle of the Mauritanian National Merit and Iran's Order Pahlavi with Collar, the title of Doctor Honoris Causa of Nice University, and the Apimondia Jubilee Medal, conferred in token of homage at the 26th International Bee-Keeping Congress by the Executive Council of the International Federation of Bee-Keepers' Associations. Until his demise, these treasures were enshrined in a special Museum of National History, visited daily by well-scrubbed Romanian schoolchildren as part of the required curriculum of all Romanian schools. The rooms displaying Ceaușescu's gifts from abroad and his decorations was closed on December 22, 1989—never to reopen. Also closed to the public, after his death, was the Museum of the History of the Romanian Communist Party, whose director, Professor Ion Ardeleanu, had courageously resisted untold pressure to turn it into a Ceaușescu shrine. Ceaușescu's picture appeared only once in the museum, and as Ardeleanu showed me around the shuttered rooms for a private visit months after Ceaușescu's death, I noted that it had been removed.

Like Mao, Enver Hoxha, and Kim Il Sung, in his official photographs at least, the Conducător appeared to be subject to none of the ordinary human aging processes. In *Omagiu*, his face remained unlined, his cheeks smoothly pink, immortalized in eternal youth.

Officers from Securitate's "protocol department" saw to it that Nicolae Ceaușescu, at least on Romanian TV and newsreels, always appeared in the most favorable circumstances. This, as one long-suffering film editor assigned to the "Ceaușescu beat" for twenty years, told me, represented hours of work every day editing film to Securitate's satisfaction. "All of Ceaușescu's involuntary pauses, hesitations, stutters, and grimaces had to be removed before anything could be shown," she said, and all discarded snippets of film were collected by Securitate and destroyed. In the last few months of Ceaușescu's reign, she noted, his public appearances were marked by a considerable increase in stuttering and faulty delivery—a sure sign that he was under increasing stress. There were also standing instructions that Ceaușescu's small size (five feet six inches) should never be emphasized on film. When state guests taller than he were shown in his company, they had to be filmed in such a way that the differences in height were minimized. Lanky heads of state like de Gaulle and Giscard d'Estaing were never shown standing next to the Conducător. As an additional precaution, all cameramen assigned to Ceaușescu were chosen for their short size. "They all had to be smaller than Ceaușescu himself," she said.

In the spate of books, such as Omagiu, glorifying Ceaușescu that appeared with increasing frequency and in a multiplicity of languages from 1978 onward, the opinions of "other world personalities" testified to his extraordinary gifts. The Soviet working people, said Leonid Brezhnev, "assess highly the wonderful gains of the [Romanian] working class." Kim Il Sung, a connoisseur in such matters, chose the exhortatory style: "You, dear comrade President, the eminent leader of the Romanian people, outstanding militant of the international communist and working-class movement, carry out an ample activity on an international plane as a militant of world peace." Queen Elizabeth, who had acted as host to Nicolae and

Elena at Buckingham Palace in June 1978 and never quite forgave either Prime Minister James Callaghan or his foreign secretary, David Owen, for insisting that she do so, was quoted (in her speech at the banquet in his honor) as saying that "we in great Britain today are impressed with the resolved stand you have taken for supporting this independence. Consequently, Romania holds a distinct position and plays a significant part in world affairs. Your personality, Mr. President, as a statesman of world-wide repute, experience and influence is widely acknowledged." Margaret Thatcher was "impressed by the personality of President Ceaușescu and I am left with particular impressions about him as the leader of Romania, a country willing to develop her co-operation with other nations."

"By his profound understanding of the world's major problems, President Ceaușescu can contribute and does contribute to the settlement of mankind's most urgent global problems," said former president Richard Nixon. "President Ceaușescu's influence in the international arena as leader of Romania is outstanding," said President Gerald Ford. "His prestige has gone beyond the boundaries of Romania and Europe," said President Jimmy Carter. "The whole world appreciates him and regards him with admiration." Erich Honecker, the president of the republic of Zimbabwe, and a French writer called Pierre Paraf ("President Ceaușescu is well known to French public opinion; he enjoys great prestige. His concept of foreign policy strongly expresses the Romanian people's will to promote peace and understanding with all nations") all joined in the same duly recorded, laudatory chorus.

From the mid-1970s onward, one of the main tasks of Romanian ambassadors abroad was to provide the Ceaușescus with acknowledgments by foreigners of their greatness, in the form of published quotations or words of praise from prominent individuals, academics, and institutions. Răzvan Theodorescu, the Romanian TV boss in the immediate post-Ceaușescu era, recalled coming across a Romanian news item from Sicily, where the Syracuse Academy had issued a flowery greeting, extolling Ceaușescu as "one of the world's

greatest leaders and thinkers." Years later in Naples, an in-
quisitive Theodorescu tracked down the Syracuse Academy to
a modest Naples apartment, where a little old lady running a
tiny coaching establishment turned out to be the Academy's
owner and sole full-time employee. She said she had been
approached by a Romanian diplomat, who had offered her a
small financial inducement to agree to the publication of the
eulogy, which he himself had drafted.

What kind of man could bask in this kind of acclaim, allow
such books to be published, and take such praise at its face
value? How could Nicolae and Elena Ceaușescu have failed to
recognize the artificial smiles of their admirers, or that in the
long run, out of sheer frustrated rage, the Romanian compulsion to kiss the hand would be superseded by a savage compulsion to bite it? How could they have agreed to endless
prime-time TV coverage of their daily ceremonial rounds,
usually extending to a full two hours, while ordinary Romanians tried to warm themselves in front of their TV sets in the
penumbra of forty-watt bulbs? Did the Ceaușescus ever pause
to wonder what ordinary people *really* thought of them, compelled as they were to "freeze" in the streets four times a day
for thirty minutes at a time to allow the nine-car Ceaușescu
cortege to proceed from the Spring Palace to the center of
Bucharest and back, at a time when gasoline was restricted to
thirty liters a month or private cars banned altogether? And
what kind of insecurity was it that compelled the Ceaușescus to
go to such lengths to prove to their people that they deserved
such adulation? All personality cults are grotesque, but this
one involved a sadomasochistic twist, for as conditions inside
Romania worsened, Romanians not only had to endure new
privations but also had to praise those responsible for inflicting
them in increasingly fulsome terms.

For all the wealth of psychological explanations and character dissection that followed the death of the Ceaușescus, a
sense of bewilderment prevails in Romanian circles. Not only
absolute but also relative power corrupts, and even in democratic societies, where politicians are supposed to remain aware
of such pitfalls, most of our political leaders live in a world of
such privilege, so divorced from ordinary day-to-day preoc-

cupations, that they tend to forget how the other half lives. The Ceauşescus went much further: Their feudal behavior was reminiscent of the *voievodates* and the Phanariots' brutally high-handed treatment of Romanian peasants in the days preceding independence.

One senior State Department official, accompanying Ceauşescu on his last visit to the United States in October 1987, under the Carter presidency, and observing him at close quarters, said he conveyed, irresistibly, the aura of a Latin American dictator, a *caudillo*, rather than that of a communist leader. By this time, Ceauşescu had lost whatever shrewd peasant common sense he had once had, walking out of a dinner in New Orleans because the cardinal also present insisted on an invocation before the meal. The gesture caused much adverse publicity and reflected Ceauşescu's absurdly inflated self-importance. "He imposed his ideas arrogantly and stupidly, with no trace of the kind of sensitivity a visiting president should have displayed," William H. Luers, the State Department official of ambassadorial rank who accompanied them throughout, said.

Ceauşescu was equally absurd in overreacting to a jocular statement by the (then) mayor of New York, Edward Koch, who visited him on his last afternoon in New York after a group of Hungarian exiles had demonstrated outside his hotel. "Mr. President," Koch told him in lieu of an apology. "Last night some friends of mine were down there demonstrating against you, and they tell me you don't give freedom of religion and cultural freedom to your Hungarians living in Transylvania. Is that right, Mr. President?" As Ambassador Luers recalled, "Ceauşescu went white, turned to me, and said, 'What does the State Department have to say about this? How dare he talk to me like that?' and I said, 'Well, the federal government has its policies, and the mayor has his say.' " Incensed by what he regarded as Koch's lack of respect, Ceauşescu gave orders that the presidential party should leave for home immediately. He was unable to do so, however: Elena Ceauşescu was closeted inside Cartier, where she stayed for three and a half hours—until, in fact, the schedule called for them to leave.

One clue to the Ceauşescu personality-cult phenomenon

undoubtedly lay in the past. Nearly five centuries of Turkish and Phanariot rule encouraged the tradition of subservience to authority, and some of the adulatory prose in the Romanian press referring to Ceauşescu could have been lifted verbatim from Romanian editorials of the 1930s and early 1940s praising the virtues of King Carol II and the first Conducător, Marshal Antonescu, in almost equally nauseating terms. At first, embarrassed Romanian officials excused the more extreme manifestations of the Ceauşescu cult by stressing the strong religious sentiments of the rural population and the lack of sophistication of many of the newly literate Romanians. By the 1970s, the ridiculous catchphrases—"Genius of the Carpathians," "Source of our light," the "Danube of thought," "Builder of the outstanding stage in the millennia-old existence of the Romanian people," "Creator of the epoch of unprecedented renewal," "Treasure of wisdom and charisma"—had become the norm.

Romania's tribal past also had something to do with it. The earliest Romanian political leaders, after 1857, had combined the responsibilities of clan as well as party leadership. The Brătianus, for example; enjoyed the unquestioning loyalty of their supporters. The behavior of these nineteenth-century Romanian politician-overlords, many of them aristocrats, was more akin to that of feudal overlords than to Western parliamentary figures, and the habit of unquestioning obedience to the head of the clan outlasted the end of the monarchy and the advent of communism. There was something in the Romanian persona that accepted such hero worship as normal, just as there was something in the flowery "latinity" of the Romanian language that lent itself to the most extravagantly worded expressions of fawning adulation. "We Romanians," Nadia Bujor, a niece of the Ceauşescus (and a psychologist), told me months after her uncle's death, "have always looked for a strong father figure."

Michael Shafir, noting with surprise the Romanian "creative intelligentsia's" relative passivity as far as this personality-cult phenomenon was concerned, found an answer not only in "the long-entrenched Ottoman tradition of dissimulation" but in "deep-rooted traditions of corruption, nepotism, and bribery." *"Que voulez-vous?"* Raymond Poincaré once asked a Romanian court of justice while arguing a case for one of his clients. *"Nous sommes ici aux portes de l'Orient!"*[1] Deference, dissimulation, and conformity were (with a few notable exceptions, such as in the case of the fearless writer Paul Goma) the hallmarks of Ceauşescu-era intellectual life. "Not even today," said Liviu Turcu, a former senior Securitate official who defected to the United States in 1987, "am I able to explain how so many intellectuals, and good journalists, fought each other in exhausting the Romanian dictionary to find the most impressive words in an attempt to please Ceauşescu."

Even Romania's most prestigious scholars found themselves caught up in personality-cult rituals. Unable or unwilling to risk ignoring them, they compromised. As Dan Berindei, a leading historian, admitted, "I too was placed in a position where I had to quote from Ceauşescu's works in order to publish my books. There were several ways of getting around it. One could quote something unexceptional, like his statement that 'whoever ignores history is like a child who grows up without knowing its parents' or that 'truth must be respected even if it is not palatable.' As in the works of Mao Tse-tung, one could find practically anything in his collected speeches suitable for quotation, if one looked assiduously enough."

"Quoting Ceauşescu was a form of ritual mass," said Mihnea Gheorghiu, another leading historian. Subsections of the Central Committee spent months, and sometimes years, examining the contents of books awaiting publication, and it was known the manuscripts devoid of the mandatory number of Ceauşescu quotes would be rejected out of hand. Even the U.S. ambassador to Bucharest, David B. Funderburk, whose Ph.D. thesis, "British Policy Toward Romania 1938–1940" was published in Romanian translation while he was nearing the end of his ambassadorship there, came under repeated pressure to insert quotations and footnotes culled from the Conducător's collected works and to acknowledge Ceauşescu's greatness. He refused.

Virgil Cândea, the general secretary of the International Association for Southeast European Studies, confirmed to me that the highest priority in the state-controlled Romanian publishing industry was the publication of the Ceauşescu speeches and his wife's papers on chemistry research, actually written, of course, by others. For this reason, there was a marked decline in the numbers of overall titles printed from 1975 onward. Works of fiction were singled out for publication that slyly, often for no dramatic reason, highlighted the youthful activities of a young revolutionary activist called Nicolae Ceauşescu or otherwise obliquely paid homage to his achievements; writers awaiting publication for their books cynically submitted servile articles to *Scînteia* and other newspapers in the hope this would accelerate their chances of publication. The only way of getting permission to stage an exhibition of Romanian medieval art, Cândea said, was to relate it in some way to Ceauşescu himself, "so we would have a poster made showing him visiting a medieval monastery."

In order to prosper, both intellectuals and Party members found it easier to go along with the system. Few challenged it. As Gabriela Adaineşteanu, a leading writer and member of the dissident Social Dialogue group, put it, "There were no clear-cut censorship rules. Much depended on the courage of the individual publisher and the celebrity of the author. The better known you were to the public, the more accommodating the people running the system would be." In later years, Ceauşescu constantly proclaimed that there was no censorship of any kind in Romania. In a sense he was right, though the "cultural committee" at the Culture Ministry established publication priorities. Self-censorship seems to have been the order of the day. The author of a book on the art of photography, Eugen Iarovici, recalled that Ion Iliescu, his publisher at Editura Tehnică, cut out some paragraphs in his manuscript dealing with image building and the role of photography in propaganda. "I knew better than to raise any objections," he said.

The timidity of most publishers, and the general bitterness resulting from the Ceauşescu personality cult, indulged in at one time or another by so many Romanians of note, has had the effect of tearing Romania's intellectual community apart, and its feuds have become as bitter as those affecting the senior generation of surviving Romanian communist leaders. As the Ceauşescus and their mythmakers knew, the insidious process of compromising artistic virtue for contingency's sake could have been designed specifically to foment rivalries and petty jealousies. Inside almost every Romanian intellectual exists the memory of servile acts perpetrated for career reasons, and all over Romania there are neighbors, colleagues, and rivals who remember witnessing them. One was forcibly reminded, for example, that Cândea, general secretary of the International Association for Southeast European Studies, for all his criticism of Ceauşescu after December 25, 1989, had acted as watchdog and was widely believed to have had a cozy relationship with Securitate. After *Ostinato*, a semi-autobiographical novel by Paul Goma (published in France and Germany in 1971), had been indefinitely held up in Romania, Cândea told a French TV interviewer that no censorship decision had been involved, for "censorship does not exist in Romania." The typographers had simply decided not to print the book. In the same way, in June 1990, equally virtuous typographers decided, under President Iliescu, not to set the type for Romania's uncompromisingly critical newspaper *România Liberă*.

Even among genuine dissidents, who were beaten up by Securitate thugs or went to jail rather than submit to the system, there was little solidarity. Thus, the writer Alexandru Ivasiuc, although jailed for a time for his opinions, had no hesitation in turning informer, according to his old friend Paul Goma. Ivasiuc's behavior showed how powerful Securitate and career pressures could become.

"We had been cellmates in 1957–58," Paul Goma recalled, "and the kind of relationship we had then should have ensured our friendship for life. He had been sentenced for five years, I for two. But after our release, our paths diverged. I was sent to the countryside for five years of 'internal exile.' I asked for a job as librarian in a village, but this was refused. A former political prisoner could not hold down any kind of job, however small, involving ideology. I became, eventually, a factory worker in Braşov. Ivasiuc's subsequent career was very different. After a mere two months' internal exile, he was allowed to live in Bucharest, where his career took off. After a short spell as a factory worker, he joined the ranks of the *nomenklatura*, was hired as a translator by the U.S. Embassy in Bucharest, obtained a Fulbright scholarship, and eventually became secretary of the writers' union and head of a film and publishing company. After I had submitted the manuscript of a novel to him, he denounced me to the authorities, claiming that my novel was *à clef*, with thinly disguised portraits of Elena Ceauşescu and other leading figures of the regime."

The U.S. Embassy appointment was a clear indication, to Goma and his colleagues, that Ivasiuc had chosen the path of cooperation with the Ceauşescu regime, for it was unthinkable that such a job could be made available to a Romanian national without the compulsion to report on his dealings with his U.S. colleagues. The Ivasiuc phenomenon was not an isolated case. Translators inside embassies, posts in the department of tourism involving contacts with foreigners, and all foreign trade ministry appointments were known to be jobs that involved close relations with Securitate. Many distinguished intellectuals, including some whose outspoken writings and opinions had led to prison sentences in the 1950s, were lured into collaboration with the Ceauşescu regime through such bread-and-butter assignments, for few writers could afford to make ends meet from their books alone. The lure of foreign travel, lucrative jobs, and access to above-average apartments proved difficult to resist. Westerners, according to Goma, were frequently taken in, unable to gauge the extent of Romanian deception. "For me," said Goma, "a Romanian Fulbright scholarship automatically carried a Securitate label."

Thus, the same climate of suspicion and distrust that had been a feature of the Romanian Communist party since its creation also spread to the intellectual community during the Ceauşescu era. In Czechoslovakia, Václav Havel was not an isolated phenomenon but a symbol of widespread Czech intellectual resistance, centered around Charter 77, the committee set up to monitor respect for human rights after the 1977 world summit meeting in Helsinki. In Romania, however, no such movement emerged, on that scale at any rate. As Paul Goma, who tried to organize a dissident forum, recalled, he met with point-blank refusal from his colleagues when he first started canvassing for signatures. As a last resort, and deliberately drawing attention to his isolation, Goma wrote directly to Ceaușescu, care of the "Royal Palace," asking him to add *his* signature to Goma's appeal for a Romanian-type Charter 77 movement, "since," as he put it, "it consequently seems that only two persons in the country do not fear Securitate: Your Excellency and myself. . . . Should Your Excellency send a similar letter, a declaration of support to Charter 77, I am deeply convinced that millions of Romanians would follow." As Goma wryly recalled later from his Paris home, "I mentioned in my letter to him that since my own wife had signed as a cosignatory; perhaps his wife would care to sign too, so that we would appear in the letter as two cozy couples." This extraordinarily brave gesture of Goma's, amounting to foolhardiness, caught Ceaușescu off balance. "We waited and waited," Goma recalled. "Nothing happened for two months." Goma was eventually beaten up and then offered the choice of either going to jail or being expelled. He chose Paris. Years later, along with Virgil Tănase, another leading Romanian literary exile, he became the target of a bungled Securitate assassination attempt that became a cause célèbre, covering both Securitate and Ceaușescu with ridicule.

Inevitably, memories of that period still condition relationships between the minority of writers and intellectuals who openly challenged the Ceaușescu regime and the majority who chose some form of collaboration. As Professor Dan Berindei noted, it was impossible to get a book published before December 25, 1989, that *didn't* have references to Ceaușescu in it, just as it was impossible *after* December 1989 to publish anything that *did* contain such quotes. Berindei himself remains a controversial figure to many Romanian intellectuals, and Goma has no hesitation in labeling him an "opportunistic collaborator." In post-Ceaușescu Romania, such backbiting has become standard behavior.

I asked Chris Thau, a Romanian-born British filmmaker who worked for Romanian TV until his departure from the country in 1978, to explain how Romanian TV bosses could possibly have decided that the activities of the Ceaușescu were worth two hours of film daily on prime-time television. Things didn't happen that way, he explained. One official inside Romanian TV had probably suggested a ten-minute résumé, on film, of the Ceauşescus' official daily engagements. Another official, wanting to look good in the eyes of his superiors, assumed responsibility for the original suggestion and increased the screening time to thirty minutes. After sycophant after sycophant in the higher echelons of Romanian TV had vied with one another in demonstrating who was the most loyal, dedicated follower of the Ceauşescus, the program ended up two hours long. This, he said, was what happened in the Ceauşescu era, not just in television but in all fields of government planning. With all out to prove that they were the most loyal, most subservient, most servile protagonists of the Ceauşescu regime, there were no limits to the absurdities, or the disasters, that ensued.

Dan Petrescu recalled that when Ceauşescu paid a visit to Iaşi late one summer, local organizers planted rows of trees on either side of the road leading into town. The trees were planted too late and died before Ceauşescu's arrival. A squad of workers set to work painting the leaves green. Unlike in Czechoslovakia, where from 1968 to 1989 the nation's most talented writers either went to jail or were assigned manual laborers' jobs, Romanian poets and writers, including former dissidents, were assiduously wooed by the government, often with success. Adrian Păunescu, in the 1960s Romania's most gifted young poet, ended up staging huge *son et lumière* pageants glorifying Ceauşescu, became his occasional confidant, and praised his genius to the skies in *Omagiu.* Memories of such humiliating compromises are still vivid, and explain the distrust Romanians continue to have for one another.

Excess bred excess. The humorless Ceauşescu had no sense of the ridiculous. In Elena's case, she was also devoid of a sense of shame, for her plagiarism of other people's work and her thirst for honorary degrees—which psychologists explain in terms of a pathological quest for acceptance—amounted to piracy.

Whatever their persistent divisions and hatreds, all Romanians agree on one thing: that Elena Ceauşescu was Nicolae's

evil genie. Former members of her personal staff acknowledge that the only creatures she appeared to have genuinely
loved were her two pet Labradors, Corbu and Sharuna. Her
nagging was constant. As Colonel Maluţan, the helicopter pilot, put it, "Anything and everything unpleasant that happened was our fault: the lint on the carpet inside the
helicopter, the rough ride occasioned by bad weather. She had
no confidence in anyone, she hated everybody." In public at
least, she came across as her husband's most loyal, most ad-
miring supporter, but in private her contempt for the human
race extended even to him. "He was afraid of her, I'm convinced of that," says Professor Ion Ardeleanu. "If he was late
for a meal or a meeting with her, he would look at his watch
and begin stammering and sweating." Another former member of the Ceauşescu team recalled that Elena Ceauşescu used
the two favorite weapons of nagging wives: "without me you
would be nothing" and "I am the only person you can trust."

Elena Ceauşescu had been a member of the RCP's Bucharest Municipal Committee since 1968, but by 1972 she had
become a member of the Central Committee and a year later
was on the Executive Committee. In 1979 she became an ex-
officio member of the cabinet, through her chairmanship of
the National Council of Science and Technology, and by 1980
she was first deputy premier and the most powerful figure in
Romania after Nicolae himself. More important than any of
these titles, however, was her Party appointment in January
1979 as chairman of the Central Committee commission for
state and party cadres, which meant in effect that she controlled every single senior Party and government appointment, whether to district secretariats or within the Romanian
civil service. She was as unpleasant in her dealings with Party
and government underlings as she had been with her
ICECHIM staff: "She was a nagging shrew," said former
health minister Eugen Proca. "She was totally negative. She
was mean; she always had to get her own way. She was
Ceauşescu's devil. As with a mentally unstable person, you
went around her, you tried to avoid her. He was someone you
could talk to, he had the human touch, but she was unadulterated evil. She was very vain and almost illiterate. I saw her

as a mixture of Imelda Marcos, Evita Perón, and Chiang Ching. How on earth, you may well ask, did those two climb so high? They had stamina and strength. They knew how to select people and work the system."

Elena's nagging extended to all those who came into contact with her, whatever their status. A former photographer recalled that an assignment to photograph Elena Ceaușescu was a traumatic experience, for she was never satisfied and berated photographers constantly. "Why did you make my nose so big? We give you all this expensive equipment and look at the mess you make of it." Her contempt extended to everyone. Those unlucky enough to incur her wrath would find themselves on a blacklist, banned from working in the media. Her stinginess, her former headwaiter said, was legendary. She would carry out spot checks on kitchen stores and have servants' quarters searched, to see whether pilfering was going on. Such was her suspicious nature that when she sent specially made yogurt to her son Nicu in Sibiu, she had the jars padlocked, so that the curds could neither be stolen nor poisoned.

"When she came back from Greece once, she gave me a small box containing ten pieces of Turkish delight," her former headwaiter said. "I was given to understand that this was a most signal honor. I wasn't expected to give them to my family to eat. They were to be preserved, as a sacred memento."

Elena's determination to set herself apart from all other members of the Ceaușescu family was brought home to Mircea Codreanu, a diplomat in the Romanian embassy in Washington at the time of the Ceaușescus' October 1970 visit to the United States. "She had insisted on being taken to fur shops in Manhattan and had ordered well-known jewelers to come to her New York residence to display their wares," he said. Later, he escorted Elena Bărbulescu, one of Ceaușescu's sisters, on a similar trip. "She was a decent, modest woman," Codreanu recalls. "All she would buy was one rather inexpensive gold ring. I said, 'Why don't you take something more expensive?' She replied, 'Elena doesn't allow us to wear anything that might show her up.' "

Her craving for international recognition and foreign honors was far greater than her husband's, and a substantial part of the advance work involved in the Ceaușescus' official visits abroad had to do with the attribution of honorary degrees in recognition of her research as a "prestigious scientist." "Being an ignorant, uneducated, primitive kind of woman, she really thought that if she had some titles after her name, it would change her image," says Codreanu, who was later sentenced to death for alleged espionage and freed only after the Ceaușescus' demise.

On the eve of the Ceaușescus' visit to Buckingham Palace, at the behest of the Callaghan government, the Romanian advance party made a strong pitch to obtain an honorary F.R.S. (Fellow of the Royal Society) for her. Oxford and London universities were also approached for honorary degrees but turned her down, so she had to settle for an honorary fellowship of the Royal Institute of Chemistry and an honorary degree from the Central London Polytechnic. At a public ceremony, Professor Sir Philip Norman, vice-chancellor of London University, praised her contribution to macromolecular experimental chemistry, especially in the field of "the stereospecific polymerisation of ijisoprene, on the stabilization of synthetic rubbers and on copolymerization." As Mircea Corciovei, one of ICECHIM's scientists who had actually contributed to this research, said later: "We were told: No paper can be written or published, no conference delivered without Elena Ceaușescu's name appearing in first place. We never saw her, we never heard from her at any time during our research or afterward. She never even acknowledged our existence. We were producing papers with words which, we knew, she could not pronounce, let alone understand."

Such foreign awards, and the panegyrics of leading Western statesmen concerning Nicolae Ceaușescu, were duly headlined in the Romanian press and on TV, further contributing to low morale and a state of hopeless passivity among intellectuals. "Every time there was another honorary degree," said Berindei, "everyone's spirits fell." What is largely ignored, in immediate post-Ceaușescu Romania, is that those very same people who attack Western leaders and intellectuals for their idolizing attitude toward the Ceaușescus were, many of them, equally craven. An exception was the Romanian academy, which to the very end fought a rearguard battle against Elena Ceaușescu's determination to dominate it. A member since 1974, she had plans to become its president, but the academicians balked at that. As a result, she broke its power, setting up a string of new, rival academies, each devoted to a special field of study and staffed with her own nominees.

There were differences between Elena and Nicolae. As Professor Gheorghiu put it, "He had a way with people, he flattered them. He would say things like: 'You may be an outstanding surgeon, but you don't know anything about leadership.' He liked to put his pet intellectuals on display when he received distinguished foreign guests, like Averell Harriman. It was his way of saying, 'Here is my intellectual stable.' " "As long as you pretended that an idea was his in the first place, you could occasionally get him to agree to implement it," said former health minister Proca. With Elena Ceaușescu, on the other hand, there could be no dialogue. She got her own way by bullying and the use of the implicit threats.

The litanies of praise for Elena became as established as in any religion. Leading poets vied with each other in reaching for new hyperbolae. A typical sixtieth-birthday homage, the work of a leading Romanian poet, was dedicated to "the first woman of the country, the homage of the entire country. As star stands besides star in the eternal arch of heaven, so, beside the great man, she watches over Romania's path to glory." In the media, it was customary to qualify her not just as Comrade-Academician-Doctor-Engineer but as the front of "prodigious political activity who has played a decisive role in the assertion of Romanian science, education, and culture." Fed such garbage, Romanians reacted with gallows humor when they felt the coast was clear: Ceaușescu's Romania became *Ceauschwitz, Ceaushima, Paranopolis.*

As Ceaușescu's personality cult developed, the quality of middle- and upper-level leadership changed. From 1968 to 1971, many self-respecting Romanians believed the lip service increasingly paid to Ceaușescu's genius was worth the benefits.

Even after 1971, those who found the degree of servility
intolerable—to the point of resigning and severing all contact
with the regime—were few and far between. The résumé of
the current president, Ion Iliescu, is typical. An early protégé
of Ceauşescu, singled out for lightning promotion for the
purges he carried out among the student population while
head of the Young Communists' League, he was part of the
"charmed circle" of intimates until autumn 1971, when he was
bold enough to criticize some aspects of Ceauşescu's cultural
policy. At the time he was a key Central Committee member,
responsible for cultural affairs. After 1971, he was demoted,
and moved "laterally." His later career included posts as regional secretary in Timişoara and other districts, and minor
ministerial posts (water supply). By December 1989, he
headed a leading technical publishing firm, Editura Tehnică.
"Ceauşescu's approach to dissidents was a subtle one," said
Emanuel Valeriu. "There was a saying among us: He kept
everyone circling inside the goldfish bowl."

Few of the fish were actually removed, but the charmed
circle became, increasingly, the jealously guarded preserve of
sycophants and relatives. "Socialism in one family," Romanians called it. Elena apart, key posts were occupied by Ilie
Verdeţ, a brother-in-law; Manea Mănescu, another brother-
in-law; and Corneliu Burtică, a nephew. Gheorghe Petrescu,
Gogu, the Blockhead of earlier days, became a deputy premier; Ilie Ceauşescu, an elder brother, became deputy minister of defense; Nicolae-Andruţa, another brother, lieutenant-
general, and a key figure in the Interior Ministry. Several
brothers-in-law became ministers or members of the Central
Committee. Nicu, the turbulent younger son, became first the
leader of the Young Communists' League, a C.C. member,
then district secretary in Sibiu and a candidate-member of the
innermost Executive Committee.

Charges of nepotism were of course refuted. "Everyone
who looks into the biographical data of the persons close to
Mr. Ceauşescu will see how simple and normal things are,"
wrote an anonymous hagiographer. "Everyone has found a
way in life according to his or her training, skills and professional experience. Some newsmen delight in finding out that

a person newly appointed or elected to an important leading office is a relative of the head of state and accredit untrue data, circulating incorrect information, or malevolent interpretations."

"I would like to ask you," said a journalist abroad to the Romanian head of state, "what is the role of Madame Elena Ceaușescu, who is not only your wife but also a person with a political function?" Ceaușescu's reply, quoted in the anonymous Pergamon Press biography, was not only a monument of hypocrisy but a perfect example of his inability to reply to a simple question without introducing the insufferably pompous, didactic, and interminable wooden language of Ceaușescu-speak logorrhea:

> I will answer you, starting with a more general presentation of the mechanism of societal government. A principle of collective leadership operates in the Romanian socialist society. In the deliberative bodies, the cadre and party and state, activists participate in decision making along with the wide mass of working people as this is one of the fundamental characteristics of socialist democracy in Romania. We have such bodies from enterprises, economic and social units, in which all people, from workers upward, operate. All of them work in a collective manner, make collective decisions on all problems. The government operates upon the principle of collective leadership and in the party, in between congresses, the Central Committee and the Executive Committee are the bodies that decide on all problems regarding the country's internal development and its foreign policy alike. In this framework, just like the other members of the government, Elena Ceaușescu contributes to solving the questions of our society's development.

For all the rigid controls, omnipresence of informers, and the appalling diet of "Ceaușescu thought," Romanians remained highly aware of the idiosyncrasies of Romania's first family. Through gossip and rumor, they knew all about Valentin's rift with his parents, Zoia's affairs, and Nicu's womanizing and drunken driving, the collapse of his "arranged" marriage, and his propensity to indulge in nightclub brawls. The absence of anything like a free press or free circulation of information probably led Romanians to exaggerate Nicu's villainy, as well as the frequency of Zoia's numerous affairs. All three Ceaușescu children now appear to have been the victims of the system as much as its beneficiaries. But the personality cult could brook nothing short of storybook idealism as far as the family life of the Ceaușescus was concerned. As *Omagiu* put it,

> We gaze with esteem, with respect, at the harmony of his family life. We attach special ethical significance to the fact that his life—together with that of his life comrade, the former textile worker, communist youth militant, member of the Party since the days of illegality, today hero of Social-ist labor, scientist, member of the Central Committee of the RCP, comrade Elena Ceaușescu—offers an exemplary im-age the destinies of two communists. . . . The three children of the President work, like any of us, following the example of their parents, to bring socialism to Romania. All this at-tests clearly to the truth that work and personal example are obligations in the Ceaușescu family.

Romanians in the know, reading this, were overcome by twin feelings of rage and merriment. In a country increasingly given over, as time went on, to Ceaușescu worship, the real relationships between the Ceaușescu parents and their off-spring were well known. It was common knowledge, for in-stance, that Valentin's wife, Iordana Borilă, who was half-Jewish, was banned from the Ceaușescu circle and that as a result, they were deprived of most *nomenklatura* privileges and lived in a small two-room apartment. Valentin, who surren-dered voluntarily to the newly constituted militiamen of the National Salvation Front the day after his father's flight, had by then separated from Iordana and become a member of the Central Committee. He was arrested, but his trial is unlikely. The National Salvation Front, and especially Petre Roman and President Ion Iliescu, know that their *nomenklatura* privi-leges, during Ceaușescu's lifetime, were far more important. Valentin Ceaușescu will almost certainly claim, with consider-able justification—if his trial ever takes place—that his rela-tions with his parents were adversarial and that his hatred for Elena Ceaușescu was genuine. At the Institute of Nuclear Physics, where he worked after obtaining a degree at London University, there remained substantial support for him after his father's death.

Zoia Ceaușescu's case is similar. When she was a mathematics student, she became aware of the true nature of her parents' regime and was nauseated by it. In 1974 she fled the family home, and the entire resources of Securitate were mobilized to track her down. Nadia Bujor, then Nadia Bărbulescu—Ceaușescu's niece and the daughter of Nicolae's younger sister Elena—was called in, because it was known that Zoia and she were close. "Nicolae Ceaușescu swore at me, shouting that he would send me to jail if I didn't tell them immediately where she was," she recalled. "Elena Ceaușescu was more subtle, adopting a wheedling tone, saying, 'I thought you were our friend.'" As a result of the encounter, Nadia Bărbulescu feared for her life so much that after Zoia's return to the family fold, Nadia told her they could no longer go on seeing each other. "Zoia's life as a young woman was a nightmare," she recalled. "She wanted to escape, but she knew she was trapped. However far she went, she knew the long hand of Securitate would pluck her back. She kept asking me, 'What on earth am I to do with my life?'" Nicolae and Elena Ceaușescu believed that Nadia Bărbulescu had inspired Zoia's rebelliousness. Nadia was a student at the faculty of psychology at Bucharest University and the Ceaușescus accused her of trying to "psychoanalyze" Zoia.

The impact of Zoia's *fugue* on Romania's academic life was disastrous. Zoia had been a member of the prestigious Mathematics Institute. Out of rage, because the Ceaușescus blamed it for inculcating in Zoia a "bohemian mentality," Nicolae dissolved the institute, dispersing its staff throughout various research units. As a result, as Mircea Malitza, the former education minister, recalled, "Over two hundred skilled mathematicians left the country and ended up working in the United States, probably the most massive specialized brain drain of any European country." Using her family connections, Zoia was able to help obtain exit visas for many of her fellow mathematicians from the institute, and this too infuriated her parents. Finally, in 1977, the faculty of psychology was closed down, too. Valentin and Zoia, arrested in the immediate aftermath of their father's death, were both released eight months later.

Of all the Ceauşescu children, only Nicu seemed at ease in the presence of his parents. He too was under constant Securitate watch, but because he did not openly revolt, his parents doted on him and excused his drinking, as well as his notorious playboy life-style. As principal secretary of the Party in Sibiu, in the few years before the December 1989 revolution, he appeared to have acquired a measure of responsibility. At his trial in 1990, many character witnesses testified that he had tried to alleviate local food shortages and otherwise improve the living conditions of Sibiu's inhabitants. At least some of the wilder reports of rape, sexual brutality, and sadism (one favorite rumor had it that he had had Nadia Comăneci's nails torn out because the celebrated athlete had refused his advances) were concocted by ordinary Romanians as a means of getting their own back while the country plummeted into economic and moral bankruptcy. Similarly, rumors that Nicolae Ceauşescu wore a new suit every day (and after each day's wear, had it destroyed) were meant to symbolize his wasteful extravagance at a time when Romanians searched the stores in vain for a wearable pair of shoes. As his former tailor, who maintained Ceauşescu's large but by no means unusual wardrobe, confirmed in 1990, this rumor was as unfounded as the tale, eagerly spread immediately after Ceauşescu's death, that he regularly received blood transfusions from sacrificed Romanian children—a throwback, this, to the myth of Vlad (Dracula) the Impaler . . .

Inside the hideously ornate Spring Palace where Nicolae and Elena Ceauşescu lived when they were in Bucharest, three separate apartments remained reserved for their three children, but they never stayed there or even spent the night. No other guests were ever invited, a former member of the household staff recalled. He could not remember ever seeing any of their children enter the palace, though they did surreptitiously slip inside the gates to visit their grandmother, who lived in a separate house, just by the main entrance on the left. Aged 102 at the time of the Ceauşescus' flight, she was found wandering about the palace grounds in a nightgown, her mind gone, on December 22, 1989. Taken to a hospital, she died a few days later, unaware of her son's fate. She, too, household employees confirm, had little to do with Nicolae and Elena in their last years and rarely saw them, though for propaganda purposes, photographs showing Elena and *her* aged mother and Nicolae with *his* father were regularly reproduced in the Romanian press. For the last few years, the old lady could not understand, former household staff said, why she was being kept a virtual prisoner inside the palace grounds and why her grandchildren no longer came to visit.

# CHAPTER TEN
# THE SLIDE BEGINS

I'll come right out and say it: the King of Kings preferred bad ministers. And the King of Kings preferred them because he liked to appear in a favorable light by contrast. How could he show himself favorably if he were surrounded by good ministers? The people would be disoriented.

—RYSZARD KAPUŚCIŃSKI
*THE EMPEROR*

N JUNE 1971, A YEAR AFTER THEIR FIRST TRIP TO the United States, Nicolae and Elena Ceaușescu embarked on yet another state visit—this time to China, North Korea, and North Vietnam. The consequences for Romania were to be incalculable. Receptive, as always, to outside ideas, the couple took at their face value the "lessons" of the Chinese Cultural Revolution. By this time, the world at large was starting to become aware of its appalling cost and brutality, but to a relatively unsophisticated outsider, unaware of the stresses and strains beneath the surface, it remained, outwardly at least, a formidable experiment in social engineering.

The Ceauşescus were also immensely impressed by their welcome in Pyongyang. Here, in the geometrically neat layout of the streets, the endlessly similar housing estates, the people cheering as one person, the adulation extended to them as guests of the already deified Kim Il Sung, in the spotless factories staffed by apparently contented flag-waving workers and in industrial complexes buzzing like beehives with disciplined activity, the Ceauşescus found a living example of what, as a good Stalinist, Nicolae had always aspired to: the translation into reality of Karl Marx's *Communist Manifesto*.

Despite his expert manipulation of the RCP, his elimination of all potential challengers, and his skill in exploiting Romania's "maverick" position vis-à-vis the Western world, Ceauşescu remained in many respects singularly naïve. He had the average Romanian's intense love of pageants, parades, and rallies. Culturally, his level remained abysmally low. "I never once had a personal discussion with him on matters unrelated to the work at hand," said Maurer, who, from 1962 to the mid-1970s, was one of his closest associates. "I never once heard him mention anything about art or literature. This side of things simply didn't exist for Ceauşescu." His attitude toward his fellowmen was marked by contempt and suspicion bordering on paranoia, but he believed, to the very end, that the mass demonstrations staged in his honor represented a mystical communion between himself and the people and an authentic surrender of their will. From the early 1970s onward, he started losing contact with reality. Increasingly, as he aged and as real debate within the Party withered, he came to believe in the adulatory, worshipful mass meeting as the only possible form of "communication" with "his" people, even when the rituals had become stale, overrehearsed, and based

on compulsory mobilization. All this made him highly susceptible to the mass rallies and displays staged in his honor in both
China and North Korea. The notion that these two countries
might be vast Potemkin villages for the hoodwinking of gul-
lible foreign guests did not cross his mind—though it did seriously perturb Ion Iliescu, a member of Ceauşescu's Asian
traveling party.

The China trip was important for another reason: Chiang
Ching, Mao's ambitious, ruthless wife, took a shine to Elena
Ceauşescu. Their backgrounds were very different. For
Chiang, the road to power had started when she was a pro-
miscuous little starlet trying to make her mark in the film
world by sleeping with as many Shanghai film industry ty-
coons as succumbed to her somewhat brittle charms. When
this failed to further her career, she aimed her talents in another direction, seducing Mao and making herself sexually,
emotionally, and professionally indispensable to him in
Yenan. Despite their different backgrounds, both women were
ruthless, uneducated, and anti-intellectual, quick to seize on
easy, simple formulas that cut across abstract arguments and
achieved immediate results. Both had become the indispensable consorts of powerful men. In her warped, totalitarian
way, Chiang Ching was a feminist, hugely successful in an
overwhelmingly male world, and she instilled in Elena a desire
to emulate her—and become more politically active herself.

The "achievements" of the Chinese Cultural Revolution,
with their emphasis on the "remolding of revolutionary man,"
and the eradication of individualism and of the symbols of the
past, made a deep impression on the Ceauşescus. It is easy to
ridicule this impact, to present it solely in terms of a couple of
half-baked Stalinists succumbing to a nightmare masquerading as a revolution. But this would be to forget that the
Ceauşescus were not the only ones mesmerized by the "Great
Chinese Cultural Revolution." In 1971, its fervent admirers
included not only Western students, artists, and intellectuals
but even some of the world's most respected sinologists, including a handful of prestigious Harvard academics.

What Ceauşescu saw in China confirmed many of his existing prejudices, that collection of rigidly held Marxist-

Leninist theories and opinions that, for want of another term, one can only call Ceaușescu thought. China bore out his already firm conviction that Marxism-Leninism and jingoist nationalism went hand in hand. It instilled in him the need to impose more austerity and self-sufficiency in Romania itself, as well as the need to exact stricter discipline from a Latin country incorrigibly prone to argument and individualism even after decades of communism. The "social engineering" the Ceaușescus witnessed in China and North Korea also helps to explain their later follies: Not for the first time, Ceaușescu would seize on and put into practice simple ideas originated by others, regardless of cost, to bring about the true revolution described in the *Communist Manifesto*. It is impossible to examine his later attempts at "normalization" of town and country by blending them into a soulless, aesthetically appalling "agro-industrial community," or his efforts to change the face of Bucharest by bringing it closer to his idealized vision of a symmetrical, lifeless, and artificial Pyongyang, without remembering his June 1971 Asian trip. Ceaușescu had memories of a former visit made in 1964, before becoming general secretary, when he had accompanied Emil Bodnăraș on an arms-buying trip to China and North Korea. What he observed in Pyongyang, he told his colleagues on the 1971 trip, was a transformation so vast as to be almost unbelievable. Here was an example of social engineering that had to be taken seriously, regardless of the material and human cost involved.

No sooner had Ceaușescu returned to Romania than he indicated, in no uncertain terms, that a turning away from the spirit of Dubček's 1968 reform attempts, or a "retreat from Prague," as the (then exiled) Peasant party leader Ion Rațiu put it, had begun.[1] In a series of high-level party meetings beginning in July, Ceaușescu introduced a series of measures that were described, by RCP ideologues themselves, as a "mini–cultural revolution." They included more centralized control over cultural matters, education, and the media; a new emphasis on the need for "agitprop among the masses," a call for more cultural festivals, with increasing emphasis on jingoist themes, and simple, easy-to-understand plays and pageants, including more folk dancing. Western "decadent" forms of enjoyment such as rock concerts and disco dancing were banned or severely curtailed, as was the import of foreign books and films. There was to be more emphasis, too, on Romania's unique history as a "survivor nation" battling with, and eventually overcoming, its foreign invaders.

Increasingly severe rules for the Romanian press were to follow. One of the consequences of the tightening cultural yoke was the shifting of Iliescu from his post as the Central Committee's secretary for cultural affairs to a less sensitive job, for daring to speak up against the new policy. Hardly coincidentally, Elena Ceauşescu's picture appeared in *Scînteia*, the caption referring to her for the first time not as the wife of Nicolae Ceauşescu but as "Doctor-Engineer Elena Ceauşescu, Director of the Central Institute of Chemical Research."

In the months that followed, a new body, the Council on Socialist Culture and Education, under the direct control of the Central Committee, completed the subordination of the media and publishing to the Party. Ceauşescu, even before his trip to China, had been a cultural populist, constantly reminding his docile audiences that no art or literature could afford to be esoteric in a country aspiring to "scientific socialism." After his return from the Far East, he ordered all theater companies and publishing houses to include on their boards "representatives from workers' and peasants' organizations." This ensured that there would be little support for any avantgarde works or for anything likely to contain even veiled criticism of Ceauşescu. Unlike Poland and East Germany, Romania lacked a strong tradition of satiric workshop theater and cabaret, but in any case, Securitate would have nipped a movement in that direction in the bud.

In due course, the screws would be tightened ever more efficiently. By the early eighties, all typewriters had to be turned in to the police. Their owners would then get a special license, or else the machines would be confiscated for good, without any explanation. State firms owning photostat machines were subjected to caricatural restraints in their use. Unlike in the rest of Eastern Europe, the samizdat craze never found a wide audience in Romania. Any individual purchasing reams of paper from a stationer's shop risked being routinely reported by the shopkeeper and being investigated. Intimidation, and the threat of Securitate reprisals, accounted for the population's apparent docility, amounting for over a decade to passivity. In Romania, there were no Sakharovs, no Václav Havels, and precious few of the army of anonymous dissidents who, in Poland, Hungary, Czechoslovakia, and the Soviet Union, carried the torch for cultural and political freedom during the dark 1960s and 1970s. The Romanian temperament, combined with the peculiar nature of Ceaușescu's regime, including the climate of mutual suspicion and the prevalence of informers, saw to that. Repression was total but achieved with a minimum of force, at least where intellectuals were concerned. The latent "historic" cleavage between Romania's intellectual community and the rest of the population made Securitate's task easier.

Ceaușescu, then as later, showed a far greater sophistication than Mao or Kim Il Sung in his treatment of those who dared protest his "cultural revolution" policies after his return from Beijing and Pyongyang. Though this mini–cultural revolution incensed intellectuals, Ceaușescu handled the wave of protests with considerable skill and—at least initially—soothing, kid-glove tactics. As Paul Goma recalled, the anger felt by most writers was expressed through angry speeches and bitter attacks on Ceaușescu's cultural watchdogs, like Dumitru Popescu, Dumitru Ghișe, and Vasile Ricolescu, whose task it was to implement the new decisions. "Like children, we deliberately set out to see how far we could go without getting slapped," Goma said. "Our meetings inside the writers' union building were uproarious, and almost caricaturally free. We insulted the Ceaușescu lapdogs, we called them murderers, cultural gravediggers, shits. They blandly turned the other cheek. I remember, after a meeting in the writers' union that had almost degenerated into a brawl, leaving the building with Ghișe, and saying to him, Well, have you phoned for the 'raven' [the slang Romanian word for the paddy wagon] to take us away? 'Not at all, comrade.' he replied. 'You were right to let off steam. Say anything you want inside the writers'

union, but remember, if you people open your mouths outside the building, things will be very, very different.' "

The same approach to dissent applied, to a lesser extent,
to the Party itself. Within the Central Committee and its various subcommittees a form of "parliamentary immunity" existed. Iliescu was shifted to another job but was neither
arrested, interrogated, nor persecuted. Ceaușescu instinctively
understood that the Romanian temperament would accommodate itself to this more ambiguous form of repression. Indeed, even as Ceaușescu teetered, in later stages, closer and
closer to clinical madness and paranoid megalomania, the
same cautious instinct prevailed. After his extraordinarily courageous, cheeky letter to Ceaușescu in 1977, Goma waited for
some kind of retaliatory measure. But the reason for the com-
paratively mild Securitate response, Goma felt, was that
Ceaușescu did not want to antagonize President Jimmy Carter,
with whom he had established cordial relations and who was
known to be a firm believer in human rights. In the years
leading up to the December 1989 revolution, there were to be
hideous exactions, beatings, and several examples of mass
deportations of rebellious coal miners and trade unionists.
But these brutal measures—duly recorded by Amnesty
International—were selective, designed to strike fear into the
minds of the population as a whole, to "kill the chicken to
frighten the monkey." The regime became increasingly repressive, but Ceaușescu's apologists could claim that there
were fewer political prisoners in Romania than in Yugoslavia.
As many intellectuals were to say again and again after December 1989, "Gheorghiu-Dej was far more brutal in his use
of labor camps, prisons, and summary military tribunals, but
Ceaușescu controlled us far more effectively."

Yet another measure introduced by Ceaușescu after his
return to Romania at the end of June 1971 had to do with
local state and Party administration. From mid-1971 onward,
district Party leaders and their staffs were kept on a very short
leash indeed. They were subject to sudden job changes. These
were so rapid and unpredictable that no official could be sure
of remaining at his post for more than a few months. Party

nominations to districts and other middle-level posts resembled a game of musical chairs, increasingly controlled by the whims of the Conducător and, after 1979, by those of his wife.

There was undoubtedly an element of sly planning to the paranoid way appointments were made and unmade from July 1971 onward. Ceaușescu obviously feared that any local communist official staying in one place too long could conceivably acquire a power base of his own and in time become more responsive to the needs of the local people than to Ceaușescu's own *diktat*s. There arose, of course, unforeseen consequences: As the economic crisis deepened, abuses of local power and opportunities for petty corruption increased. The officials' shorter tenure of office only increased their greed.

The tightening of the screws was not only ideological. At the July 1972 Party congress, Ceaușescu began setting targets for agricultural and industrial production at an unrealistically high level. More ominously still, the pace was to be achieved not with more money or investment but through a more efficient use of existing resources. Here again, the stick-and-carrot inducements were not at first unbearably repressive. It was only by stages, as the economy plummeted, that the workers' living standards dropped alarmingly. The introduction of piece rates, designed to cut absenteeism and idleness and reward the truly motivated worker, was negated by caricatural "profit-sharing" rules that in fact introduced an element of medieval serfdom to factory life. Workers were bound to their factory for an initial five-year period, and during this period half the "profits" resulting from the factory's balance sheet were held in a blocked account. Should a worker leave, he lost his share. But workers could be shifted at will by the state to other factories, without being allowed to quit and with no other form of compensation.

Ceaușescu's rigid belief in Stalinist economic principles and his increasingly idiosyncratic implementation of them were bound to lead to disaster. What is surprising is that his failures were papered over for so long. The December 1989 "revolution" might have occurred earlier had he not benefited from two powerful supporters: international banking consortiums and, until 1976, the shah of Iran. The former stood in line for the privilege of extending loan after loan to gallant little Romania, the maverick state that had dared defy the Soviet Union. The latter presented Ceauşescu with an inestimable gift, a barter agreement for Iranian oil at a fixed price. But the loans raised resulted in factories producing a range of goods so shoddy and obsolete that no developed country would even look at them, while the shah's departure led to a drastic revision of the Iranian deal. From 1976 onward, Romania began paying hard-currency world prices for oil, not only from Iran but also from the Soviet Union, and the factories built with bank loans were huge energy consumers. One aluminum complex at Slatina consumed almost as much electric power as the entire city of Bucharest.

Ceauşescu's decision to expand Romania's oil refinery capability also ended in disaster: By 1979 the huge, expensive installations were functioning at 10 percent of total capacity. Other dismal failures included the Danube–Black Sea canal, which turned out to be a white elephant, and expensive highways, which became monuments to a materialist heaven that never took shape, for by the 1980s oil shortages were such that private cars were banned for months at a time and gasoline rationed.

Olivia Manning in 1939 and Ivor Porter in 1944 had both commented on Romania's abundant food markets and the profusion of high-quality, cheap vegetables. By stages, Romania's food production also shrank, owing to the rigid Stalinist orthodoxy with which quotas were determined and official price ceilings imposed even on food grown in private plots. The situation deteriorated to such an extent that by 1981 bread rationing had been introduced for the first time since the war, and "hoarding" of foodstuffs had become a serious criminal offense. Commuter factory workers who happened to live in rural areas were forbidden to buy food in the towns they worked in.

The severe food shortages—leading to hours of standing in line daily for basics, and consequent factory absenteeism— were bad enough. What was even worse was that Romanians had to listen to Ceauşescu's interminable lectures about the

need for a balanced diet and his complaints that "Romanians
eat too much." On paper, Romanians had nothing to find fault
with. Statistics showed a steady annual increase in all forms of
food production. The official figures were false in many respects, for they were an estimation of amounts produced, not
amounts consumed—and most of the high-quality food, from
the late 1970s onward, was earmarked for export to repay
Romania's massive foreign debts. The food statistics were no
more reliable than those showing the number of copies of
Nicolae Ceauşescu's collected works sold throughout the country. As Dumitru Ghişe, the former boss of the Humanitas
publishing house and former cultural watchdog, explained,
with a straight face, after Ceauşescu's death: "Every copy of
Nicolae Ceauşescu's collected works, once distributed to the
bookshops, was automatically decreed to have been sold on
delivery." Their purchase, by Party members, factories, and
institutions, was mandatory, a form of poll tax. The percent-
age of sales of Ceauşescu's collected works, he added, "was
increasing year by year right up to 1989."

The final insult would come in 1985, with Ceauşescu's
proclamation of the ideal "scientific" diet for Romanians.
This—on paper at least—afforded every Romanian 54.88 kilos of meat, 114 eggs, 20 kilos of "fruit and grapes," 45.30
kilos of potatoes, 114.50 kilos of flour, 14.80 kilos of sugar,
9.60 kilos of edible oil, and 1.1 kilos of margarine a year. In
reality, of course, supplies fell far short of these figures, and
Romanians were not amused by pictures of Nicolae and Elena
Ceauşescu standing in front of heavily stocked buffet tables on
their birthdays.

The Ceauşescus, in fact, had become, by the 1970s, extremely calorie-conscious. Aware that she was putting on
weight, Elena went on a strict diet in the early seventies, and
Nicolae followed suit. His tastes were, in any case, uncomplicated. He enjoyed simple peasant food, delighting in snacks of
tomatoes, goat cheese, and scallions. All the Ceauşescus' edi-
bles came from a special "organic" state farm, and both a
dietician and a food taster were constantly in attendance. Even
on his foreign trips, Ceauşescu traveled with his own food
supplies. Microscopic portions of everything he ate were first

routinely sent to a laboratory for analysis and stored there for twenty-four hours. Nicolae and Elena almost invariably ate lunch together, without guests. Elena's nagging at the table was dreaded. A former headwaiter recalled that she was never satisfied with the food provided. "She would say, 'The spinach, it tasted better when I used to cook it myself for my husband,' and he would pat her hand and mutter, 'Forget it, my dear, forget it.' "

Elena's tantrums and tyrannical behavior toward the numerous household staffs maintaining their palaces around the country were legendary. In the huge Villa Forişor,[2] where Ceauşescu had added a fifteen-room wing they never lived in ("because Elena couldn't stand the smell of fresh paint," a housekeeper there told me), she would slip hairpins under carpets and into corners to monitor the thoroughness with which the servants cleaned the place. Nicolae must have been aware of the strains imposed on their personal household. As guests of Todor Zhivkov in Bulgaria, the Ceauşescus and the same headwaiter witnessed Zhivkov's daughter give one of her staff a terrible, foul-mouthed dressing down. In one of his rare informal moments, Ceauşescu, in an aside to the same headwaiter, whispered, "And you thought *we* were difficult!"

In the ritual phraseology of sycophantic scribblers like Gheorghe Iordache and the strongly anti-Semitic poet Corneliu Vadim Tudor, the Ceauşescu years were "years of light." This phrase became something of a joke when, to save fuel, electricity and hot-water supplies were curtailed, apartment buildings remained barely heated in winter, refrigerators and vacuum cleaners were banned, and only forty-watt bulbs were sold. Checks were instituted to see that the rule—one bulb, one room—was not broken.

These were inconveniences that Romanians got used to, and could survive. Worse were the sudden power cuts that forced coal miners to climb up ladders in the dark at the end of their shifts or compelled surgeons to abort surgical operations at the last moment. More terrible still was the fate of infants whose life-support machines were suddenly disconnected, the patients whose iron lungs suddenly stopped, those over sixty considered too old for any major surgery and left to die, and women factory workers whose pregnancies were humiliatingly monitored to ensure they would not have abortions. Those with Party or Securitate connections, of course, were treated differently. All this was well known to Romanians, but as Nadia Bujor, Ceauşescu's niece, put it, "Words had no bearing on our direct lives. There was life as it was supposed to be, and there was life as it really was." As the Romanian-born writer Richard Wagner wrote in *Exit*, "In a regime that occupies the language you cannot express opinions."

A chilling example of the transformation of the RCP into a mindless "claque" occurred at a Party congress in 1979. On the very last day of the congress session, its chairman called for a unanimous vote by acclamation confirming Nicolae Ceauşescu in his post as general secretary. A frail old man then rose. He was Constantin Pîrvulescu, then eighty-four, a lifelong communist, and he shouted that he had repeatedly asked to speak during the congress but had been ignored. The chairman objected, saying the proceedings were closed, but Ceauşescu was heard to say, "Let him speak."

Pîrvulescu walked to the rostrum. "Yesterday," he said, "you allowed that clown Păunescu to have lots of time on this rostrum. Am I not as important as he?" He then announced that he would vote against Ceauşescu's reconduction. "I am amazed at the way this congress has been prepared," he said. It had been organized "solely to reelect Ceauşescu. The major problems of the country have not been discussed."

Taking their cue from Elena Ceauşescu, the entire congress gathering rose and began applauding Ceauşescu with rhythmic fervor for minutes on end. Some of the delegates started screaming insults at Pîrvulescu, who replied with stinging contempt, repeating: "I will not vote for Ceauşescu." The scene was filmed by a Romanian TV cameraman but was never shown on Romanian TV, nor did the official minutes of the congress make any mention of the incident. What caused some Party "reformists" to look askance at Pîrvulescu's plucky one-man stand was his own background. As Professor Ardeleanu pointed out, Pîrvulescu had a lifelong association with Soviet-style communism. From 1917–20, he served as a Romanian volunteer in the Red Army, followed by a long (1924–28) spell in a Soviet revolutionary school, and an official acknowledgment of his pro-Soviet stance in 1958, when he was the sole member of the Central Committee to advise Gheorghiu-Dej *against* asking Khrushchev for the withdrawal of Soviet troops.

What happened next to Pîrvulescu illustrated the extent, as well as the limits, of Ceaușescu's retaliatory action. He had Pîrvulescu expelled from his large, comfortable apartment and moved instead to a tiny, hideously cramped flat in a small provincial town, at the same time maintaining him under house arrest. When the news clip showing the disgraceful conduct of congress members of the meeting appeared on West German TV, Ceaușescu was furious. The cameraman suspected of smuggling the tape out of Romania was fired, and also became a Securitate target. The indomitable Pîrvulescu survived: Speaking on Romanian TV shortly after Ceaușescu's death, he recalled how embarrassed he was, after his 1979 intervention, when the chief Soviet delegate to the congress ostentatiously shook his hand.

Ceaușescu's measures in the Pîrvulescu case showed that while he became increasingly sensitive to criticism, he preferred intimidation to elimination. So cowed was the Romanian establishment that—overnight—Pîrvulescu became a pariah. Rumors even circulated, possibly spread by Securitate, that he had been "eliminated." The Pîrvulescu incident did not attract a great deal of international attention. *Le Monde* was one of the few newspapers that referred to it at length. More significant even than Ceaușescu's selective punishment of Pîrvulescu was the reaction of the politically sophisticated "class." In East Germany or Czechoslovakia, Pîrvulescu might well have become a symbol. In Romania he became a nonperson.

The passivity of the *nomenklatura* and of professional groups of all kinds remains baffling. "On fundamental matters, Ceaușescu and his wife used to take decisions by themselves without prior consultation with our collective [i.e., the Executive Committee]", said Emil Bobu, his prime minister right up to December 22, now serving a life sentence. "They would both say: 'This is the way it should be'—and there could be no argument. It was almost impossible for someone outside his family to influence him in any way."[3]

But even certain members of his family found it impossible to communicate with the Ceauşescus. "There were times," said Zoia Ceauşescu[4] after her release from jail in 1990, "when I felt that the only people who dared disagree with him were Nicu [her younger brother] and myself. I tried to convince them in vain of the lengths of the lines in the city of people queuing for food. They would never listen to me."

Similarly, as David and Sheila Rothman wrote in *The New York Review of Books*, "Had the medical profession and its leading members ever taken a stand about the gynecological examinations, we asked, or, for that matter, had they criticized any of Ceauşescu's other brutal medical and social policies? Not that anyone could recall."[5]

What is astonishing is that Ceauşescu's personality cult and the slavish behavior of all those associated with the RCP, the government, and the administration was ignored, and even condoned, for so long, and that Ceauşescu's apologists included Western politicians, businessmen, writers, and journalists, some of them of repute. It was perhaps inevitable that those with vested interests in Romania should ape their Romanian counterparts, but with hindsight, it was surprising to discover the lengths to which they went, in the interests, of course, of "cordial relations," i.e., trade imperatives. Lord (Harold) Wilson, who was associated with a British company called Rindalbourne Ltd., which did considerable business with Romania, seldom missed the occasion of congratulating Ceauşescu on his birthday in fulsome terms. In 1987, he cabled him that "only those who have had the responsibility of leading a government can appreciate what this entails. You have raised the Romanian nation to a unique role in the world." In 1988, when Ceauşescu's international reputation was at an almost all-time low, Wilson wrote him that "I am looking forward to renewing our friendship."

John Simpson, the BBC's senior foreign affairs editor, first into Ceauşescu's office with a film crew during the 1989 "revolution," was handed an expensive Mont Blanc pen as a memento—a gift from the British Labour party. Needless to say, an official denial was issued from the Labour party head-quarters, which failed to cut any ice with Simpson: The pen was still in its gift-wrapped box with a formal presentation note.[6]

There was no lack of apologists, either, among authors and journalists. In 1983, at a time of hideous hardship, an anonymous English-language (but Romanian-financed) book entitled *Ceaușescu: A Man for Europe's Unity and Peace* claimed that

> By virtue of the care for a good supply of the people with all the necessary goods, for the improvement of trade, of public services, price stability, the population often meet Nicolae Ceaușescu in the town's shopping centers, when opening new shops, when examining the supply of the market with goods. On these occasions, President Ceaușescu listens to what they say and what else should be done, and, when possible, takes measures on the spot to improve things. These signs speaking by themselves to the honest-minded man that the final scope of building a new society in Roma-nia according to President Ceaușescu's view is the man and his interests, the satisfaction of his spiritual and material demands, the realization of his ideals of progress and civilization.[7]

And what is one to make of the fulsome biography of Ceaușescu by conservative *Figaro* journalist Michel-Pierre Hamelet, and of his even more fulsome *La Vraie Roumanie de Ceaușescu* (Editions Nagel, 1983, with a preface by French Sen-ate president Alain Poher), which extolled the harmonious relations between workers and the state, taking all official sta-tistics at their face value, or of the 1988 biography of Ceaușescu by Robert Govender,[8] which begins:

> Romania has recorded phenomenal progress both domesti-cally and internationally. . . . It is one of the most remark-able achievements of our times. . . . Ceaușescu slashed the military budget and with the money saved strengthened child welfare benefits.

Such benefits, in fact, were the lowest in Europe, exclud-ing possibly Albania, and successive health ministers had at-tempted, without success, to get Ceaușescu to spend more on social security. Proca had tried to get postnatal benefits for Romanian mothers extended from three to six months, but Ceaușescu had refused. Romanian doctors did their best to bend the rules to help their patients, and Ceaușescu complained to Proca once that in hospitals, there was a conspiracy to get around the no-abortion laws, by adding to the list of afflictions endangering expectant mothers' lives and requiring abortions as preventive measures. "It was true," Proca said, "that we doctors did our best." But the Ceaușescus, especially Elena, he added, were exceptionally vigilant. They assumed that everyone was out to cheat them.

Romanians, Mr. Govender went on,

> know that they have a right to a good health service, the right to material and cultural security in old age and the right to child, maternity and sick benefits. These are the birthrights of every Romanian citizen. . . . The 20th century is low on great and responsible statesmanship, but fortunately there is a handful of outstanding statesmen who have not lost sight of the fact that the pursuit of happiness under conditions of security, friendship and prosperity is the inalienable right of all human beings. Few will dispute that the name that stands out in this select group of giants among world statesmen is that of Nicolae Ceaușescu.

Quoting Ceaușescu's concern for "the new human type we intend to mold in our society [who] must be devoted to creative work with a high sense of responsibility for the country's general interest and a lofty moral standing and elevated spiritual life," Govender explained that the Romanian media's role was to "serve the cause of the people and the nation's interest. To a society such as ours, which has been breast-fed on 'page three' girls and social tittle tattle masquerading as news the Romanian example seems hard to follow," though not, apparently, by Robert Maxwell, whose interview at the end of the anonymous Ceaușescu Pergamon Press biography began with the following question or, rather, assertion: "Dear Mr. President, you have been holding the highest political and state office in Romania for almost 18 years, a fact for which we warmly congratulate you. What has—in your opinion—made you so popular with the Romanians?"

More amazing still was the letter, in the London *Times*, written by the late Mervyn Stockwood, then bishop of Southwark, just before the Ceauşescus' state visit to Britain in 1978. He wrote that

> Whether or not we favor a communist economy there has been a marked improvement in the standard of living since Mr. Ceauşescu came into office. There has been a marked improvement in housing, education and health services. Of course there is a long way to go before Romania catches up with the West, but each year I have noticed a higher standard of living.

After praising Ceauşescu as "a brave man" for speaking up against the Soviet invasion of Czechoslovakia, he tackled the tricky issues of human rights and religion.

> First, human rights. A Romanian thinks twice before he goes into active opposition. However the country has no long tradition of unfettered freedom. The present Communist Government is not the first to use methods that are repugnant to us in Britain but which we ourselves have used in the past. . . . A human right about which most of us feel strongly is the freedom to travel and it is not easy for a Romanian to get a visa to go to the West. When I have discussed this matter in official circles, I get a reply on these lines: "You in Britain spend thousands of pounds training doctors and surgeons and you let them go to the United States because the salaries are so much larger. Well, that's your business, but we can't afford to do it. We spend large sums of money to train skilled men to serve our country, not the U.S." Even so, there are irksome restrictions which are not necessary. People in the West who have friends in Romania should be allowed to stay with them without let or hindrance, as guests in their homes and vice versa.
>      Much the same line is taken with regard to hooliganism and violence. "We are trying to create a better life for our people. We don't want our work spoilt by these anti-social elements." So what is a human right when it comes to smashing or taking stern action in the interests of the majority to prevent smashing? Of course there is no simple answer . . .
>      As far as religion is concerned, although a Marxist state, Romania is a deeply religious country. It is said that 50% of the population, most of them Eastern orthodox, go to church on Sundays. Not only are the churches crowded but

so are the theological colleges. The attitude of the government is ambivalent. Although it is officially opposed to all
religions and in its schools it puts forward a non-theistic
interpretation of life, it is, by British standards, exceedingly
generous to the Church and indeed to all faiths. It contrib-
utes to the salaries of the clergy. It helps maintain the buildings and erect new ones.

   My guess is that Ceauşescu is so determined to push
ahead with his new Romania that he does not intend to
become involved in an unnecessary fight which could en-
danger patriotism and turn friends into enemies. . . . Meanwhile one is grateful that the terrible persecution of the
Church at the time of the Russian occupation is over and
that the Christian faith provides an inspiration and an influence for millions of the Romanian people. We in Britain
might well be envious!

The fact that within Romania Christmas Day was a working day like any other, and that the Romanian Foreign Ministry tried to pressure resident diplomats in Bucharest not to
send Christmas cards but only New Year's cards to Romanian
friends    and    contacts    "to    avoid    offending    President
Ceauşescu," seems to have passed Bishop Stockwood by. In
addition to his double standards and inaccurate assessments,
Stockwood also failed to differentiate between the persecution
of the Catholic Church in Romania (not just at the time of the
Russian occupation, but much, much later) and the singularly
privileged, indeed cozy, relationship that existed between
Ceauşescu and the Romanian Orthodox Church. The leaders
of all established religions sat in the Great National Assembly
as ex-officio members. The Interior Ministry, which was responsible for the Romanian Orthodox Church promotions
and finances, invariably designated docile priests for key jobs,
and indeed used them, through Securitate, to proselytize Romanian communities in the United States and Canada in favor
of the Ceauşescu regime. Many of the Romanian Orthodox
Church priests in exile were strongly anticommunist, and
some were former Iron Guard sympathizers, but they proved
highly susceptible to arguments—by visiting priests, also with
controversial Iron Guard pasts—who praised Ceauşescu to the
skies as a nationalist and "one of us." In this way, noted Ion
Pacepa, Romania's foreign intelligence chief and a close con-

fidant of Ceaușescu's, who defected in 1978, Securitate infiltrated many exiled Romanian communities.

A powerful secret police had been a characteristic of prewar Romania. Gheorghiu-Dej had expanded it, turning Securitate into a major instrument of government, at the same time attracting senior communists, many of them intellectuals, into its ranks. As Romania's problems multiplied, the Ceaușescus increasingly relied on Securitate not only to act as watchdog, but to indulge in a variety of fund-raising activities. Ceaușescu's background inclined him to believe in a conspiratorial theory of history. Securitate fed this paranoia. It became, in the eyes of ordinary Romanians, an all-seeing, all-knowing, tentacular monster supervising every aspect of their day-to-day lives. One should not fall into the trap of attributing to Securitate alone the twists and turns of Ceaușescu's policies. His domestic shortcomings were ignored or downplayed for so long precisely because, in the international arena, he displayed a shrewd understanding of the forces at work. His views were warped, his attitude toward individuals invariably tinged with contempt, and his beliefs in the Stalinist ethos never wavered. But he exploited Romania's vocation as a deliberately maverick communist state, coexisting with Arabs and Israelis, courting capitalists and emerging third world leaders alike, with considerable brilliance. Only once the Soviet Union emerged from its long torpor did Ceaușescu become obsolete.

# CHAPTER
## ELEVEN
# FATAL
# ATTRACTIONS

How wonderful international life is! It suffices to recall our visits: airports, greetings, cascades of flowers, embraces, orchestras, every moment polished by protocol, and then limousines, parties, toasts written out and translated, galas and brilliance, praise, confidential conversations, global themes, etiquette, splendor, presents, suites, and finally tiredness, yes, after a whole day tiredness, but how magnificent and relaxing, how refined and honored, how dignified and proper, how-exactly-international!

—RYSZARD KAPUŚCIŃSKI
*THE EMPEROR*

■

N 1978, SHORTLY BEFORE THE CEAUȘESCUS' state visit to Great Britain, General Ion Pacepa defected to the United States. This was probably the single most shocking blow suffered by Ceaușescu until his humiliating flight on December 22, 1989, and subsequent arrest.

As head of the DIE (Departamentul de Informații Externe), Romania's equivalent of MI6, Pacepa had unlimited access to Ceaușescu and saw him on an almost daily basis. Separate from and to some extent competing with Securitate, the DIE was at once a dirty-tricks department, a recruiting center for agents, and an intelligence service offering analysis on every facet of world affairs. Like the CIA and MI6, the DIE was not supposed to concern itself with domestic matters, but it did maintain a close watch on Romania's foreign community, recruiting foreign agents not only abroad but also at home. Pacepa himself was no intellectual lightweight but a highly sophisticated analyst, and his defection was a blow Ceaușescu never overcame. Overnight, whole networks were closed down, DIE officers sacked, investigated, or pensioned off, their place taken by far less qualified Securitate staffers, many of whom were not even fluent in the language of the country they were assigned to.

Pacepa's lengthy debriefing in the United States may have yielded a great deal of valuable material on DIE activities all over the world, but many experts found his book, *Red Horizons*, published in 1987,[1] disappointing despite its sensational revelations about the Ceaușescus' life-style and personal habits. Written in the breathless style of tabloid journalism, with occasional flashbacks, it was Pacepa's day-to-day, almost minute-by-minute chronicle of his last month (March 1978) in office immediately prior to defection. He also provided a gossipy, insider's look at the vagaries of a first family so caricaturally nasty and prurient that the Ceaușescus emerged not as real-life people but rather as two-dimensional villains straight out of a James Bond movie. Blowsy Elena Ceaușescu was portrayed as an insatiable sexual predator, forever dragging Nicolae off to bed, reveling in surreptitiously taken films of leading establishment figures having sex with their legitimate or ancillary partners, gorging herself on caviar and champagne, and uninterested in anything but her accumulation of mink coats and honorary doctorates. Ceaușescu came across as a petulant charlatan, obsessed with dirty tricks of all kinds, from sexual blackmail of foreign diplomats to the acquisition by stealth or trickery of high-tech secrets to be duly sold to the Soviet Union for hard cash.

While there is no doubt that surveillance and a rapacious acquisition of goods occupied much of the Ceaușescus' time, Pacepa's account trivialized them, inevitably provoking unanswered questions about Pacepa himself. Was the entire book a crude piece of CIA-inspired disinformation propaganda? The book was so caricatural that it was difficult to take its portrait of the Ceaușescus seriously. Perhaps one of the reasons for its inadequacy was the exaggeratedly colloquial tone of the reconstituted dialogue of the Ceausescus and their henchmen. It was like reading a history of the Nixon presidency based exclusively on the vocabulary of the Watergate tapes. Another deficiency of the book was that Pacepa could write only of his own encounters with Ceaușescu, and these dealt, quite naturally, exclusively with espionage and dirty tricks—Pacepa's specialty. Presumably, when Ceaușescu was not so engaged, other facets of government preoccupied him, but there was no indication of this in *Red Horizons*. Finally, for all his willingness to tell all, Pacepa was less than frank about himself. One did not become head of Romania's espionage service under Ceaușescu without providing the notoriously suspicious Conducător with proof of one's utter devotion and reliability, but Pacepa, in the book, was remarkably discreet about his own past.

The fact is that for all the mediocre seaminess revealed in *Red Horizons*, Ceaușescu *was* taken seriously by the outside world, becoming the third best known personality in European communism after Khrushchev and Brezhnev, eventually outshining even Tito. In 1969, when Richard Nixon visited Ceaușescu in Bucharest, he became the first U.S. president to make an official visit to a Warsaw Pact country. Ceaușescu visited the United States in 1970, 1975 (the year Gerald Ford visited Romania), and 1978. No other communist head of state could come anywhere near Ceaușescu's travel record, either in the West or in the third world. In part, this was because from 1965 onward, Romania was a one-man show, and since Ceauşescu viewed the business of diplomacy as a series of personal gestures, he saw his role as that of the indefatigable traveler. The fact that he and Elena were insatiable in their quest for international recognition helped, as did Ceauşescu's thirst for the praise of foreign leaders to instill in the Romanians a sense of his grandeur, and prove to himself that he deserved his unique Conducător status.

Heads of state who met Ceauşescu from the early 1970s on all noted a marked change in the couple's personalities. On Ceauşescu's first official visit to Paris, in 1967, said former president Giscard d'Estaing, he made a "mediocre" rather than a "bad" impression. In 1978, on the Ceauşescus' later visit to France, Giscard was president and found Nicolae Ceauşescu "loathsome, arrogant, convinced at all times that he alone was right." In 1979, when Giscard made a return visit to Romania, his earlier conviction was reinforced: "He gave the impression that he felt he was dealing with corrupt fools." One farcical side to the Romanian trip amused Giscard and his wife, Anne-Aymone, considerably. When they arrived at their state guesthouse in Bucharest, they were greeted by a small crowd, shouting, "Hoorah! Hoorah!" Then, when they visited Sibiu and stayed in the former royal palace there, another small crowd was stationed outside the palace gates, also shouting, "Hoorah!" The Giscards noted in Sibiu that these were the same people, bused in for the occasion.

But it must also be said that for all his Stalinist rhetoric and intellectual shortcomings, Ceauşescu *did* acquire a vision of the outside world, or at any rate fooled observers from de Gaulle to Nixon into believing that he had such a vision. Though based to a very large extent on the ideas of others, his theories of national independence enabled Romania, for almost two decades, to play a role quite out of proportion to its size. As early as June 1966, he had called for the abrogation of both the Warsaw Pact and NATO. His blueprint for a Balkan nuclear-free zone attracted the sympathetic support of maverick Greek premier Andreas Papandreou. Though his interest in the Middle East was self-serving, his views were listened to with attention by Arabs, Israelis, and Western statesmen. His refusal to condone the Soviet invasion of Afghanistan in 1979 (Romania abstained at the UN) or to condemn it was a shrewd piece of fence-sitting. The mileage he obtained out of his decision to ignore the Soviet veto and send a Romanian team to the Los Angeles 1984 Olympics was considerable. As former ambassador Funderburk wrote, "Romanians became virtual heroes in the eyes of Americans at exactly the time when Ceaușescu was actually moving closer to the Soviets and enforcing harsher human rights violations and an anti-religious campaign."[2] The State Department, he added, intent on differentiating between "good" and "bad" communist leaders, didn't want to know. What riled Funderburk most was that both Pacepa, in his CIA debriefings, and his own reliable intelligence sources within Romania confirmed that Ceaușescu's decision to "defy" the Soviet Union by sending a team to Los Angeles in fact had full, if tacit, Russian approval—the Soviet rationale being to convince the world that Romania really *was* a maverick, independent communist state.

But for all Pacepa's account of Ceaușescu's deviousness in his relations with both Arafat and the Soviets, there transpired the ambition of a man eager to leave his mark on history by contributing to a Middle East settlement through Romanian good offices, expecting international recognition from such an initiative. Ceaușescu's obstinate and unsuccessful insistence that Arafat should establish a Palestinian government in exile was not in itself entirely inept. There was something almost pathetic in Ceaușescu's determination that *he*, and not Jimmy Carter, should be acknowledged as the middleman in any Middle Eastern settlement. He had, after all, been among the first to spot Arafat and take him seriously, inviting him to Bucharest as early as 1970.

The Western world suffered no illusions as far as the Ceaușescus' dark side was concerned. Even within the communist bloc, their obsession with security and fear of assassination provoked mirth. Their food tasters and personal cooks and their insistence on providing their own bedding on foreign trips (even to Buckingham Palace and Blair House), their inability to make small talk, and their rigid formality on all occasions made them ghastly guests. "Among heads of state and heads of government," said Giscard d'Estaing, "a Ceauşescu visit was regarded as an unavoidable calamity."

Giscard experienced such a calamity twice. The first time, on their visit to Paris in 1978, the French president's officials responsible for state visits discovered to their horror afterward that at the Residence, Marigny, opposite the Elysée Palace, where the Ceauşescus had been staying, considerable damage had been done—electric and phone wiring ripped from the walls, presumably by Ceauşescu's security men looking for bugs. In addition, the Ceauşescu party had walked off with a number of household objects—clocks, ashtrays, and other easily removable artifacts—simply plucked from tables and walls and stolen from the presidential guesthouse. Shortly afterward, President Giscard d'Estaing met Queen Elizabeth, and—knowing that the Ceauşescus would shortly be visiting Buckingham Palace (in June 1978)—warned her of the Ceauşescus' party's tendency to make off with anything they could pack away in their suitcases. He also warned King Juan Carlos, for the Ceauşescus were soon due to visit Spain. Queen Elizabeth instructed her palace staff to keep a watchful eye on the Romanians, and pilfering was kept to a minimum. The queen was grateful for the warning, above all appalled that Ceauşescu ("that frightful little man," she called him in private) should assume that his Buckingham Palace quarters would be bugged. She watched with wry amusement as Ceauşescu held early-morning staff meetings with his suite in the Buckingham Palace gardens, presumably to avoid electronic surveillance, Ceauşescu striding ahead, his aides following like ugly ducklings.

It was only with extreme reluctance that Queen Elizabeth had agreed to act as hostess to the Ceauşescus. The Callaghan government had convinced her that this had been a condition of his coming to Britain in the first place and that the importance of imminent aircraft and arms sales to Romania made such hospitality mandatory. Similarly, Giscard had been compelled to invite the Ceauşescus as part of a trade deal involving Bull (the French computer firm) and Renault.

Queen Elizabeth was always remarkably well briefed on the countries whose leaders she was compelled to entertain, and by 1978, the Ceauşescu personality cult was in full swing and his incipient megalomania reported on and analyzed by Britain's Foreign Office staff. There were other, more personal reasons for her reluctance. Ceauşescu was the leader of the party that had expelled King Michael of Romania, a distant kinsman, and persecuted his followers immediately after his return to Bucharest from London, where he had attended the royal wedding of Princess Elizabeth and Prince Philip in 1947. The RCP had also taken the credit for the king's August 23, 1944, anti-Nazi coup.

Britain's royal family is so professional in its social savoir-faire that it can cope with almost anything, but the strain of attempting to entertain the Ceauşescus proved an almost unsurmountable challenge. Photographs of the Ceauşescus in the company of Queen Elizabeth and Prince Philip, however, reveal Nicolae and Elena's delight with their hosts. It was, said one former courtier, the first time they had been seen to smile since Pacepa's defection.

At the time of the Buckingham Palace visit, Romania was chiefly perceived as the country that had recently suffered a devastating earthquake, leading in turn to an unprecedented exercise in international aid. The Ceauşescus had been on another official trip—to Lagos—when it had occurred, in March 1977, and had promptly flown home, where Ceauşescu personally took charge. The damage had stimulated Ceauşescu's interest in urban renewal and, by extension, the transformation of town and country alike. Ironically, it was the widespread natural destruction of city landmarks and historic buildings that caused him to embark on a manmade urban and village devastation with such a vengeance that his public image altered drastically. Before 1977, he had been known mainly as the maverick nationalist communist leader of a small Balkan country who had successfully challenged the Soviet Union and gotten away with it. After 1977, he began to be perceived as an urban rapist, Dracula driving a bulldozer. As Mark Almond pointed out in *Decline Without Fall*, "To seek to comprehend the enormity of Ceauşescu's upheaval through

comparisons with the activities of Western socialist town-
planners and corrupt developers is to see events in Romania
through a trivialising lens."[3] True, but correspondents who
began by recording the wholesale destruction of Byzantine
churches and eighteenth-century mansions ended by focusing their attention on broader issues, including the ban on
divorces and abortions, though it was not generally realized
that stringent anti-abortion and anti-divorce rules had been
in force since 1966. Needless to say, Securitate used these
restrictions to admirable effect: The promise to facilitate a
divorce or to cast a blind eye on an abortion was a sufficient
inducement to lead to the recruitment of thousands of Securitate informers.

"The 1977 earthquake was the trigger," said Professor Dan
Berindei. Ever since his return from Asia in June 1971,
Ceauşescu had been haunted by the memory of orderly
Pyongyang, with its endless wide avenues and mile after mile
of identical apartment blocks. Such architecture is repulsive to
those of us for whom cities are living and varied repositories
of the past. Much of old Barcelona is, by town-planning standards, a slum, but the destruction of the back streets giving on
to the *ramblas* would be a cultural as well as an architectural
tragedy.

The Ceauşescus had no such aesthetic preoccupations, and
their view of foreign architectural landmarks had been largely
from the windows of limousines speeding through cities on
their many official trips. The combination of cultural and aesthetic illiteracy, rigid Marxist-Leninist orthodoxy, and an in-
nate taste for "gigantism" was to be devastating.

As Professor Trond Gilberg has pointed out, Karl Marx
was a product of the Industrial Revolution and a committed
urbanite who "spoke disparagingly about the 'idiocy of rural
life.' "[4] Under communism, Karl Marx had prophesied, the
distinction between town and country in an industrial society
would eventually become blurred. Ceauşescu's "narrow view
of Marxism"[5] led him to apply Marx's theories and the Stalinist industrialization doctrine with extreme crudeness (in one
speech he defined the task as that of "radically wiping out
major differences between towns and villages"). Aesthetic and

historic considerations simply didn't matter. Long before 1977, Ceaușescu had approved the slogan "systematization, modernization, civilization" to destroy the "breeding ground of bourgeois liberalism" perpetuated by "forms of private property," and even before the 1977 earthquake some steps had been taken in this direction. Whereas the communist authorities in postwar Warsaw deliberately decided to restore the old city, which had been completely razed by the Nazis, in loving detail, Ceaușescu not only set about destroying historic villages and regrouping its inhabitants into jerry-built suburban slums, but also began the process—interrupted only by his death—of flattening part of historic Bucharest.

In the countryside, village householders were given short notice to evacuate their homes, which were then bulldozed. They were rehoused in concrete boxes, often with communal kitchens, toilets, and washing facilities. Some five hundred villages were razed in this way, and thousands more were due for demolition. The aim was to do away with "archaic" village life and get rid of the difference between factory and agricultural workers. Needless to say, cooped up in apartment blocks, people were far easier to keep under surveillance than had they continued living in individual houses. As a result of production bottlenecks, cheap materials, inadequate budgets, and corruption, the new "village suburbs" were abysmally built, often with no plumbing or running water. In these new Ceaușescu complexes, it was impossible to keep rabbits, chickens, ducks, or geese, which had been a small mainstay for many Romanians as the food situation steadily deteriorated.

In the towns, "systematization" and "modernization" took another form. From 1977 onward, the piecemeal demolition of churches occurred under militia guard, for some conservationists, churchgoers, and architecture students did try to picket the demolition sites. But the most spectacular destruction of an entire Bucharest district was first planned in 1978 and had nothing to do with the aftermath of the 1977 earthquake.

Ever since he had become general secretary, Ceaușescu had dreamt of a single monumental edifice that would house all of Romania's major Party and state institutions under a single roof. In 1978 he set up a competition for a "People's Palace" to fulfill this purpose. A little-known young architect straight out of architecture school, Anca Petrescu, then only twenty-five, armed with an iron determination matched only by her indifference to Bucharest's historic past, bulldozed her way past other established architects and attracted Ceaușescu's attention. No relative (the false rumor was based on the similarity of her and Elena's names, for Petrescu is a common patronymic), she won the competition for the People's Palace by concentrating her efforts on a spectacular papier-mâché model, itself of vast size.

"I knew Ceaușescu favored traditional architecture with a French neoclassic flavor," Anca Petrescu said. Among the other entries were several modern designs, including a Crystal Palace-type plan (for it was known that Ceaușeseu had seen illustrations of the long-defunct building and been impressed). The rival architects were no match for Anca Petrescu—she lobbied Ceaușescu's aides with superior skill and greater persistence. The deciding factor was her insistence that the People's Palace (after Ceaușescu's death it was renamed House of the Republic) should not only occupy most of Arsenal Hill, but that its 200-meter-long, 100-meter-high facade face a monumental "Victory of Socialism Boulevard." The latter was designed to be at least as long as the Avenue des Champs Elysées (it ended up even longer), requiring the total destruction of the Uranus district and its replacement by soulless concrete apartment blocks in the pure Pyongyang tradition.

Though groundbreaking did not actually start until 1984, plans for the transformation of the Uranus district started as early as 1978. The enormous cost included the bill for a vast underground shelter and a small underground two-person railway train for the Ceaușescus' exclusive personal use—there were no plans to link the palace to a public underground station. While the People's Palace budget was being elaborated on, health minister Proca was trying to get Ceaușescu to increase the postnatal benefits available to Romanian mothers, which were the lowest in Europe. Proca wanted to increase the paid leave for working mothers giving birth to a child from three to six months and resigned when this was refused. The cost involved would have been half a billion lei. The cost of the People's Palace was estimated at twelve times as much—at least 6 billion lei.

From the start, Ceauşescu was obsessively preoccupied with the project. The birth of Romania's "new man" was proving unexpectedly difficult, and Ceauşescu's social engineering, like his Stalinist economics, was running into unforeseen problems. As the Romanian economy floundered, as his other plans for heavy industry, oil refining capacity, and agro-industry plunged disastrously into the red, as the euphoria of the early 1970s waned, then died, the Ceauşescus' hold on events faltered. Statistics had to be systematically faked, and Nicolae and Elena were reduced to berating fearful officials for their nonfulfillment of grandiose and unrealistic plans. Here at least was a project over which they were able to maintain full control, whether it was the shape of the public fountains adorning the Victory of Socialism Boulevard, the size of door handles, or the gilt inlay patterns of Elena Ceauşescu's cherrywood-paneled offices. Anca Petrescu's team of architects at Nicolae and Elena's beck and call could be relied on to fulfill their dream: the posthumous legacy to Romania of the largest single building in the world. That it caused the destruction of almost a quarter of the city of Bucharest and had no functional meaning—for council of state, presidency, Central Committee, and council of ministers were all housed in perfectly adequate, if admittedly separate, buildings—meant nothing to the Ceauşescus.

For Mariela Celac, an architect not connected with the project but who knew the area well because as a child she had visited her music teacher there, the rape of the Uranus district was "an act of sheer violence." Here, she said, had stood houses in excellent shape, many with gardens. There had been a monastery with chestnut trees, schools, tram lines, small shops, and churches. "I tried to imagine what was going on inside Ceauşescu's head," she said.

Ironically, what began for the diminutive Anca Petrescu as a triumph over her better-established colleagues soon turned into a nightmare, for the Ceauşescus turned out to be extraordinarily difficult, indecisive patrons. Unlike Hitler, who at least chose an advocate of gigantism—Albert Speer—and allowed him to get on with it, the Ceauşescus showed the same suspicious, niggardly attention to detail at all stages of planning and construction of the People's Palace that they displayed in the supervision of their own domestic life. "He was," Anca Petrescu recalled, "an impossible benefactor." Every Saturday morning, once work was in progress, he and Elena spent two hours on the site, only part of their weekly schedule devoted to construction, for they also took in other building projects in Bucharest. "He was always very formal, very businesslike, never praising anyone," Petrescu remembered. "He had more regard for the workers than for the architects, shaking hands with craftsmen, talking informally to the foremen. He was a very civilized man."

But for all of Ceauşescu's unquestioning belief in the Leninist need for ruthless, forceful change, he proved a remarkably indecisive patron, constantly dithering, unable to make up his mind, but at the same time unable to formulate his likes and dislikes articulately. "We knew he was unable to gauge the effect of a column or a door if shown only a reduced model, so we had to build actual full-size papier-mâché models of columns or windows, and even then he was incapable of taking a decision," Anca Petrescu recalled. The columns were first Doric, then Ionic, then Doric again. In the earliest model, the roof had been flat, "but he wanted a dome, like the roof of a university." As an afterthought, he insisted on adding another two stories, for offices. Windows and doors originally oval-shaped at the top became rectangular at his insistence. He ranted and raved when he discovered that the two additional floors were dark, with low ceilings, and ordered more windows built to let in natural light. He personally designed the huge, twisted metal flagpole on the top of the roof, a shape of surpassing, disturbing ugliness (which was removed after his death). Above all, he was unable to master problems of perspective and scale. Because the project itself grew and grew, and the space around it grew larger, Anca Petrescu said, "the palace itself began to look smaller, so he now wanted it bigger. His sycophants would back up all his requests and chorus their approval of his successive demands and changes of mind."

Mariela Celac, who observed from afar some of her colleagues associated with the project being driven to the verge of a nervous breakdown by the Conducător's constant orders and counterorders, remains convinced that Ceaușescu himself never perceived his behavior as abnormal and that what appeared to others to be indecisiveness was in fact one of the many manifestations of his growing paranoia.

The House of the Republic is not only the largest building in the world but almost certainly the ugliest. It was not entirely architect Petrescu's fault. Though abominably heavy, the original model had some kind of symmetry. Ceaușescu's insistence on major alterations and his choice of designs was invariably ghastly. For all its cost, the overall effect was one of shoddy compromise. The vast hall "for signing treaties" contains the world's largest and most ostentatious chandeliers, but the concrete balcony flanking this huge room is already crumbling. Successive amendments to the original plan add to the lack of proportion of the whole; attempts to save money resulted in breeze blocks replacing stone, colored stone replacing marble (though so much real marble was required as well that for several years there was none left for headstones in Romanian cemeteries). There were cracks in the facade, and the building was impossible to heat adequately in winter, for Ceaușescu rejected as unaesthetic the presence of radiators or heat ducts.

Had Elena Ceaușescu alone been responsible for the planning of the People's Palace, things might have moved along more quickly. Pahun N. Pahun, a resident of Petrești, recalls that when Elena visited her village in 1986, she stayed in her limousine. "We could see her pointing at one old building after another," she said. The following day a demolition team moved in and razed to the ground all those she had fingered. Elena Ceaușescu had decided in her own inimitable way to apply systematization, modernization, and civilization to her native village.

The modern buildings meant to turn Petrești into a showcase new town were in terrible taste. The palaces and hunting lodges erected in every province for the Ceaușescus also reflected a parvenu, petit-bourgeois mentality. The Palatul Primăverii (Spring Palace) residence, in the "forbidden district" of Bucharest, was furnished in a style that can best be described as an amalgam of the Saudi Arabian French Renaissance and Scottish Baronial styles, with a touch of the Kremlin added. Room after room consisted of long dining tables and uncomfortable, heavily embroidered armchairs. The Ceauşescu suites, with their gold-plated bathroom fittings, were both ornate and uncomfortable, the beds as hard as boards. Large mirrors in Elena's bedroom had carved gold, silver, and semiprecious stone motifs encrusted in their ornate frames, monuments in a museum of kitsch. When I visited Palatul Primăverii, an inventory was in progress, and the bedroom suites reserved for Zoia, Valentin, and Nicu (perpetually empty, for they never came) were full of junk—trinkets amassed by Elena and never thrown away: vases, pottery, mirrors, cheap jewelry. The overall effect was of a seedy booth on Portobello Road or the Paris *marché aux puces*. In Elena's bathroom there were three weighing machines: one was the old-fashioned kind, with movable weights. The other two had digital figure panels, and did not work. Both his and her suites had huge walk-in closets. In an annex there was a huge indoor swimming pool decorated with gaudy mural paintings. As in the other palaces, there was a room to screen movies in. There were very few books, and the entire building had a curious, never-lived-in look. There were never any guests at the Spring Palace, an employee said. The garden was magnificent, surrounded by a low wall. Security was so tight in the district for several square miles around the residence that the Ceauşescus needed neither barbed-wire enclosures nor electrified fences to feel safe.

Whenever the couple traveled, the household staff moved too. The waiters, cooks, and bodyguards rarely had a day off, and one of the security guards was also a trained projectionist. The Ceauşescus, their former headwaiter recalled, were especially fond of the *Kojak* series. They also enjoyed an old kitsch French film series starring Michele Mercier called *La Marquise des Anges*, about the adventures of a shapely lady in prerevolutionary France. Movies they saw again and again included *Room at the Top*, a special favorite; *The Great Gatsby*; and the filmed version of Françoise Sagan's *Aimez-vous Brahms?* The staff was allowed to watch, but only from the projectionist's cabin. They also, the headwaiter implied, were not averse to "films about physical love"—soft rather than hard-core pornography.

Hunting and shooting on a lavish scale had been the favorite pastime of leading communists like Tito and Brezhnev, aping the traditions of the tsars, but Ceauşescu surpassed their excesses. Because the main purpose of RCP regional first secretaries was to please the Ceauşescus, their overriding concern, after the stage management of welcoming pageants, was to provide Nicolae Ceauşescu with adequate hunting and shooting facilities. From the 1970s onward, huge tracts of land were earmarked for his exclusive use, and by the time of his death, Ceauşescu had the largest hunting estate in the world at his disposal. In the Timişoara area alone there were 2.5 million hectares fenced in for his exclusive use. He possessed twenty-three hunting lodges around the country, including fifteen "country palaces," furnished in the Spring Palace style but with a profusion of stuffed mounted trophies and antlers.

In the Azuga district, between Sinaia and Braşov, there were no less than *three* hunting lodges reserved for the Ceauşescus' exclusive use. Their favorite, a huge Swiss-style wooden chalet, was permanently guarded by Securitate. Orders were that no one was ever to be allowed inside apart from the Ceauşescus and their occasional guests. Zoia once drove up there and was turned away at the door. She had been sightseeing in the vicinity and had simply stopped by for a glass of water.

The housekeeper at this particular chalet remained an unabashed fan of Ceauşescu but, like almost everyone else, loathed Elena. "He was a kind man," she told me. "Once, a Securitate dog bit Corbu [Ceauşescu's favorite Labrador], and when Ceauşescu found out that the Securitate squad there had shot the Securitate dog [for this act of lèse-majesté], he became very angry indeed." She recalled that once, through no fault of her own, smoke from a crackling fire in the sitting-room fireplace filled the room. "Elena immediately started screaming, accusing me of sabotage, of trying to poison 'the Comrade,' " she said. "She threatened to turn me over to Securitate. Nicolae Ceaușescu said, 'Don't make such a fuss, dear, smoked meat lasts longest.' "

The Ceaușescus' hunting and shooting budget was huge. Wild animals, some of them imported, were carefully bred and fattened on meat and corn. One former hunting-estate manager in Ceaușescu's employ said that at a time when farmers' lambs were dying of malnutrition because of drought and lack of feed, he was giving corn to herds of wild boar and meat to bears. "Ceaușescu was a very ferocious hunter," he said. "With his Holland and Holland guns, [the make favored by the British hunting and shooting aristocracy] he shot huge numbers of animals in a very short space of time."

The estate manager recalled a hunt during which Ceaușescu shot sixty-six black wild mountain goats, a rare and protected species. Near Sinaia he rode a ski lift to shoot the bewildered animals from above. A professional hunter attached to the Ceaușescu household was responsible for providing Nicolae with an endless supply of game: Wild goats were imported from Austria; bears, from Alaska. In Rîușor, in Argeș county, a full-time vet was employed to look after the animals and feed them cheese, fish, meat, apples, and carrots. A research institute called ISCAS undertook a five-year study to discover whether polar bears could survive in the Romanian mountain climate (they all died). Because of work pressures, Ceaușescu's hunting expeditions rarely lasted more than a couple of days, but they were organized on a huge scale. In 1983, the professional hunter recalled, it had been necessary to deploy two planes, four helicopters, and six Range Rovers for Ceaușescu and his guests. With practice, Ceaușescu had become an excellent marksman, but his targets were always carefully set up: Fed on a special diet, the bears that were his favorite target were practically zoo animals. They would be drugged and beaters would drive them to the spot where they presented the easiest target. At all times, the fiction was that these were wild animals and that only Ceaușescu's skill as a hunter enabled him to kill them.

As with the People's Palace project, it is difficult not to view Ceaușescu's passion for killing animals (which increased in the last ten years of his life) as an escape from the more intractable problems facing him. In the rows of slaughtered animals was proof of his mastery over at least some of the elements around him. Vasile Maluțan, the Ceaușescus' personal helicopter pilot, recalled that hunting trips were a nightmare for him and his crew, because they often went without food while Ceaușescu blazed away for hours at a time, and if Ceaușescu stayed overnight, they usually had to sleep, sometimes in freezing cold, in their parked helicopters. (This indifference to the Ceaușescus' subordinates' welfare extended to Romanian journalists who traveled with them abroad: Their food allowance in the United States came to $8 a day.)

Ceaușescu collected hunting trophies with the same assiduity that Elena collected honorary degrees, and there was a friendly feud between him and Todor Zhivkov, the Bulgarian communist leader, over who had the finest collection of trophies. Ceaușescu, by December 1989, had accumulated 244 trophies for deer and 385 for bear. He shot thousands of animals a year, a former employee said. He particularly enjoyed using the rifle with a powerful telescopic sight presented to him by Queen Elizabeth, because it reminded him of his finest hour.

# CHAPTER TWELVE
# SECURITATE

And as a consequence of Our Benefactor's concern to develop the forces of order and thanks to his great generosity in that area, the number of policemen multiplied during the last few years of his reign, and ears appeared everywhere, sticking up out of the ground, glued to the walls, hiding in offices, lurking in crowds, standing in doorways, jostling in the marketplace. To protect themselves from the plague of informers, people learned—without anyone knowing how or where, or when, without schools, without courses, without records or dictionaries—another language, mastered it and became so fluent in it that we simple and uneducated folk suddenly became a bilingual nation. . . . One tongue served for external speech,

the other for internal. The first was sweet and the second bitter, the first polished and the second coarse, one allowed to
come to the surface and the other kept out of sight."

—RYSZARD KAPUŚCIŃSKI
*THE EMPEROR*

**A**LL THOSE WITH EXPERIENCE OF EASTERN
Europe prior to the collapse of communism there,
when the satellites were still unadulterated police
states, recall the huge resources devoted to surveillance. Tourists may have been relatively immune so long as they did not
use their status to try and contact dissidents. But whether in
East Germany or Czechoslovakia, Bulgaria or—until 1986—
even Hungary, a system closely based on the pre-Gorbachev,
totalitarian Soviet model was in force, affecting embassies, hotels, foreigners of all kinds and, of course, nationals of these
countries as well.

Nowhere, perhaps not even in the Soviet Union under
Stalin, was this apparatus as all-pervasive as in Romania under
Ceauşescu. The Romanian secret police dominated every facet
of Romanian life. It was more feared than Ceauşescu himself,
and enjoyed the truly sinister aura that always eluded the
Soviet KGB. The reason was not simply that Securitate and
the RCP itself, at all levels, collaborated in a unique way, but
that Securitate, a far more flexible, many-faceted organization
than the KGB, infiltrated many more areas involving state
activities of all kinds. The Romanian Foreign Trade Ministry,
for example, was not simply a hotbed of Securitate agents. It
*was* virtually a self-contained Securitate ministry. Securitate
also ran its own network of trading companies, holding companies abroad, and even banks. It also relied heavily on an
information network from within the RCP.

Silviu Brucan, the veteran communist (and former Stalinist) who had been shunted aside in the mid-1960s and became
a leading dissident in the seventies and eighties, spending
some time under house arrest as a result, took issue in *The
Independent*, the London daily newspaper (Nov. 28, 1987),
"with a misconception prevailing in the West that this regime

owes its survival to the repressive organs of the state. . . . In fact the main instrument of power has been the Communist party, with security forces playing only a marginal role and dealing with especially deviant cases." So devious and so tentacular was Securitate's hold on the country, so expert was it in disinformation, that Western intelligence specialists on Romania wondered at the time whether even this Brucan letter, written at considerable personal risk, might not have been a Securitate ploy. Securitate was so omnipresent that it became a kind of bogeyman, its admittedly considerable power exaggerated in the minds of ordinary Romanians. The leading dissident architect Mariela Celac was taken on a tour of a large factory in the 1980s and shown proof of Securitate's efficiency in monitoring all factory workers. All telephone conversations in and out of the factory were taped, and she was shown cassette number 6432. "What was so absurd," she said, "was that though they probably typed up all phone conversations, probably no one read the result or analyzed their contents. The fact that everything was taped was enough to keep everyone cowed. The instrument they used was the people's sense of fear." She was also amusingly critical of the somewhat simplistic Western perceptions concerning the workings of the secret police. "I think in the West you have a somewhat romantic view of the system," she said. In her own case, when she started speaking out against the wholesale destruction of the Romanian architectural environment, "I don't think a phone call from a Party boss or from a Securitate official was required to get me fired from my job. My employers fired me as a kind of Pavlovian reaction."

Liviu Turcu, the senior Securitate official who defected in 1987, put it, "Imagine a huge apparatus spreading rumors, fear, and terror, an atmosphere in which common people feel that if they try and do the most insignificant thing identified as an act of opposition to Ceauşescu, they will disappear. It was psychological terror that paralyzed the Romanian population, and the most outstanding piece of disinformation was the rumor, deliberately spread by Securitate itself, that one out of every four Romanians was a Securitate informer."

From 1978 on, Romania was in the grip of an increasingly

intractable economic crisis for which there was no possible solution as long as Ceauşescu clung to his Stalinist principles and one-man rule. The first coal miners' strike, in the Jiul valley, occurred in September 1972, after a dispute over work schedules and reduced pensions. A far more serious strike, in August 1977, affected 35,000 coal miners, and during the Securitate repression that followed, two engineers who had sided with the workers died in "accidents." The attempt to set up a "free" trade union ended with its ringleaders being sent to psychiatric hospitals by Securitate. Others were charged before courts for "crimes against socialism." Yet another strike occurred in Jiul in October 1981. Securitate did more than simply put down the malcontents with riot troops and selective savagery. So many miners and their families were moved to other areas that Paul Goma, who has kept in close touch with dissident workers, believes that the composition of the Jiul work force was entirely transformed from 1981 onward. Former army men and Securitate agents nearing the end of their contracts were then drafted into the Jiul area as coal miners and foremen, which would explain why the miners allowed themselves to be used, by Iliescu, to terrorize students and political opponents on the streets of Bucharest in June 1990.

In contrast, Mariela Celac and almost all other dissidents agree that the repressive measures taken against isolated intellectuals operating, as it were, in a vacuum, were far less harsh than those taken against any form of *organized* opposition. The harassment was psychological as much as physical. Several times Mariela Celac was notified that she was required to be at a certain address for questioning, was kept waiting, and was then questioned repeatedly by individuals who were clearly aware of her activities. But she was invariably allowed to leave. Dan Petrescu, one of the two known dissidents of the town of Iaşi, was treated similarly but said that after the questioning sessions were over, the Securitate officials engaged in "normal conversation" and banter and even revealed some embarrassment at having had to harass him.

Professor Dinu Giurăscu, a well-known historian (who obtained asylum in the U.S. in 1988 but has since returned to

Bucharest University to teach after a stint at the University of Texas) explained how, after notifying his Securitate contact of dinner invitations at Western embassies—to do otherwise was to invite harassment and, perhaps, house arrest—he endeavored to give them an edulcorated version of the conversations with his foreign hosts. "Occasionally," he recalled, "I felt I was doing good—by highlighting, for instance, our talks about the need to enable Romanian students to take scholarships abroad, and the damage done to our academic standards through our enforced isolation." His hosts, of course, knew of his constraints and even joked about it. The Securitate contact he reported to, an elderly man who regarded the whole routine as somewhat boring, relayed such reports without unduly bothering him. "There was no major problem when I was the only Romanian guest at such functions," he said. "The trouble arose when there were several of us, for I had no way of knowing how zealous the others would be in their debriefings or whether they were agents provocateurs."

By 1980 Romania was no longer responding to Ceaușescu's directives. His speeches reflected this, containing as they did interminable statistics proving that under his enlightened leadership things had never been better, and invective against those subordinates and Party cadres responsible for "shortcomings." In 1982, while making one of his spot-check visits to a Bucharest market, Ceaușescu sacked his accompanying agriculture minister on the spot, blaming him for the inadequate choice of food available to Romanian housewives. Such Haroun al Rashid behavior may have been good propaganda, but it underlined the fact that as far as food shortages were concerned, Ceaușescu had no real solutions, only dramatic gestures.

As control slipped from Ceaușescu's grasp, Securitate became increasingly not just a repressive apparatus for keeping malcontents in line, but a method of government. It might not remedy any of the problems inherent in Stalinist economic planning on the 1970s oil crisis, but it could at least enforce obedience. More important still, it acted as a watchdog, and would be able to warn Ceaușescu if his closest cohorts were plotting against him—for Ceaușescu knew from past experi-

ence that the post of general secretary, once things started to
go wrong, was very precarious indeed. Had he not himself
witnessed, or participated in, the downfall or disgrace of
countless colleagues and superiors, from Ștefan Foris to
Pătrășcanu to Ana Pauker to Drăghici to Apostol? Had he not
posthumously destroyed the reputation of his own immediate
predecessor, Gheorghiu-Dej?

Securitate surveillance extended, abroad, to Romanian
ambassadors suspected of undue "liberalism." Corneliu Mănescu, one of Romania's brightest diplomats, ambassador to the
UN and later foreign minister, confirmed in a January 1990
TV interview that "finally, almost everywhere, our embassies
became the domain of Securitate." There was supposed to be
an agreement between the Interior and Foreign ministries on
the relative numbers of genuine diplomats and Securitate
agents, he said, but by the mid-1970s the proportion of Securitate staff had increased "unduly." They were adept at keeping Romanian diplomats under surveillance, Mănescu added,
but hopelessly inept as diplomats.

Another ambassador to Washington, Mircea Malitza, recalled to me that in order to prevent him from socializing with
Americans, Securitate saw to it that he was kept systematically
short of funds for any kind of formal entertainment. He got
around this by skimping on other expenditures and confining
his invitations to the U.S. press to informal, inexpensive break-
fasts, which Washington-based correspondents used to attend
regularly, to the local Securitate men's fury.

The funds spent on Securitate were incalculable, and
Ceaușescu may well at times have wondered where all the
money went. "I calculated," said Silviu Brucan, "that simply
keeping me under watch and guard in my house, what with
staff, cars, and overtime, was costing them 200,000 lei a
month."

It had always been a favorite trick of Securitate to use
non-Romanian thugs to beat up dissidents abroad. It was also
capable, at times, of a laughable Inspector Clouseau type of
bungling—as when it tried to eliminate the two best-known
Romanian writers in exile, Virgil Tănase and Paul Goma, in
1981. Haiducu, the agent sent to hire the killers to do the job

in France (for there, too, Securitate policy was to have non-Romanians directly involved in dirty tricks whenever possible), immediately turned himself over to the highly efficient French security service, the DST (Direction de Sécurité du Territoire). The dissident writers were kept under wraps, and Ceaușescu was led to believe that one assassination at least had taken place. Only months later did the "turned" agent, Haiducu, reveal all—to Ceaușescu's intense embarrassment. The incident gave President François Mitterrand the pretext he needed to cancel his official visit to Romania slated for 1982.

Securitate documents—especially those on the intimate life-styles of RCP colleagues closest to them—became the Ceaușescus' favorite reading. When Elena Ceaușescu's Spring Palace safe was opened after her death, it was found to contain, along with jewelry, a number of sealed envelopes containing lengthy, updated Securitate reports on a number of senior Romanian personalities in frequent contact with her. One of Securitate's top priorities was to keep permanent tabs on the three Ceaușescu children. Its surveillance activities sometimes took on a surrealist aspect.

Ex-king Michael recalled that his own home in Switzerland, and the comings and goings of his wife and daughters, came under Securitate scrutiny, despite the fact that he scrupulously abstained from any political activity. Some obscure Securitate functionary in a low-grade dirty tricks department delighted in sending the ex-king and his family anonymous letters, threatening them with death and kidnapping. "Some of these letters purported to come from former Iron Guards," ex-king Michael said, "but their communist phraseology and stilted Marxist vocabulary gave the game away." Neither ex-king Michael nor his family changed their life-styles as a result, except for requesting that all parcels and unrequested deliveries (including flowers) be sent for prior examination to the local police station in Versoix, near Geneva, where they live. "We were not too keen to give our address and telephone number to strangers and sometimes made a point of taking alternative routes by car into town," he said. The efficient Swiss police also kept a discreet watch on the ex-king's house in Versoix, with occasional car patrols.

From the day ex-king Michael was forced to leave Bucharest to the time of the December 1989 "revolution," he received neither phone calls nor mail from Romania, but immediately afterward he was deluged with telegrams, letters, and phone messages of goodwill. Even a year after Ceauşescu's death, the amount of fan mail he received continued to be impressive. It was clear, said ex-king Michael, that despite Ceauşescu's attempt to turn him into a nonperson, there were people who remembered his role in August 1944. After Ceauşescu's death, a stream of visitors, including many young people, began calling on him. "They know almost nothing about their country's past," ex-king Michael said, "but they seem exceedingly anxious to find out what really happened." (As a British subject—a courtesy passport was granted to him and his family at the direct request of Queen Elizabeth—ex-king Michael needs a visa to visit Romania, and this has not yet been granted by the Iliescu regime, though he did slip into Romania for a few hours at the end of 1990 before being expelled. Denied a visa in April 1990, he toyed with the idea of producing his former Romanian passport [which expired in 1954) and explaining that he had been unable to renew it, "owing to past circumstances."] Princesses Sophie and Margarita visited Romania in January and September 1990, with a view to setting up a foundation to restore Romanian historic monuments, fight pollution, and contribute to better public health. They were received with enthusiasm by four Romanian cabinet ministers, but for four days the telephone in the house they were staying at went dead. "Old traditions," said one veteran Romanian ex-communist experienced in Securitate's ways, "die hard."

Silviu Brucan, for one, had direct experience of the thoroughness with which Securitate operated. After the "revolution," he obtained Ceauşescu's personal copy of the Securitate report on himself. His dossier was beautifully prepared, in form and size resembling a bound film script. It bore top-secret and *exemplar unic* ("one copy only") mentions and was identified as Ceauşescu's personal copy because of its large-type format. (Nicolae Ceauşescu was short-sighted but hated wearing glasses, even in private. Reports submitted to him were typed in special characters, not quite capitals but lower-case letters three times the usual size.) The report on Brucan, saved accidentally by a Romanian worker who was part of a force that set to work burning Securitate documents after Ceauşescu's death, was so complete that it contained details of his past life that he himself had forgotten about. The one-hundred-page document showed that he had been under permanent surveillance for decades and that some of his closest acquaintances had furnished Securitate with information they could have gotten in no other way. Brucan also laid hands on a shorter document. When events of unusual interest occurred that might intrigue Ceauşescu, Securitate prepared bound booklets for him. The booklet on Brucan concerned a telephone conversation he had with a BBC journalist in 1989. It was not printed but written by a professional calligrapher, employed full-time by Securitate, and penned with such exquisite skill that when Brucan showed it to me, I could not believe, at first, that it was not a high-quality facsimile printing. Only slight traces of ink on the reverse side of the pages proved it to have been handwritten.

Among the truckloads of similar documents burnt in March 1990 there were hundreds of "eyes-only" reports on top RCP officials, for Ceauşescu, like Stalin, not only spied on his enemies and putative opponents but also, and especially, on his colleagues. The electronic surveillance of ministers, regional secretaries, senior army officers, and government officials was routine. Whole floors in hotels were given over to monitoring, and tourist-bureau jobs were known to be a Securitate preserve, which might explain why some of the Bucharest Inter-Continental dining-room staff, unchanged since the events of December 1989, have remained so surly in the post-Ceauşescu era.

Securitate informers and part-time officials were said to have numbered one in ten, and possibly even one in four, of Romania's total population. Perhaps Securitate's greatest disinformation coup was to deliberately spread the rumor that all Romanian telephones were constructed with built-in bugs and that Securitate thus had the capacity to listen in to over ten million phone conversations. Professor Dan Berindei told the story of meeting a former student in the street, who told him he was working "in the security field" and suddenly asked him, "Hey, do you want to listen to your neighbors, the Popescus?" On him, Berindei said, he had a device that picked up their conversation inside their apartment. He demonstrated how well it worked.

What is certain is that at one stage or another in their lives and careers, Romanians in all walks of life were approached, usually by educated, charming strangers who knew all about them, and urged to establish a loose but regular Securitate connection. Often, the targets were not by any stretch of the imagination connected with security in the conventional sense of the term. One leading architectural draftsman so approached asked his interlocutor what on earth he could possibly contribute. He was told, "Yours is a field we don't know very much about." The aim clearly was to bring about a state of affairs where, whether in hospitals, schools, universities, publishing, banking, theaters, or film studios, Securitate would know at any given moment where individuals' loyalties lay. "We Romanians," wrote Paul Goma, "live under Romanian occupation, more efficient than a foreign one."

In Pacepa's *Red Horizons*, there is ample evidence of Ceaușescu's obsessive concern for electronic surveillance devices, and there's no doubt that in time he would have bugged the entire country. But he didn't really need to. Romanians *were* convinced that their phones and bedrooms were bugged, that listening devices were present everywhere on such a scale that no one was immune from surveillance.

What set Securitate apart from totalitarian secret police in other countries was the level of its informers or, to use the less demeaning French term, *honorable correspondants*. There were of course the usual "street committee" watchdogs appointed by the Party, usually moonlighting for Securitate as well. But there were also doctors, film directors, and writers with known or suspected Securitate affiliations, so much so that a favorite topic of conversation, far more fascinating to Romanians than any who-is-sleeping-with-whom gossip, consisted of speculating on who in one's entourage was likely to be working for Securitate. Known informers included leading intellectuals, like the translator of the French poet Henri Michaux, and almost certainly the noted dissident writer Sasha Ivasiuc. So vast was the cross section of Romanians who had been involved at one time or another with Securitate that in the immediate post-Ceaușescu era, a convenient way of eliminating potential rivals within the National Salvation Front was to invoke their past Securitate connections.

This happened only a few weeks after Ceaușescu's death. One of the most prominent members of the original National Salvation Front caucus that assumed control of Romania after December 22, 1989, was Dumitru Mazilu, a lawyer attached to the United Nations who had submitted an anonymous but singularly eloquent diatribe against Ceaușescu's methods to the UN in 1988 and been placed under house arrest as a result. Mazilu clashed with Iliescu over the circumstances of the Ceaușescus' trial and execution, furious that he had not been consulted and aware that it had thrown considerable discredit on the new regime. On January 12, 1990, he took part in an anti-NSF street demonstration. The protesters were demanding the restoration of the death penalty (which the NSF had abolished after the Ceaușescus' deaths), but Mazilu's real purpose in joining the demonstration was to denounce the NSF's intention of transforming itself into a political party. Mazilu was compelled to resign shortly afterward: A file leaked to *România Liberă* revealed that Mazilu had been a member of Securitate. "I knew Mazilu when he was a Securitate colonel," Silviu Brucan told the media. The *România Liberă* report was that Mazilu had headed Securitate's staff college. Mazilu claimed that he had merely taught law at the interior ministry's "university" in the early 1970s, and then only for a few months. He denied ever holding military rank.

The whole episode showed how easily skeletons in cupboards could be made to rattle. All Romania's new power holders had to do was to reach out into the past, with the help of remaining Securitate files, for not all were destroyed after Ceaușescu's death. Not surprisingly, the post-Ceaușescu-era National Salvation Front politicians were, like Brucan, eager to retrieve, and destroy, their own.

Securitate survived the revolution with surprisingly little

damage. Its name has changed to SIR. (Romanian Intelligence Service), its ranks have closed, and its members now wholeheartedly serve the Iliescu regime. Their loyalties to the "new men" in power are indisputable: They have nowhere else to go.

They provide the regime with a weapon of considerable potency, for Securitate attracted some of the brightest, as well as the most opportunistic, government servants. For many of them, theirs was the equivalent of a well-rounded university education, and as Dan Petrescu, a former schoolteacher from Iaşi turned dissident, noted, many of the brightest kids in his school desperately longed to be recruited. Though Securitate had its complement of thugs and torturers, it was a highly sophisticated directorate. Whenever possible, Ceauşescu saw to it that beatings, murders, and the cruder forms of intimidation were carried out not by Romanians but by "client" bullyboys, usually Palestinians. This was to give rise to the completely unfounded rumor that during December 22–25, 1989, the hit squads and snipers operating on Bucharest streets were part of an "Arab commando."

By the mid-1980s, it had become clear to several senior Securitate executives that the Ceauşescus were becoming a liability. By 1989, with *perestroika* in full swing, it was also clear to many that Ceauşescu was doomed. Securitate had long since given up warning the Ceauşescus of the real attitude of the Romanian people toward them. General Iulian Vlad, its exquisitely dressed head, always in immaculately cut civilian suits, would no more have considered providing them with such reports than a Caligula aide would have dared inform the mad emperor of the true feelings of the Romans. Sycophancy and a desire to stay out of trouble and avoid personal disgrace gradually led Securitate to provide the Ceauşescus only with what they wanted to hear, and in any case, in the last few years of their reign, Elena Ceauşescu's office monitored all reports headed for the presidential "in" tray. She withheld any that she considered were inappropriate or reflected adversely on her husband's prestige. In the end, this unique instrument of intelligence, intimidation, and repression became virtually useless as a barometer of public opinion.

Even General Vlad, however, was not able to keep the truth of the Timişoara crisis from the Ceauşescus, though he did emphasize its ethnic nature, hint at foreign involvement, and at first consistently downplay its significance for the rest of the country.

The trouble started, in this attractive Transylvanian town, on a relatively small scale at first, on November 17, 1989, when a small crowd of the faithful gathered outside the house of a popular Calvinist local minister, László Tökes. Because he was a vocal critic of the Ceauşescu regime and a Hungarian-speaking nationalist, Tökes had for many years been a considerable embarrassment to Securitate, which had finally convinced his religious superiors to move him to a less "visible" rural parish. At the time, and it was only the first of many hyperbolic distortions, rumor had it that Tökes was about to go to prison or into internal exile. *Libération*, the well-informed Paris daily, which had reported on Romania more thoroughly and aggressively than any other European daily, even mentioned that he faced "deportation." It was a measure of the ambiguities of Romanian manners and morals that dissidents, then and later, felt compelled to present the Tökes case in an exaggeratedly dramatic light.

The truth was very different, and Ceauşescu might well have argued, had there been anyone left to argue with, that he had absolutely nothing to do with Tökes' displacement and that legal right was on his side. For it was not the government or Securitate that had ordered Tökes' removal from Timişoara but his own bishop. Because Tökes had refused to leave, the bishop had called in the local police to expel him from his church-owned house, claiming that after being notified of his new posting, he was nothing more than an illegal squatter. It was this admittedly halfhearted attempt by the local police to evict Tökes that provoked the initial November 17 demonstration.

The Tökes affair was proof of Ceauşescu's past skills as a manipulator. Unlike Poland, where the Catholic Church had acted as an opposition "shadow cabinet" ever since the communist takeover there, Romania's religious leaders had enjoyed a cozy relationship with Ceauşescu, sitting in the Great

National Assembly as ex-officio members. As Paul Goma noted,[1] it was useless trying to enlist most of the clergy, whether Orthodox or Protestant, into any anti-Ceauşescu action, "for their immediate reaction was to call Securitate." Ambassador Funderburk, attending a midnight Easter mass in a Romanian Orthodox Church, walked out when the officiating priest "mentioned Ceauşescu's name in the same breath as Jesus Christ."[2]

Picketing of the Tökes house continued throughout November. On November 27, the Fourteenth Romanian Communist Party Congress got under way in Bucharest, and those foreign observers who had predicted this might become the occasion of a Party revolt against the Ceauşescus were proved wrong. Though the Berlin Wall had fallen only days before, the disintegration of the communist eastern bloc was only briefly and euphemistically mentioned. The congress was chiefly noteworthy for its delegates' ostrichlike behavior. They sat through interminable speeches by the Conducător, who reported in glowing terms on the state of the country and the achievements of "scientific socialism." Though the continuing picketing of the Tökes home in Timişoara must have been disquieting, no mention of it was made during the proceedings, which were marked by "prolonged, spontaneous applause" for Ceauşescu's speeches. Among the uniformly sycophantic speeches of delegate after delegate were muted references to "certain trends in neighboring socialist countries taking the capitalist road and returning to capitalist values." Though he never said so directly, Ceauşescu clearly believed by now that the Soviets, as well as the "Western imperialists," were out to get him.

His defiance of Moscow at the congress had a quixotic side to it. In two separate speeches, he demanded the abrogation of the German-Soviet pact of 1939, "including the secret dispositions" that had led to the Soviet annexation of Bessarabia by Stalin in 1940. In earlier days, this feisty, defiant nationalism would have earned him not only the applause of the RCP congress delegates but the approval of the Western world as well. Nothing illustrated Ceauşescu's retreat from reality more than his inability to understand that such crude anti-Soviet verbal antics no longer inspired respect, or even much curiosity. He failed to understand that *glasnost* and *perestroika*, and especially their knock-on effects on Eastern Europe, had shifted interest away from Romania. No longer was there a role on the world scene for a maverick anti-Gorbachev Stalinist leader of a small Eastern European country in appalling economic trouble. Insofar as there were any Western preoccupations concerning Romania, they centered on the question, In the changing Eastern European context, how long will Ceauşescu last, and how will he end?

If any of the RCP delegates at the congress were aware of this, they didn't show it. Not a single voice was raised among the 3,308 conference members to vote against the reelection of the Conducător, and there was not a single abstention. Afterward, a huge crowd gathered outside the square facing the old royal palace, and the Ceauşescus made one of their time-honored balcony appearances, basking in carefully stage-managed adulation. The crowd shouted, "Ceauşescu and the people," "Independent socialism," and "No to interference," the three slogans the Central Committee's propaganda department had decided were the most effective in both boosting the Ceauşescus' morale and implying that everything working against them was the work of foreign agents.

The defection of Nadia Comăneci, the Olympic gold medalist, on November 26 and her arrival in New York on December 1 got far more coverage in the Western media than had the Fourteenth RCP Congress. And it was the Tökes affair, still brewing throughout November and the first two weeks of December (though never once mentioned during the congress proceedings), that was to be the spark that lit the final blaze.

On December 16, 1989, a large crowd, including women and children, once again gathered in front of Tökes' house to block his eviction. That night, large crowds of young people, some of whom had been picketing the Tökes home, marched through the center of Timişoara. At first they chanted pro-Tökes slogans, but soon the crowds were shouting, "Down with Ceauşescu," "Down with communism," and "We want democracy." Police and firemen with hoses closed in on the demonstrators, but the town was now in an uproar. Another group of determined protesters, alerted by the earlier turmoil, now marched on Timișoara town hall and on the local RCP headquarters, trashing files, throwing portraits of Ceaușescu and communist literature out of windows, and setting fire to them in the street below. Police and armored cars opened fire, killing scores of people. Securitate men collected the corpses, spiriting them away, while the increasingly bold crowds shouted "Give us our dead."

News of the dramatic events in Timișoara on the night of December 16 spread like wildfire, leading to exaggerated accounts of casualties. With the collapse of communism in neighboring Eastern European countries, Romanians only had to tune in to East Berlin or Hungarian frequencies to learn what was going on. Largely fed by rumor, encouraged by East German, Hungarian, and Yugoslav radio reports, the news spread of 4,000, then 6,000, and then even of 40,000 dead in Timișoara. Corpses would later be displayed on television, from December 22 onward, allegedly victims of Securitate torture. These were in fact bodies dug up from the paupers' cemetery in Timișoara or taken from hospital morgues after natural deaths, but the psychological effect on Romanians would be colossal. Though casualty figures were grossly inflated, anti-Ceaușescu riots broke out, that same December 16 evening, in Arad and other Transylvanian towns. For the first time, Ceaușescu became aware not only that a full-scale revolt against him had begun in Timișoara, and was brewing in other parts of the country, but that the army had failed to act decisively against the rioters.

Refusing to allow anything to interfere with his foreign travel, Ceaușescu maintained his decision to visit Iran the following day. But before leaving (late on the night of December 17), he held an angry postmortem on the Timișoara events with members of the Party's "political executive." The tape-recorded proceedings were remarkable for several reasons, not least for the evidence presented of Ceaușescu's interpretation of the Tökes affair. "The pretext [for the riots] has been the so-called reform-church minister, who has been punished by his own church authorities, and has been transferred to another county," Ceaușescu began. "He didn't want to vacate the house. The bishop went to the courts, who decided to move him." So far, Ceaușescu had the details pat, but he was unable to admit to his subordinates that the Tökes affair was a pretext—that the real target was Ceaușescu himself. "Here we have the involvement of foreign circles," he went on, "of foreign spy agencies, beginning with Budapest. . . . Moreover, it is known that both in the East [i.e., Moscow] as well as in the West everyone is saying that things ought to change in Romania. Both East and West have decided to change things and they are using any means possible."

Ceaușescu then launched into a furious attack on all those who had allowed the protest to escalate into a riot, and especially on General Vasile Milea, the defense minister. "The Defense Ministry authorities and those of the Interior Ministry had a defeatist attitude. Last night I spoke to them and told them to put on a show of strength with tanks during the day. . . . I gave the order for this, but you organized a parade. . . . The motorized units should have been in the center of the town. That's what a show of strength means! Where was the show of strength I ordered? The same thing should have happened with the Interior Ministry troops. My impression is they were not armed."

Interior Minister Tudor Postelnicu confirmed this was the case.

Ceaușescu exploded: "Well, why not? I told you they should all be armed. Who gave such an order? Some hooligans get into the county Party HQ, assault soldiers and officers, and they do nothing? What did your officers do, Milea, why didn't they intervene immediately, why didn't they fire? They should have fired to bring them down, to warn them, and then to fire at their legs. . . . You don't put an enemy down with sermons, you have to burn him. Socialism is not constructed with false information and with devotion but by fighting. We must battle to construct it. At the moment in Europe there is a situation of capitulation, of signing pacts with imperialism in order to wipe out socialism."

Ceaușescu ordered General Vlad, the Securitate chief, to join the meeting. When he showed up, a few minutes later, he too faced a furious Ceaușescu. "Why weren't they armed?" Ceaușescu asked him.

"I thought it wasn't necessary," Vlad replied.

"Why didn't you report this and tell me?" Ceaușescu shouted back. "I talked with you the whole night. From this moment onward," he announced, "if the Political Executive Committee agrees, we will dismiss the defense minister, the interior minister, and the head of the security forces. From this moment I am taking over command of the army. Prepare the decree for me. . . . We cannot carry on like this. All night I stood and talked to them every ten minutes, only afterward to realize that they had not done what I ordered."

General Vlad came in for even harsher treatment a few minutes later. "Don't you know what state of emergency means?" Ceaușescu asked him.

"I know, comrade, I gave the order," Vlad replied.

"Not even now are you telling the truth," Ceaușescu told him. "Had one of them fired, they would have fled like partridges." Elena Ceaușescu chipped in, "You should have fired on them, and had they fallen, you should have taken them and shoved them into a cellar. Weren't you told that? Not one of them should have got out."

Abjectly, all present agreed they had acted improperly. Ceaușescu extracted from them a pledge to act decisively in the future. "I assure you, comrade secretary general," said Interior Minister Postelnicu, "that such a situation will not occur again. Please place this trust in me and let us allow the facts to speak for themselves." Milea admitted that "I did not appreciate the danger from the beginning." Vlad assured Ceaușescu that "hearing the tasks you have given me, I will proceed in such a way as to merit your faith."

Grudgingly, Ceaușescu withdrew his decision to dismiss them all. "Good," he said. "Shall we try once more, comrades?"

What Ceaușescu failed to realize was that—even as the meeting was winding up—key figures in the Executive Committee were already preparing to betray him. For General Milea continued to refuse to allow troops to fire on civilians, and General Vlad had no intention of obeying Ceaușescu's orders either. He saw that his leader's future was bleak in any case: If the demonstrations were put down with maximum force, as Ceaușescu demanded, he might gain a short amount of time but would shore up more hatred. Vlad knew he was being maintained at his post only on sufferance, that the next time around Ceaușescu would get rid of him, as he had almost done that day. And Vlad at least had no delusions about "foreign agents." On the basis of the extensive Securitate antennae throughout the country, he was aware of the extent of ordinary Romanians' discontent. At the meeting, he had narrowly averted disgrace and, possibly, arrest.

It is difficult to interpret the groveling admission to Ceaușescu by the Executive Committee members of their failings as anything but a way of getting themselves off the hook, of buying time, and of extricating themselves from a hopeless situation. One cannot be certain that from December 17 onward, Milea and Vlad "betrayed" Ceaușescu. But Milea's "suicide" four days later, and Vlad's cool appearance at the Defense Ministry, at the Central Committee, and at the Romanian TV center's headquarters right up to December 24—the day before the Ceaușescus were shot—indicated that he and at least some elements of Securitate had been in league with the National Salvation Front from the very beginning of the Bucharest riots, if not before, and that they had been in all likelihood part of the conspiracy that existed before the popular uprising began. The really important question was: How long had this conspiracy been in existence, and were the people of Romania, who rose in their tens of thousands against the hated couple, maneuvered into doing so?

# CHAPTER THIRTEEN
# PLOTS

Let's admit that in the last years of his reign Our Benefactor
had fewer successes and more problems.

—RYSZARD KAPUŚCIŃSKI
*THE EMPEROR*

THE ROMANIAN POPULAR UPRISING OF DECEM-
ber 1989, seen live on TV all over the world, and the
Ceauşescus' flight and subsequent execution have taken
on a mythic quality. Some images of the events that took place
and were seen on TV screens between December 22 and December 26 will remain in our minds with the same intensity as

the famous Tet 1968 photograph showing South Vietnamese General Lo An executing a Viet Cong prisoner on a street in Saigon. Throughout Eastern Europe, where the totalitarian Marxist-Leninist tyranny had already suffered terminal blows in Poland, Czechoslovakia, and East Germany, the fall of the one remaining Stalinist attracted immense attention, and led to immediate rejoicing. So the outcry was all the more strident when it became clear not only that the casualties, among the revolutionaries, were far fewer than had earlier been claimed but that the uprising itself was not quite the simple, idealistic revolution it was first perceived to be.

This new information in turn led to two somewhat outrageous, and untenable, premises. The first (peddled initially in the French media, and then in a book by Michel Castex, an AFP correspondent) was that the entire "revolution," with its inflated casualty figures, had been masterminded by the Soviet Union, eager to bring about Ceaușescu's downfall, which had used docile East German and Hungarian news agencies as conduits for exaggerated casualties and other forms of disinformation. The other was that the uprising was not spontaneous at all but part of a carefully prepared plot involving a number of civilian and military personnel in high places.

As we shall see, plans to overthrow Ceaușescu had indeed existed for a long, long time in the minds of a small handful of Romanians. But it would be grossly inaccurate to adhere to the cynical theory that the uprising, from beginning to end, was a carefully staged event. It is true, however, that what began, first in Timișoara and then in Bucharest, and other major towns, on December 21, as a series of spontaneous demonstrations was very quickly channeled in a certain direction by a small group of sophisticated plotters who had bided their time for just such a moment as this for at least five years.

To make sense of the events of December 1989, and understand why the Ceaușescus' flight was in a sense preordained, one must go back at least twelve years, to the time of the severe 1977 Bucharest earthquake. The Ceaușescus were in Africa, on one of their numerous state visits. Instead of initiating relief operations immediately, the staff Ceaușescu had left behind in Bucharest spent almost all its time, in the hours that immediately followed, arguing among themselves over the terms of the telegram to be sent to him announcing the disaster. Precious time was lost while they considered each phrase, each nuance, each adjective—both in order to minimize the disaster and to imply that his team was competent to deal with it.

To a handful of disgruntled former power holders, like generals Ionita and Militaru, convinced since the mid-1970s that Ceauşescu was leading the country to ruin and wondering how to get rid of him, the lesson was clear: No decisions of any kind were likely while the Ceauşescus were out of the country. So if there was to be a putsch, it had to occur while they were on one of their foreign trips.

Securitate kept strict tabs on all leading members of the Romanian establishment, especially those who had fallen from grace. But even among such people there were occasional opportunities to meet each other casually from time to time without attracting their minders' attention. Even within Securitate there was a very small minority that was sufficiently disaffected by the country's downward slide to turn a blind eye to malcontents' talk. And there was even a handful of Securitate men prepared to become messengers, and even contemplate playing an active role in an anti-Ceauşescu conspiracy. There were, in fact, several conspiracies, from 1971 onward. They all remained theoretical except for the last, which took advantage of a popular uprising to impose a leadership that had been passively plotting for years.

As early as 1970–71 and again in 1975–76, three army generals, including the defense minister, Ion Ioniţa, had secretly discussed the possibility of a coup but rapidly decided its chances of success were nil. Then, in the early 1980s, a handful of former establishment figures, both civilian and military, began talking to each other in extremely guarded terms about the unthinkable: getting rid of Nicolae Ceauşescu. It was not the first gesture of revolt.

The senior-most military member of the tiny group that began discussing the possibility of a coup in 1983–84 was the same Ion Ioniţa, once a close friend of Ceauşescu's. He had good reason to be disgruntled, for Ceauşescu, as was his habit, had made him take the blame for a number of spectacular government failures that were none of his responsibility, before finally easing him out in 1976. Ioniţa, was convinced that not only Ceauşescu, but also his "kitchen cabinet" of close associates who pandered to him and isolated him even further from reality, had to be ruthlessly dealt with. Another senior army officer who shared this view was General Nicolae Militaru, a retired army chief of staff, who still wielded considerable moral authority among senior officers. A third military figure was even more determined to get rid of Ceauşescu: He was former major-general Ştefan Kostyal, the same Kostyal who, as a young communist, had shared a prison cell with Ceauşescu in the 1930s. Kostyal had been the only one of this group to suffer physically at Ceauşescu's hands: After his forced retirement from the army (for marrying a Russian), Kostyal, a tough-minded Magyar with an impressive military bearing, demanded a hearing before an army commission in 1971 and—with almost foolhardy courage—launched a brutal, detailed attack on Ceauşescu's policies. Needless to say, the system immediately struck back: He was taken off the army reserve, his pension was stopped, and he was sent into enforced exile in the remote countryside as a manual worker for several years.

Kostyal's case attracted negligible attention because the official line (successfully spread, through rumor, within the Party and of course by Securitate) was that Kostyal was nothing more than a Soviet agent. It was a shrewd way of discrediting him, for Kostyal, as a veteran communist, had remained, like many other members of the old guard, including Pîrvulescu, a faithful supporter of Soviet policy. In his address to his army colleagues in 1971, he had stigmatized Ceauşescu's "erratic" (i.e., anti-Soviet) foreign policy.

A handful of civilians was also involved in the conspiracy, liaising with Ioniţa. The leader of this group was Silviu Brucan, editor of *Scînteia* under Gheorghiu-Dej, then his ambassador to the UN and to Washington until 1963.

As a veteran communist, Brucan was skilled in clandestine ways. He also had a somewhat dubious reputation as a former Stalinist with the habit of twisting facts to his advantage. He alleged, for instance, that he had refused to serve Ceaușescu from 1965 onward because he distrusted him, even in the early days of his rule. Experts like Professor Ardeleanu and erstwhile colleagues and Party members like Malitza, however, point out that it was Brucan's Stalinist reputation, and his close links with Ana Pauker and the so-called Odessa group, that had led to his 1963 retirement. With age, however, Brucan had mellowed; he valued his contacts·with the United States and Western European academics and intellectuals and, perhaps initially out of pique at his exclusion, began speaking out, sometimes at considerable personal risk, against Ceaușescu's policies, also establishing links with Western diplomats in Bucharest and with visiting Western journalists.

Through trusted messengers and go-betweens, Brucan, Ionița, and Militaru were able to exchange their highly subversive views, and even evolve a series of contingency plans. All started with the premise that the faithful clique around the Ceaușescus—men like Ilie Ceaușescu, Bobu, Postelnicu, and Ion Coman, the Central Committee member charged with liaison over justice, Securitate, and army matters—had to be neutralized, and that a coup could take place only while the Ceaușescus were out of the country. For this reason, the plotters needed some cooperation from the Ceaușescu inner circle, the RCP's Executive Committee, as secrecy concerning the Conducător's travel plans, at home and abroad, was such that even army generals were never told too far in advance what they would be.

They started drawing up lists of army officers likely to cooperate and ended up with several names. Asked whether General Victor Stănculescu[1] was among them, Kostyal replied tartly that to have approached Stănculescu would have ensured the plot's immediate failure. "He was very close indeed to General Ilie Ceaușescu, the brother, and functioned within the army as the family's eyes and ears," said Kostyal. But, he added, there was at least one member of the Party's Executive Committee who *did* provide them with useful advance information about Ceaușescu's travel plans, and some generals who refused to participate in the plot agreed to keep quiet about it.

Another important plotter was a Securitate colonel called Virgil Măgureanu, with links high up in that organization.

Among the contingency plans made were the seizure of the TV and radio stations, which, the plotters believed, would be followed immediately by truly spontaneous mass street demonstrations throughout the country. But they were under no illusion about the risks involved. On the irrecuperable pro-Ceaușescu side, they felt, was a force made up of Securitate and elite troops numbering at least twenty-five thousand. On the plus side, the plotters were assured of the cooperation of a unit manning an arms and munitions warehouse in Tîrgoviște.

At this stage, in 1984, the plotters had no intention of doing away with the communist regime as such. Rather, their intention was to restore a communist legitimacy that, they felt, Ceaușescu had usurped by changing the rules of the game. Traditionally, the First Secretary was elected by the Central Committee, but Ceaușescu had ensured that his would be a lifelong appointment by getting the more docile Grand National Assembly to vote, again and again, for his reelection.

The conspirators debated among themselves over the choice of a possible successor to Ceaușescu who would introduce "communism with a human face" and restore Party "legitimacy." Ion Iliescu, who had been shunted aside at the end of 1971 and, after a series of respectable but second-echelon jobs (minister of water, regional secretary in Timișoara), ended up as chief executive of a publishing house, Editura Tehnica, became by consensus their candidate. Approached through an intermediary and sounded out, Iliescu gave a somewhat ambiguous reply: He would not take any active part in the conspiracy, but if it succeeded he was willing to serve if asked. Kostyal admitted that the plotters' clandestine discussions with Iliescu were episodic, and very vague indeed.

The 1984–85 plot collapsed without a semblance of action. The reason was that, inevitably perhaps, too many people came to know of it. According to Brucan, two army generals, Gomoiu and Popa, betrayed their colleagues to Securitate. The conspirators had respected elementary need-to-know rules, and only Kostyal, Militaru, and Brucan were supposed to be aware of the overall plan. The two "informers" knew only that something was being prepared to coincide with Ceauşescu's trip to West Germany in October 1985 and that an infantry division stationed in Bucharest was involved. At the very last minute, before leaving for Bonn, and acting as though it were a spontaneous decision, Ceauşescu petulantly ordered the division out of Bucharest to help farmers with their wheat harvest. At the same time, he summarily retired their commander. This was enough to nip the entire proceedings in the bud.

Later, however, Kostyal was to discover—from the detailed questions Securitate would ask him—that his interrogators knew far more about the plot details than anyone could possibly have known without being directly involved. The real traitors, Kostyal remains convinced to this day, were a group of so-called dissident Securitate officials, civilian and military, unwittingly brought into the plot by Militaru. The latter, Kostyal is convinced, was not himself aware of their deviousness. These so-called Securitate dissidents began feeding back to Ceauşescu the various features of the conspiracy as they were being planned. Securitate, Kostyal told me in October 1990, in fact conducted a brilliant disinformation exercise. "Nicolae Ceauşescu," he said, "knew everything about it from the very beginning. Virgil Măgureanu, the Securitate official most closely linked with the 1984–85 plot, was nothing more than an informer. He and other Securitate officers pretending to help us had in fact been playing a double game all along." Additionally, Kostyal believes, one of the objects of the Securitate exercise had been to advance the name of Iliescu and promote him as a "liberal communist." Ironically, immediately after Ceauşescu's downfall, Măgureanu would become the boss of SIR, the post-Ceauşescu regime's version of Securitate and, as a result, one of the most powerful men in Romania.

Almost incredibly, after 1985 the only conspirator to suffer at the hands of Securitate was Kostyal, though Brucan and Ioniţa were given a strong verbal warning to stop seeing each other. Securitate men called on Kostyal in his small Bucharest flat and arrested him for "illegal possession of foreign currency"—about two dollars' worth of foreign coins, his son's childhood collection. The fiction, which Ceaușescu was careful to preserve at all times, was that in Romania, there was no such thing as a political prisoner. Once more Kostyal was sent into exile in the country in Curtea de Argeș.

By 1989 Kostyal was back in Bucharest but still under heavy Securitate surveillance. "A Securitate man had the key to my flat," he said, "and would come and go as he pleased, drinking my *țuică* [Romanian plum brandy] in the bargain." In February 1989, Brucan was the instigator and one of the six cosignatories of an open letter to Ceaușescu—also signed by Apostol, Bîrlădeanu, Mănescu, Pîrvulescu, and Răceanu— criticizing his rule. Despite the considerable surveillance that ensued, Brucan was still able, clandestinely, to resume his connection with General Militaru, through third parties. By 1989, of course, the situation had changed considerably. Not only had General Ionița died (in 1986), but most Romanians (unless they belonged to the small, elite top *nomenklatura*) were living miserable lives—without light, food, and other bare essentials. Even Securitate men and RCP officials were experiencing the disastrous consequences of Ceaușescu's austerity measures and indifference to his fellow citizens' living standards. Outside Romania, the Warsaw Pact countries were preparing to make their definitive break with communism. The conspirators knew any action on their part would inevitably trigger a popular explosion.

Militaru, himself under routine surveillance, managed to contact, through intermediaries, some twenty generals and other senior officers in the Romanian navy and air force in the first six months of 1989, and also to liaise with Brucan. Kostyal's movements were considerably restricted, his phone and apartment bugged, a Securitate car outside his apartment building twenty-four hours a day. Unable to move much, he decided to go on record to remind Romanians that he remained a staunch anti-Ceaușescu figure. He began writing an "open letter to Ceaușescu," hoping at first to get it published either in the Paris newspaper *Libération* or in a German paper. His link was Doctor Zorel Filipescu, a senior health official and the father of a well-known dissident. But plans to contact either newspaper failed, and the letter, deliberately unfinished, lay openly on Kostyal's desk, where, he knew, Securitate officials would read it and photograph it. There was a rationale to this defiance: Kostyal believed that the Securitate men around him would think that he was simply planning a media coup on the lines of the Brucan letter—not that he was involved in something clandestine. Both Militaru and Brucan were again in touch with Iliescu but found him, this time around, even more cautious and elusive. Time and again, through a go-between, Kostyal urged Militaru and Brucan to convince Iliescu to display a more active, gutsy approach to the plot. "What are we waiting for?" he asked Militaru in a message smuggled out in March 1989. "Let's do it!" Iliescu, Kostyal recalled, kept saying the time was not ripe. In April 1989, Kostyal tried once more to get things going. "If Iliescu won't help," he told Militaru and Brucan through a go-between, "let's drop him and do it ourselves." Militaru was noncommittal.

Kostyal continued drafting his open letter to Ceaușescu. He deliberately incorporated many of the points he had made before the army committee in 1971, knowing that some army men at least would spot the similarities and draw the necessary conclusions. He wanted to inspire Romanian army officers, to remind them that a challenge to Ceaușescu was feasible, that he, Kostyal, had already been forced to resort to such action twenty years previously, long before conditions in Romania had reached their present abysmal state.

On June 2, 1989, Securitate pulled Kostyal in for questioning. This time he was ready for them. Recalling the trumped-up charges of hoarding foreign currency in 1984, he told the man in charge: "If you're going to arrest me, at least arrest me for the right reasons, and let's talk about Ceaușescu," then lost his temper and warned him that one day he too might face arrest. Kostyal was promptly charged with "insulting a state official." There followed a cat-and-mouse game. Kostyal was questioned at length at Securitate headquarters at Rahova during the day but allowed to go home at night. The following morning he was brought in for questioning again.

This went on for two weeks. Then he was held in Rahova overnight and questioned more brutally. Securitate's questioning was unfocused. His interrogators clearly had no idea that Kostyal was an integral part of a conspiracy to overthrow Ceauşescu, but they were intent on discouraging him from indulging in any further anti-Ceauşescu activity. "What the hell's the matter with you?" one Securitate man asked him. "Do you really want freedom on the Hungarian model, with all those queer bars in Budapest?"

Kostyal's wife was at this time in Russia, but she returned to Bucharest, and the day she came back, Kostyal was released. It was as though Securitate feared she might appeal to Soviet embassy contacts to initiate inquiries about him, and Securitate had always been sensitive to approaches of this kind. From the moment she returned, Kostyal said, he went to the Soviet embassy daily, not to meet any diplomats—he had no contacts there—but to read the papers and spend some time in the library. The rationale for this was that Securitate might *think* he had Soviet embassy connections who would raise questions concerning him if he "disappeared." "It was a form of self-protection," Kostyal said. "Brucan had British and American diplomats call on him regularly, to ensure that he was alive and well. This was *my* way of making Securitate aware that someone might inquire about my whereabouts if anything were to happen to me."

In October, Securitate told him not to leave town or attempt to meet anyone. He tried to stage an "accidental" meeting with Radu Filipescu in a supermarket. It was unsuccessful: He found himself surrounded, in the shop, by the same Securitate men who had routinely followed him in the past. They greeted him with great hilarity. "Hello, what are you doing here? Fancy seeing you here! What a surprise!" Kostyal's wife decided to take another trip to Moscow.

Privately, Kostyal was dismayed by the apparent passivity of the other co-conspirators, especially Iliescu. He couldn't understand why nothing was happening, and had almost completely given up on Iliescu, obscurely feeling that he was being left out of things, that the others felt he was too extreme, too aggressive. He toyed with the idea of trying to slip out of

Bucharest undetected and make for Timișoara, where he had many friends, but he decided against it. He felt he would only put them at more risk.

Days slipped by, the riots began in Timișoara, and still nothing was happening. On December 20, Kostyal's wife phoned him to say she would be returning to Bucharest the following day. On December 21, followed by the inevitable Securitate car, Kostyal went to the airport to meet his wife. She was not on the plane, but while he was at the airport, he learned of the start of the revolution: It was the sole subject of conversation among the crowd at the airport. Like thousands of other Romanians, Kostyal roamed the streets that day—the Securitate car, meanwhile, had vanished—reveling in the dictator's discomfiture. He didn't stay far from a phone for long, though. He was sure his co-conspirators would call. His telephone, however, remained silent.

The following day, there was still no sign of a Securitate car outside his apartment. In the morning, Kostyal walked to the square in front of the Central Committee, less than five hundred yards from his flat. He arrived just as Colonel Maluțan's overloaded helicopter was taking off from the roof with the fleeing Ceaușescus and their two henchmen, Bobu and Mănescu, on board. Someone in the crowd recognized him and shouted: "That's Kostyal, he's against Ceaușescu!" but Kostyal shook him off. "I didn't want that kind of recognition," he said. "I wanted results."

Recalling the 1984–85 plan, Kostyal knew that by rights the conspirators should be gathering in the Defense Ministry building. He drove there, showed up at the main entrance, and demanded to see the ranking officer in charge. "Who shall I say?" asked the NCO at the entrance. "General Kostyal," he said. He was ushered into the presence of General Stănculescu, who had one leg in a plaster cast from ankle to knee. "Everything is calm, the troops are back in barracks," Stănculescu said, addressing him as he would a superior. Kostyal went straight to the point. "Where is General Ilie Ceaușescu?" he asked. "In his office," Stănculescu said. "I couldn't believe it," Kostyal recalled later. He went to see for himself, and indeed found Ceaușescu's brother at his desk in his usual office as if nothing untoward were happening. Returning to Stănculescu's office, Kostyal said, "Put that man under arrest." Stănculescu stalled. "We'll do it by and by," he said. "No, you'll do it now," Kostyal told Stănculescu. "What's more, you'll send out a transport, and bring Iliescu, Militaru, and Corneliu Mănescu [a former minister, and a co-conspirator] back to the Defense Ministry." Again Stănculescu stalled. There was no transport available, he said. Besides, he didn't know where these people lived. He said his own movements were restricted, because of his leg injury.

By this time, Kostyal was convinced that Stănculescu was simply "waiting," as he put it, "to see which side would come out on top." While he was talking to Stănculescu, an officer came in to tell the general he should watch TV—Militaru was on the air, live, broadcasting from the TV headquarters. Kostyal told the officer to phone the Romanian TV station. "Tell General Militaru that General Kostyal is at the Defense Ministry and he should join me here straight away," he said. Stănculescu was complaining again about his "injury." He had broken an ankle, he said, and moving about was painful. Kostyal believes to this day that Stănculescu had an army nurse put a cast on his leg to fake an injury. Earlier in December, Stănculescu had been sent by Ceauşescu to Timişoara to put down the riots, and had faithfully carried out his orders: Timişoara was one of the few places in Romania where the army, as opposed to Securitate, fired on civilian crowds of demonstrators—though not, as Ceauşescu pointed out in his angry December 17, 1989, postmortem, vigorously enough to stem the tide. Stănculescu had then been brought back to Bucharest, after the suicide of General Milea, the defense minister. Kostyal believes it had been Ceauşescu's intention to appoint Stănculescu to succeed Milea, had he not been forced to flee. With a cast on his leg, Stănculescu could claim to be sick and thus avoid carrying out his duties. As eyewitnesses later confirmed, Stănculescu had been among those urging the Ceauşescus to leave by helicopter in December 1989, and had accompanied them to the rooftop of the Central Committee building.

Shortly afterward not only Iliescu and Militaru, but also

General Iulian Vlad, the overall Securitate chief, showed up in Stănculescu's office, along with a small group of people. Flanking Iliescu were two civilians Kostyal had never seen before. "You don't need bodyguards," Kostyal told Iliescu. "Get them out of here." "No, no," Iliescu said. "They're with me, they're part of my team." Kostyal was told their names were Gelu Voican and Petre Roman. Roman, of course, was soon to become prime minister, and Voican was the mysterious figure who was to have a hand in Ceaușescu's December 25 trial, but Kostyal had never met either before.

Petre Roman's account (to the French media) that he happened to find himself inside the Central Committee building "by accident" cut little ice with experts. From the start of those hours inside the Central Committee building, then at the TV headquarters, Iliescu and Roman seemed to enjoy considerable, almost *shorthand*, rapport with each other. They knew each other professionally: Roman had authored a couple of short books for Editura Tehnica, headed by Iliescu, and this had given them a "legitimate" reason for meeting in Iliescu's office, which was routinely monitored, like all such places, by Securitate. Their backgrounds—both sons of prominent Stalinist Romanian communists—were strikingly similar. Ceaușescu was known to have been in awe of old-time "International Brigades" types like Walter Roman, perhaps because their adventurous past was in such contrast to his own, somewhat plodding beginnings. As Professor Ardeleanu put it, "Ceaușescu couldn't refuse a thing to people like Walter Roman." If anything, Petre Roman's youth had been even more privileged than that of some of the Ceaușescu nephews and nieces. As Nadia Bujor, one of them, put it, "*I* never had the privilege of living in France for five years, coming and going as I virtually pleased." President François Mitterrand is said to have shown considerable impatience with fawning French television reporters who failed to question Petre Roman's version of his past. Within the Ceaușescu "system," anyone able to spend five years in France must have given cementlike guarantees to the regime ("*des garanties en beton*"), the shrewd, cynical French president told an aide.

From the start, Kostyal recalled, he had the feeling that

Iliescu did not want him around, that he was "undesirable," and that despite his 1984 and 1989 role in plotting Ceaușescu's downfall, a new set of people, Roman and Voican among them, was working closely with Iliescu with the express task of shaping the embryo National Salvation Front to their own ends. There followed a confused debate in the vacant office of the defense minister, with a number of persons, all unknown to Kostyal, arriving in turn from the Central Committee building, including a Romanian TV camera crew, which filmed the whole scene—though nothing of this meeting was ever shown on Romanian TV.

His past shilly-shallying over, Iliescu had clearly made up his mind to take overall charge. A recurring topic was the name of the organization, with Iliescu at its head, that, in Iliescu's own words, would "take the nation's destiny in hand." Kostyal suggested calling it the Popular Front, but Iliescu rejected this. The National Salvation Front, he said, was a much better title. It so happened that Kostyal had heard, on Radio Free Europe, broadcast appeals that emanated from a National Salvation Front and wondered at the time whether the idea came to Iliescu from hearing this on RFE.

There and then, Iliescu and his friends began selecting individuals to serve on the NSF. Various names were mentioned, including that of an army general called Burcă. Iliescu said he would be a good man to serve as defense minister. Kostyal again objected. He recalled that Burcă had refused to join the 1984 conspiracy, though he had not betrayed it.

Kostyal also had a heated exchange with Iliescu over the future of the Romanian Communist party. Iliescu and his friends wanted it dissolved. Kostyal, as he put it, wanted it to "come to an end in an honorable way." He suggested convening a special congress, as Dubček had in 1968, to reform the Party from within. This too was rejected. The group that had arrived with Iliescu was planning its return to the Central Committee building in the center of town. No one invited Kostyal to come along. "You'd better stay here," Militaru told him. "Join us later if you want to." Stănculescu left with Iliescu and, as Kostyal later put it, "stayed with them for evermore." Somewhere along the way, he shed his cast, for there was no sign of it on December 23 or subsequently. Kostyal was deeply hurt at being shunted aside in this way.

Swallowing his pride, Kostyal showed up at the Central Committee building later that day. At first, none of the hastily improvised revolutionary guards would even let him into the Central Committee building. Finally, he talked his way through and went in search of Iliescu, Militaru, and the nucleus of the National Salvation Front group he had been with at the Defense Ministry. Everything was in a terrible state of confusion, he recalled. "I was told they were on the sixth floor. They weren't. There was a war atmosphere, young soldiers with their rifles at the ready at the windows, blasting away at nothing and wasting a lot of ammunition on imaginary targets."

On the fourth floor, Kostyal found bodyguards with armbands protecting some kind of an operational headquarters. They wouldn't let him through either, but eventually he talked his way past them. "There was no sign of Iliescu inside," said Kostyal, "but I did find General Vlad, Avram (a former industries minister), and an Iliescu aide, N. S. Dimitru."

Isolated sharpshooters were still active in the city and army tanks and armored cars were firing back at them, wasting a great deal of ammunition. Kostyal pointed out to Dimitru that the soldiers, instead of taking potshots from the windows, would be better employed guarding the building's tunnel approaches, for deep down in these tunnels, Kostyal knew, were offices with sophisticated phone and radio links, food and ammunition depots, "and I was afraid some of Securitate's fifth-division shock troops could be preparing a counterattack." Vlad's behavior was ambiguous, Kostyal recalled. "He was pretending to be a loyal servant of the revolution but in my view was also deliberately spreading confusion." Vlad was in touch with a General Muceanu, in charge of anti-aircraft defense out at the Băneasa airport area, and giving him hell on the phone, accusing him of being a traitor to the cause. "I know Muceanu," Kostyal told Vlad. "His heart's in the right place, he's no traitor."

On the spur of the moment, and realizing there was no role for him in Bucharest, Kostyal volunteered to go out to

Băneasa, remain with Muceanu, and help him out. Orders had gone out that all aircraft were to remain grounded, and Muceanu had his hands full. He was also, he feared, under threat from diehard pro-Ceaușescu Securitate troops. Kostyal drove to Băneasa and stayed there until December 26, giving Muceanu a hand. During those first three days, he said later, there were sporadic attacks on the loyalists at Băneasa, and a Securitate operation—balloons launched to simulate helicopters and confuse radar—caused considerable confusion.

While Kostyal had been looking for the conspirators in vain on the afternoon of December 22, Iliescu and his nucleus of National Salvation Front members *were* meeting in the Central Committee building, inside a room Kostyal never found. A tape-recorded account of the proceedings, made without the knowledge of the group, revealed indescribable confusion, with Iliescu constantly trying to speak to Stănculescu (who was somewhere on another floor, presumably already making plans for the Ceaușescu trial) on the telephone without success and Roman criticizing the earliest National Salvation Front proclamation ("there's nothing in it for the people outside the building"). At the height of the hubbub, a bodyguard on the landing shouted through the closed door: "Apostol's here. He wants me to let him in." A voice (Iliescu's?) shouted, "Oh God!" and Petre Roman said, "Whatever you do, don't let *him* in!" It was on this tape that General Militaru could be heard talking about the National Salvation Front, saying, "But this organization is six months old, it existed six months before the revolution!" At this stage, of course, many "spontaneous" would-be leaders or participants in the revolution were still vocal—men like the poet Mircea Dinescu, the famous actor Ion Caramitru, who would briefly become Iliescu's vice-president, and other accidental and temporary participants like Major Lupoi, an army architect who had made his way to the Central Committee in uniform as early as December 21 "simply to ensure there was an army presence," unaware of course of the already existing conspiracy.

From the tape-recorded proceedings, Iliescu, at this stage, was concerned solely with the mechanics of taking over power with a semblance of legitimacy—and with the help, of course, of the group around him, some of whom (particularly Roman) appeared to be on intimate terms with him. The veteran economist Bîrlădeanu was present, worrying about Romania's foreign image. "We need to say we are maintaining our alliances and that we won't change." He was worried that Gorbachev might get the impression Romania was leaving the socialist camp. Iliescu replied: "I've already contacted the Soviet Union and already briefed them on the situation, so they should tell Moscow who we are and what we want."

He was almost certainly referring to the Soviet embassy, and his remarks did not necessarily imply Soviet involvement in the plot. On the contrary, they seemed to confirm that the USSR (whose ambassador, at the time the Timișoara riots began, was on leave) was *not* directly mixed up in the conspiracy. It was, however, proof that Iliescu was known to the Soviet diplomats. This too was hardly unusual: As a senior but passively dissident Romanian communist, Iliescu was someone any self-respecting diplomat would have his eye on and try to cultivate. Roman was also very much in the limelight in the taped discussions. Someone tried to cut him down to size ("Nobody knows who you are"), and Roman retorted, "Yes they do. I was the one who read the proclamation on TV, and I know people at the Hungarian embassy. I've even spoken to the Hungarian defense minister." Iliescu then focused attention on the other immediate need—to promulgate amnesties and release political prisoners. The National Salvation Front caucus was not alone in the crowded room. There was Brucan, a member of both the 1984–85 and 1989 conspiracies, and there were students, ordinary people who had demonstrated in the streets, well-wishers, and critics. The noise was deafening. At one point a young man's voice could be heard, saying, "The new government must include people who actually started and took part in the revolution." He was shouted down and eventually hustled out of the room.

At this stage, one of those present relayed the rumor (perhaps initiated as a result of a misunderstanding of Kostyal's remarks) that Securitate had set off a large time bomb that was ticking away somewhere in the building. "Let's get out of here," Roman could be heard to shout. The meeting broke up in disorder, and the National Salvation Front caucus moved to the Romanian TV center. The Central Committee building was still crowded with hundreds of people, mostly demonstrators from the square below. Nobody bothered to warn these innocents of the (fortunately imaginary) bomb.

General Vlad was arrested, at Brucan's insistence, on December 24. A month later Kostyal, who had returned to his Bucharest flat from the airport after December 26, was summoned to the Defense Ministry. Along with four other reservist ex-generals, he was formally reinstated as a retired major-general and was told he was entitled to a pension. This was calculated on the basis of his pay when he was summarily retired and came to some 4,500 lei a month. The Securitate colonel who had interrogated him almost daily in the summer of 1989 was forcibly retired. He currently draws a pension of 6,500 lei a month.

In February 1990, Militaru and Kostyal talked on the phone and patched up their differences. By now Kostyal accepted Militaru's claim that he had been outmaneuvered during the revolution and unable to act differently. He voiced the fear that Iliescu was trying to remove him. "Hang in there," Kostyal told him. "Don't let them kick you out." But the following day, Iliescu, increasingly concerned about the frequency of anti–National Salvation Front riots, summoned Militaru and asked him to resign, pretexting that Militaru was himself somehow implicated in some of the riots. "The man who put him up to it," said Kostyal, "was Stănculescu. A Iago is even more dangerous in revolution than in love."

# CHAPTER FOURTEEN

# SCHIMBAREA DOMNILOR, BUCURIA NEBUNILOR *

*A Change of rulers is the joy of fools*
— OLD ROMANIAN PROVERB

**A**LL REVOLUTIONS DEVOUR THEIR CHILDREN, but Romania's was more anthropophagic than most. Because of its ambiguous, somewhat suspect origins, after swallowing them, it promptly spewed them up. The gradual disillusion, coming as it did in the wake of so much initial relief, hope, and excitement, was unbearably painful for ordinary Romanians.

Their letdown was understandable. They had suffered abominably from an evil-minded, paranoid, and petty couple, who had relied on a huge security apparatus to spread fear and psychological terror around them. It was ironic that in the end, Ceauşescu became the victim of his own system, disinformed about the degree of loyalty and obedience of his people by the very same highly professional Securitate disinformation apparatus he had helped create. Even more ironic was the fact that, having acquired scores of palatial residences all over Romania, some of which he never even visited, he ended up spending the last three days of his life in a dingy army office room, sleeping on an army cot and using a foul-smelling communal toilet.

Other Eastern European countries could take pride in the way they had fought Stalinism and communist bureaucracies. Romanians could only rue the day they had believed in Ceaușescu as a symbol of a new "liberal" era. It took them only a few years to perceive that anti-Russian nationalism was not necessarily synonymous with liberalism and that Ceaușescu could defy Moscow and at the same time remain far more of a tyrant than the rulers of the Soviet empire he so successfully challenged.

Many Romanians, in retrospect, felt a kind of shame not only for playing along with the system but for allowing it to drag on for so long. Toward the end of his life, Ceaușescu was a demon but a passé one, something out of a hopelessly outdated demonology. As Kenneth Auchincloss, editor of *Newsweek* International and the last Western reporter to interview Ceaușescu (four months before his death), put it, "This little man walked into the room, and he had no presence at all, no aura, no eloquence. The impression you had was of a pathetic figure, completely cut off from the realities of Romania, living in the past, in a dreamworld."[1] To *Newsweek*, Ceaușescu flatly denied there were any shortages of any kind, or any discontent. He was sufficiently aware of Stalin's evil influence (as far as the West was concerned, at any rate) to insist that his remarks praising Stalin as a man of order be "off record," but this was probably the only evidence of his link with reality. He only really livened up when talking about the glorious days of 1968–70. Turning to Auchincloss in his garden at Brașov, he reminisced endlessly about his talks with Menachem Begin. Pointing to a garden chair, he said, "Here is where Begin sat for two days while we worked out the deal that turned into the Camp David agreements"—shamelessly exaggerating his role as go-between.

By this time, Ceaușescu was persona grata only in a handful of African and Middle Eastern countries. He must have known from the behavior of the State Department officials on his last visit to the United States (under the Carter presidency in 1978) that they wished he hadn't come and that he would never again be invited. He must also have had intimations of mortality: The week he was killed, a Securitate report, in extra-large characters, about the circumstances of the death of Anwar Sadat, the Egyptian president murdered in 1982, was to have been his bedside reading at the Palatul Primăverii.

In retrospect, it was amazing that he lasted as long as he did, for by the mid-1980s it wasn't just the ordinary population that had to conceal its hatred for the Ceausescu couple: Securitate itself had largely turned against him. In the last few months and even years of the Ceaușescu regime, the hatred had even spread to some *nomenklatura* and members of some "communist activist" groups—the bulwark on which he depended for the stage-managed pageants and mass meetings in the form of popular tribute. Toward the end, even some of the Securitate men staking out dissidents and bodyguards protecting the Ceaușescu family were returning home to ill-lit apartments, weary wives exhausted from standing in line for hours, shortages of all kinds, and the spectacle of a self-satisfied, megalomaniac couple basking in a personality cult that had become a monstrous domestic and international joke. Central Committee officials openly grumbled to visitors of their deteriorating living standards and miserable working conditions, for by the mid-1980s the Ceaușescus were committing the ultimate, unforgivable gangsters' error: They were no longer looking after their own. Greed had overwhelmed them, and after years of rule by "divine right," they had nothing but contempt for the passive people they dominated.

When the events of December 21–25, 1989, unfolded on live television throughout the world, most non-Romanians were full of misconceptions. To have sparked this kind of violence, this kind of hatred, those in the West thought, Ceaușescu must have been an ogre on a par with Nero or Caligula, a vampire straight out of a Gothic horror movie. He was not. His was a much more ambiguous form of malignity.

Possibly the most monstrous aspect of the Ceaușescu dictatorship was not its cruelty but its petty meanness. For all the
hatred it provoked, it was never a bloody dictatorship. Fear
saturated Romania like an all-encompassing fog, but there
were no gulags, little torture, and few disappearances on a
huge Stalinist scale. More heads were broken and more blood
spilled on June 14–15 by the coal miners' clubs in Bucharest
(six months after Ceaușescu's death) than during the last two
years of Ceaușescu's rule.

It was the mental rather than physical cruelty they had
suffered that caused middle-aged men to spit at Ceaușescu's
photographs and assert that he had died too easily that fateful
1989 Christmas Day. And their resentment, so long bottled
up, spilling over into rage, derived from shame and memories
of wasted years. For the supreme ignominy, in Ceaușescu's
Romania, was that all the things achievers elsewhere took for
granted—promotion, comfortable apartments, a living wage,
well-stocked shops, a modicum of social welfare—could only,
in the Ceaușescu era, be obtained in return for the loss of
one's soul. No wonder so many Romanians cooperated with
Securitate, informed on their friends and neighbors, and took
no risks. What should have been theirs by right was obtainable
only as a bonus for betraying neighbors and fellow workers,
"and the rewards were so pathetically small," said one Romanian TV journalist, reflecting on the ways he had been effectively transformed into a watchdog of the Ceaușescu regime.

For many Romanians, these are memories that will never
fade, and they are as bitter as the recollections of the survivors
of Soviet gulags and Nazi concentration camps. Both sets of
victims were hideously traumatized. The difference was that
in the case of Romania, the damage done to individuals was
mostly psychological, and not necessarily physical—except of
course insofar as the consequences of malnutrition, illegal,
botched abortions, and the death of elderly people denied
operations or treatment because of their age were concerned.
Ceaușescu must have been aware of all such statistics. But he
may well have been kept in ignorance of the orphanages full
of children with AIDS and the unwanted children kept in
psychiatric hospitals, for doctors hid things from him, espe-

cially in the later years, that invalidated the image Ceauşescu was eager to maintain of Romania as a workers' paradise.

This workers'-paradise myth was part of the Stalinist Marxist-Leninist legend. But though Nicolae Ceauşescu never lost either his contempt for organized religion or his professed concern for the working class ("I shall only answer to the Grand National Assembly and to representatives of the working class," he told his accusers in the last hours of his life), they were acceptable only as a cliché abstraction. In real life he could not abide any direct contact with ordinary workers, except in highly controlled, official situations. "I wasn't good enough for him," said Florea Ceauşescu, his first cousin, who lived down the road from him in Scorniceşti and worked all his life as a small farmer and village carpenter and cooper, the prototype of the admirable, industrious manual workers and peasant farmers Romania has produced through the ages. "After World War Two we never met."

Prior to his death, there was at least one basic unifying factor in Romania—the secret hatred felt for Ceauşescu himself. "At least," said a member of Social Dialogue, one of the worthy civic groups that has sprung up since December 1989, "we were united in our hatred of the Ceauşescus." "Now we have got rid of him, we find we no longer know how to behave, so we hate each other indiscriminately," said Ana Blandiana, one of Romania's best-known poets (and one of Romania's rare genuine dissidents), adding, "In light of what has happened since December 25, 1989, and the way the power holders have behaved since that date, I wonder whether we were right to judge Ceauşescu so harshly."

The tyrannical couple's disappearance did lead to an immediate change. Newspapers of every conceivable variety made their appearance, including the nationalist, neofascist, *România Mare*, whose editors, Eugen Barbu and Corneliu Vadim Tudor, were two of the outstanding panegyrists of the Ceauşescu era. It was as though all the Balkan demons that had plagued Romania and remained in a state of frozen animation during the period of Romanian communism suddenly came to life again.

"After Ceauşescu, any kind of a replacement looks like an

angel at first," says Gabriela Adaineşteanu, of the Social Dialogue group. But the strength of the system he left behind,
and the nature of his removal, prevented the kind of change
that took place in Poland and Czechoslovakia. To imagine
what happened in Romania and transpose events to France,
one former Romanian exile (now French) said, "imagine what
would have happened in France if there had been forty years
of Nazi rule, no de Gaulle, and a postliberation government
composed mainly of followers of Pierre Laval."[2]

The fact was that in post-Ceauşescu Romania, the police,
the judiciary, and the civil service remained largely intact—
doomed to carry on by default. This perhaps was the grim-
mest paradox of all: The fiction remained that hated
Securitate no longer existed. The new SIR *was* purged of some
of the more extreme elements, those hopelessly compromised
for their loyalty to Ceauşescu. But the bulk of the officers,
officials, and rank and file stayed in place.

They constituted both a threat and a promise to the new
power holders. Almost all post-Ceauşescu-era politicians
were afraid of these men and women, afraid of what they
remembered, and even more afraid of those archives still in
their possession. Exposure, said former Securitate expert
Liviu Turcu, "would be devastating." Routinely, he recalled,
ministers, senior officials, members of the police, the judiciary, and the Party itself were deliberately corrupted by Securitate favors and gifts on a huge scale, "to such an extent
that toward the end, bureaucrats refused to do their daily
jobs if they were not rewarded in this way." Few of the men
and women in the post-Ceauşescu regime were entirely free
of this taint or of the impact Securitate made on their lives,
if only through blackmail, to help them get a divorce, a passport, a trip abroad. "If you are talking about moral recov-
ery," says Turcu, "I believe it will take at least one or two
generations to start putting things right, and this is perhaps
Romania's biggest tragedy."

But to the new power holders, the large ex-Securitate rank
and file, with no place to go, offered promise too. Time and
again, the way dissidents were treated (as early as January, but
far more spectacularly on June 14–15, when the coal miners

rampaged through the streets of Bucharest to put down student protests and violent antigovernment rioting) was proof
that Securitate had not only survived; in its new incarnation, it
had become a loyal servant of the new regime. Naturally
enough, its methods were muted compared to the extreme
manipulation and psychological terror of the past. Still, the
unique Securitate mixture of rumor and threats remained in
effect. Very soon after the National Salvation Front reneged
on its earlier promise not to transform itself into a political
party, dissidents began receiving anonymous letters and
phone calls—a favorite Ceauşescu-era Securitate intimidation
device. Dissidents' letters were opened, their foreign mail held
up, their telephones tapped or disconnected for days at a time.
In little ways, one dissident noted, "They [Securitate] have
been intent on proving their existence." Ex-Securitate opera-
tives have almost certainly been active in spreading the notion
that in post-Ceauşescu Romania, "whoever is not for the NSF
is an enemy."

Another source of disillusion among ordinary Romanians
was the failure of the new power holders to make good an
early "revolutionary" promise to introduce a new, independent TV network. Post-Ceauşescu-era TV was curiously gray:
Whatever the importance of world events, the first fifteen to
twenty minutes were invariably taken up with the activities of
President Iliescu and his government and parliament. The
effect was like watching Czech and Polish TV newscasts of
pre-Dubček or pre-Solidarity vintage. Dissidents were rarely
given air time and there was very little in the way of free
discussion. When a meeting of dissidents held in Braşov in
September 1990 was actually televised and when the veteran
communist turned dissident Brucan was interviewed on television, these moments were so rare they were widely commented on.

Mircea Codreanu, a former diplomat, noted that had Elena
Ceauşescu lived, she should have been tried "for genocide not
of people but of culture and education."[3] The handling of news
on TV and the partiality and lack of consensus shown by *all*
newspapers and magazines revealed the extent of the damage
done, in peoples' hearts and minds. It had been naive of many

Western well-wishers to believe that the post-Ceaușescu-era regime would make a clean break with the past. The very means
whereby the new power holders consolidated their position was
reminiscent of tactics used in the past by the Romanian Communist party to railroad through decisions that would otherwise have been contested. The new National Salvation Front
power holders' "club" had its own secrets, its own exclusive
rules. As General Kostyal found out on the second day of the
uprising, doors were very quickly closed.

Some of Romania's dissidents very quickly lost their illusions. Ana Blandiana became a short-lived second vice-
president of the first National Salvation Front "government,"
then referred to as a council. After its first session, she said, it
was composed of a few well-known dissidents, a handful of
old-time communists who had become dissidents, and students
and others who had been on the streets during the revolution.
Blandiana resigned as vice-president a few days later. At the
council's second session in January, she noted, the 40-member
council had 140 members, and there were no longer any students among them—"they had been squeezed out." The new
members were from the ministries and the provinces, Blandiana noted, and "apart from delegations from Arad, Brașov,
Sibiu, and Timișoara, where dissidents had been active, "many
of the new members from other districts were former [com-
munist] activists who had the upper hand because numbers
were on their side." They docilely endorsed whatever decisions were made by their new National Salvation Front leaders, without ever criticizing them.

I was recently in a long line of cars queueing for gasoline
near Pitești, the length of the wait compounded by a power
cut. One motorist shouted, "Under Ceaușescu we had electricity but no gasoline. Now we have neither." Nobody laughed,
and people gathering around the gas pumps embarrassedly
turned away. Almost a year after Ceaușescu's death, it was still
difficult for Romanians to joke about the past because, in all
sorts of ways, it remained so present, and the elements of
comparison between the Ceaușescu era and what came later
were too numerous to ignore. For this the new power holders
must assume considerable responsibility.

More awful still was the recognition, among so many Romanians of goodwill, that within themselves something of the Ceauşescu era lived on. While attempting to interview a senior ex-minister, who is also a brilliant, British-trained medical specialist with a reputation as an Anglophile, I found myself in a hospital consulting room face to face with a frightened but at the same time angry individual who, instead of answering my questions about the Ceauşescus, about whom he knew a great deal, seemed solely preoccupied in finding out how I had come to track him down. He clearly intended to report on this intolerable invasion of privacy to the appropriate authorities. His harsh, inquisitorial tone was such that I could not refrain from pointing out, somewhat curtly, that while I would have expected such conduct during the Ceauşescu era, I was amazed that the changes in the regime since December 1989 had had so little effect on him. It seemed, I said, that Ceauşescu lived on—at any rate, in the hearts and minds of all those who had had anything to do with him. Visibly shaken, he paused. There were tears in his eyes as he said, in a completely different tone of voice, "I don't know what came over me. I don't know why I started asking you these questions. There's no reason for it. But there's something of Ceauşescu inside me that will never go away."

I remembered the cemetery of Scorniceşti, where the grave of Ceauşescu's father, Nicolae-Andruţa (the only one devoid of a cross, on his son's orders), remains smashed, as if its desecrators were trying to root out all traces of the Ceauşescu progenitors. I recalled the flat, unmarked earth plots, the graves of the Ceauşescus themselves in the Bucharest cemetery where they had been buried after their ignominious flight and horrible death. In their lifetime they genuinely believed that they would go down in history forever as exceptionally gifted innovators of a new order of society.

To some extent, this ambition had been fulfilled. In the hatred and intolerance they continued to generate after their deaths, in the divisions and conflicts of post-Ceauşescu Romania, in the mutual suspicions of a bitter, humiliated people wracked by guilt and shame, Nicolae and Elena lived on, vicariously. How long, I wondered, would it take to dissipate this heritage?

One group of citizens stood out, lucid and untainted: Whoever talked to the new breed of Romanian students came away amazed by the breadth of their vision despite years of schoolroom indoctrination, by their courage, and by their language, refreshingly free of cant and the remnants of Marxist-Leninist clichés. Perhaps, after all, the greatest crime of the Ceauşescus was a posthumous one. They had so affected the hearts and minds of the new power holders that they and the intellectuals and students, a vocal but extraparliamentary force, were locked on a collision course with little hope of a settlement that would fall short of a surrender on either side.

So Nicolae's and Elena's execution, which was to have brought down the curtain on an epoch almost all Romanians wanted to erase from their memories, became instead merely the end of the first act of a gory melodrama likely to continue for years. In an unforeseen way, the Ceauşescus had achieved their goal. They had indeed made their mark on the history of their country. Unmentioned but ubiquitous, they continued to cast their shadow over the new Romania.

# NOTES

## CHAPTER ONE

1. His ambiguous behavior resulted in his house arrest for long months afterwards.

## CHAPTER TWO

1. Ceauşescu, quoted in *Ceauşescu, Builder of Modern Romania* (London: Pergamon Press, 1983).
2. Michael Shafir, *Romania* (London: Frances Pinter, 1985).
3. Hannah Pakula, *Queen Marie of Romania* (London: Weidenfeld and Nicolson, 1984).
4. Ibid.
5. Nicolae Ceauşescu, quoted in *Ceauşescu, Builder of Modern Romania* (London: Pergamon Press, 1983).
6. Take Jonescu, *Some Personal Impressions* (London: Nisbetand Co., 1919).

## CHAPTER THREE

1. Institutul Central de Statistică, Bucharest, 1938.
2. Private interview.
3. Ion Ardeleanu, interview.
4. Hannah Pakula, *Queen Marie of Romania* (London: Weidenfeld and Nicolson, 1984).
5. Lucy S. Dawidowicz, *The War Against the Jews 1933–1945* (New York: Holt, Rinehart, and Winston, 1975).
6. Hector Bolitho, *Romania* (London: Eyre and Spottiswoode, 1938).

7. Rabbi Moses Rosen and Joseph Finklestein, *Dangers, Tests and Miracles* (London: Weidenfeld and Nicolson, 1990).
8. Clare Hollingworth, *There's a German Just Behind Me* (London: The Right Book Club, 1943).
9. Ibid.
10. Ibid.
11. Ivor Porter, *Operation Autonomous* (London: Chatto and Windus, 1989).
12. Ibid.

## CHAPTER FOUR

1. Ghiţă Ionescu, *Communism in Romania* (Oxford: Oxford University Press, 1964).
2. Rabbi Moses Rosen and Joseph Finklestein, *Dangers, Tests and Miracles* (London: Weidenfeld and Nicolson, 1990).
3. Professor Ion Ardeleanu, former director of the Museum of the Romanian Communist Party, has made a detailed study of the police reports concerning the RCP from 1934 onward, and I am extremely grateful for his kind help in this connection.
4. Ivor Porter, *Operation Autonomous* (London: Chatto and Windus, 1989).
5. Ibid.
6. Tudor Vladimirescu was a Romanian nationalist leader who led an anti-Turkish uprising in 1821 and was left in the lurch by tsarist Russia.
7. Bodnăraş died in 1979 without writing his memoirs, and after his death, his personal papers were taken to the archives of the RCP's Central Committee. After the December 1989 "revolution," all these archives in turn were handed over to the Romanian army, where they remain, still inaccessible to all but a handpicked few army officer specialists.
8. Ivor Porter, *Operation Autonomous* (London: Chatto and Windus, 1989).

## CHAPTER FIVE

1. In Romania, a *piccolo* is the term given to an assistant waiter.
2. Arthur Gould Lee, *Crown Against Sickle* (London: Hutchinson, 1950).

## CHAPTER SEVEN

1. Vladimir Tismăneanu, "The Tragicomedy of Romanian Communism," *Eastern European Politics and Societies*, Vol. 8, no. 2, Spring 1989.
2. The Maurer memoirs were never published.
3. Mary Ellen Fischer, *Nicolae Ceauşescu: A Study in Political Leadership* (London, Lynne Rienner, 1989).

## CHAPTER EIGHT

1. *Newsweek*, September 23, 1968.
2. Ibid.
3. I am grateful to Michael Shafir and his admirable study, *Romania: Politics, Economics and Society* (London: Frances Pinter, 1985), for these figures.

## CHAPTER NINE

1. "What do you want? We are, here, at the gates of the East!"

## CHAPTER TEN

1. Ion Raţiu, *Contemporary Romania* (Richmond: Foreign Affairs, 1975).
2. The Villa Forisor illustrated the insane Ceauşescu thirst for personal property: Once a modest hunting lodge under King Ferdinand and donated to the state by King Michael in 1947, it became, under Gheorghiu-Dej, a residential center for outstanding artists and writers. Ceauşescu expelled them, took it over in 1966, and rebuilt it at enormous expense, adding a swimming pool, sauna, gymnasium, and half a dozen bedrooms that were never once occupied. The Ceauşescus would go there once a year.
3. Interview with author, from jail.
4. Interview with author.
5. "How AIDS Came to Romania," November 8, 1990.
6. Interview with John Simpson. See also his *Despatches from the Barricades* (London: Hutchinson, 1990).
7. Published by World's Peace Movement, London, 1983 (no author, no address; preface by Jacques de Launay. Books of this kind have been published in most countries, contain dozens of pictures of Ceauşescu with world leaders, and, as in this typical

excerpt, invariably show signs of literal translation from the original Romanian.

8. London Unified Printers; no other facts of publication available.

## CHAPTER ELEVEN

1. *Red Horizons: The Extraordinary Memoirs of a Communist Spy Chief* (Heinemann, 1988).
2. David B. Funderburk, *Pinstripes and Reds* (Washington, D.C.: Selous Foundation Press, 1987).
3. Mark Almond, *Decline Without Fall: Romania Under Ceauşescu* (London: Institute of European Defence and Strategic Studies, 1988).
4. Trond Gilberg, *Nationalism and Communism in Romania* (Boulder, Col.: Westview Press, 1990).
5. Mary Ellen Fischer, *Nicolae Ceauşescu: A Study in Political Leadership* (London, Lynne Rienner, 1989), p. 32.

## CHAPTER TWELVE

1. Interview with author.
2. David B. Funderburk, *Pinstripes and Reds* (Washington, D.C.: Selous Foundation Press, 1987).

## CHAPTER THIRTEEN

1. The general who organized Ceauşescu's trial and execution (see Chapter 1).

## CHAPTER FOURTEEN

1. Interview with author.
2. Pierre Laval, the French wartime collaborationist leader, was executed after the liberation of France.
3. Interview with author.

# INDEX

# ABOUT THE AUTHOR

EDWARD BEHR is a veteran journalist and war correspondent turned author and broadcaster. Educated at the Lycée Janson de Sailly, Paris, Saint Paul's School, and Magdalene College, Cambridge, he has combined news reporting from the world's trouble spots (Algeria, Beirut, the Congo, Vietnam) with the writing of books on such different subjects as the Algerian war, the Chinese cultural revolution, a bestselling biography of the "last emperor," Pu Yi (which won the Gutenberg Prize in 1988 and was the tie-in book to Bertolucci's Oscar-winning film), and another on the late emperor Hirohito, published by Villard books in 1989, which was singled out by *The New York Times* as one of its "notable books of the year."

His autobiography and humorous reflections on the nature of journalism, *Bearings* (the British title was *Anyone Here Been Raped and Speak English?*), has become something of a classic, and a novel, *Getting Even*, has been translated into ten languages.

TV documentaries include a BBC-1 and PBS film on the late emperor Hirohito and *Red Dynasty*, a three-part series on BBC-2 (also shown in the U.S.) on the tragic course of Chinese communism leading to the events on Tienanman Square.

He has written film scripts (*Half Moon Street*), and his latest book is about the phenomenon of the musical *Les Misérables*. Because of his Vietnam experience, producer Cameron Mackintosh asked him to become an honorary adviser working with the creative production team of *Miss Saigon*, and he is coauthor of a book on the making of this musical, to be published in April 1991.

Edward Behr is married and lives in Paris and Ramatuelle.